CULTURE, CORRUPTION AND INSURGENCY

CULTURE, CORRUPTION AND INSURGENCY

Threats and Quest for Survival in Nagaland

Dr. Pavithran Nambiar

INDIAN INSTITUTE OF ADVANCED STUDY
Rashtrapati Nivas, Shimla

First published 2021

ISBN: 978-93-82396-77-2

Published by
The Secretary
Indian Institute of Advanced Study
Rashtrapati Nivas, Shimla-171005

Typeset at:
Sai Graphic Design, New Delhi

Printed at Dipi Fine Prints, New Delhi

Contents

Preface

Insurgency in Nagaland has exerted its impact on all facets of human life. This infringed on all human rights and forged a serious threat to national security. Though there are several factors that give impetus to this danger, this study has focussed on two elements – Naga culture and Corruption in public offices. Hence, this piece of work has primarily examined the linkage of Naga culture with the prevailing corruption in government offices, and the connection of this corruption with insurgency. There is no doubt that the Nagas *en masse* were honest, humble and freedom-loving people in olden days. During the British rule, the annexation of Naga Hills by Assam led to the formation of the Naga Club, and thereafter Naga National Council, that struggled to throw away the yoke enforced on them. After the British left India, the fight intensified and the Indian government was forced to take several stringent steps that invited criticism from different quarters. After the statehood in 1963, pouring in of huge funds for development caused heightened corruption in government offices, leading to a 'culture of corruption'. This might have gradually permeated in the life of common men, and it exceeded all limits so that people were forced to accept corruption as a way of life. As a whole, there seems to be a weak internalisation of anticorruption values, and in this context it is obvious that the people look for different avenues to become rich by any means.

Nagas have very strong intra family/clan ties and they gave utmost importance to maintaining this relationship. It appears that the kinship and social bond got embedded with corruption in public offices, and this operated as a vicious cycle, both strengthening each other. This relationship between the culture and corruption assumes significance. On the other hand, the inflow of funds enabled the insurgents, using threats, to become a stakeholder in it and this indirectly helped to strengthen insurgency. Further, it can also be seen that corruption enabled the proliferation of criminal gangs that involved in extortion, illegal tax collection, etc. Thus, the post-statehood time period witnessed enormous changes in the Naga society. And that is why the study has focussed primarily on the second half of the twentieth century. As this is a pioneer study to explore the link between culture, corruption, and insurgency, analysis of both primary and secondary data has been done to validate the findings.

April 2021 PAVITHRAN NAMBIAR

Acknowledgements

Conceptualisation and realisation of this volume, a dream, is inextricably associated with my past policing experience. I sincerely bow in front of the almighty God for being with me in fulfilling this cherished aspiration. I express my profound gratitude to the Indian Institute of Advanced Study, its Director Prof. Makarand Paranjape and his Fellowship Award Committee for considering my project worth to be conducted at this prestigious institution and reposing faith in me.

I am highly indebted to all those who come in my way and extended kind support in completing this research. I express my deep gratitude to those who agreed to take part in this project, for their time and courage in sharing their opinion. I am truly benefitted with their participation.

I owe my special thanks to all the *Fellows* of the IIAS for their constructive inputs during the presentations.

Finally, I would like to acknowledge with gratefulness, the moral support and love of my family – my wife Suhas, son Shrrirup and daughter Supprabha – who kept me going, and this book would not have been possible without their backing.

Executive Summary

- There is an obscure relationship between culture and corruption in public offices in Nagaland.
- People have accepted corruption as a way of life.
- There is 'culture of corruption' in government offices in Nagaland.
- The government officials/employees on several occasions misused their power to illegally favour their family/clan members.
- A government official not doing illegal favours to his family/clan lost his prestige in his clan.
- Those who accumulated wealth through any means were given high respect in the society.
- There is 'culture of silence' in the society.
- Corruption in government offices is one of the factors that encouraged insurgency in the state.
- Insurgents got their 'cuts' from the funds allotted to the government offices.
- Though the government has taken steps to control corruption and prevent illegal tax collection, the results were not satisfactory.
- There exists a gulf in the relationship between the government and people.
- People hesitate to raise voice against injustice, and there is power distance in the society.
- The facilitation theory is found to be significant in the relationship between culture and corruption, as well as corruption and insurgency in Nagaland.

CHAPTER I

Introduction

Culture is what we learn, how we behave and live. Certain studies conducted in African countries indicate that there is a relationship between culture and corruption. Corruption is the misuse of power through dishonest or fraudulent conduct by an individual holding an office for his/her personal benefit. Corruption leads to weak governance, which reduces the capability of the nation to fight different kinds of threats. One such threat is insurgency. The insurgent groups exploit the situation in which corruption prevails for achieving their goals. More the vulnerabilities, higher will be the insurgent activities. So, to create such vulnerabilities, such groups will make all efforts to spread their tentacles in different branches of the government, including the criminal justice system. The impact of corruption is such that the security agencies will 'look the other way', and the judiciary will deliver judgements that would favour the insurgent outfits. If at all any insurgent is punished, corruption enables them to get all the facilities in jail. Corruption lowers the morale of security personnel and forces them to fight with inadequate or low quality equipments. Corruption enables incompetent personnel to get jobs in various departments, begets further corruption, thereby efficiency of the departments goes down, and competent candidates rendered unemployed, who many times turn to violent and criminal paths. Corruption enables insurgents to make fake passports and travel across the borders. Similarly, when corrupt officials have access to nuclear materials, the consequence will be disastrous, making the role of corruption in international terror funding and attacks significant. Corruption also facilitates strengthening the ties between insurgent groups and organized crime syndicates in carrying out mutually beneficial activities like drug trafficking, weapon/explosive smuggling, smuggling of migrants, human trafficking and so on.

This study examines the relationship between culture, corruption, and insurgency in Nagaland - a Northeast Indian state. The Naga issue has been at a boiling point since long and is one of the oldest insurgency in India. The discontentment amongst the Nagas was seeded when the British took over Naga Hills in 1881. To protest against this, the Naga Club (NC) was formed in 1918, and it submitted a memorandum to the Simon Commission in 1929 rigidly opposing the British move. To continue with their fight, Naga National Council (NNC) was formed in 1946, and thereafter declared Nagaland an independent state on 14th August 1947. There are a variety of factors that encouraged the growth of insurgency beyond control, e.g. non-surrendering attitude of Nagas, geographical factors, experience of World War II, and lately - culture, corruption in public offices and so on. However, due to time constraints and limit of infrastructure, the researcher will be focusing only on two factors, i.e. culture and corruption*, and hence, is interested to study the extent to which these impacted insurgency in the state of Nagaland during the second half of 20th century, i.e. 1950 to 1999.

In many places the terms 'insurgency' and 'terrorism' are interchangeably used, and hence, there is a need to bring clarity to it. Insurgency is a rebellion or movement with mass support to overthrow the prevailing government. It is a "struggle between a nonruling group and the ruling authorities, in which the nonruling group uses political resources and violence" and is a "protracted political-military activity" that uses irregular military forces. On the other hand, terrorism is politically motivated violence or the threat of violence against non-combatants by sub-state actors to create fear in the minds of the society and government. So, terrorism can be a tactic/tool used to achieve their goal. Terrorists plan for their attacks to "have far-reaching psychological effects beyond the immediate victim(s) or object of the terrorist attack."

* The term corruption is used in the entire report to indicate the misuse of power in different ways in public offices in Nagaland.

Terrorists want to spread terror amongst the population. The terrorist's objective is therefore more about scaring civil society and making themselves known, and thus to achieve their goal[1].

Insurgency is a protracted political-military struggle directed toward subverting or displacing the legitimacy of a constituted government or occupying power and completely or partially controlling the resources of a territory through the use of irregular military forces and illegal political organizations[2].

According to Hayden[3] (2007), insurgency is best defined as an organized movement aimed at the overthrow or destruction of a constituted government through the use of subversion, espionage, insurgency and armed conflict. Terrorism can be a subset of an insurgency, or it can be an act of violence by criminals or crazies who want to strike out at anyone especially a government. E.g. Timothy McVeigh committed a terrorist act in Oklahoma City but he was not part of any insurgency. While the aim of insurgent group is to subvert or displace a constituted government, terrorists' aim is to create terror in the minds of the people and government. This objective differentiates insurgent groups from terrorist organizations.

The Department of Defense (DoD) discussed the difference between insurgency and terrorism in a US Military Academy training manual titled "Insurgents vs. Guerrillas vs. Terrorists"[4]. This document defines terrorism as 'the calculated use of violence or threat of violence to inculcate fear; intended to coerce or to

[1] Treston Wheat, 2011; The Difference between Terrorists and Insurgents, World Report News, 26th December http://www.worldreportnews.com/us-foreign-policy-archived/the-difference-between-terrorists-and-insurgents

[2] Guide to the Analysis of Insurgency, 2012, US Government https://www.hsdl.org/?abstract&did=713599

[3] Thomas Hayden H, 2007; Whast is the difference between insurgency and terrorism? 28th Feb. https://usiraq.procon.org/view.answers.php?questionID=000931

[4] US Military Academy training manual, "Insurgents vs. Guerrillas vs. Terrorists" https://usiraq.procon.org/sourcefiles/InsurgentsvsTerrorists.pdf

intimidate governments or societies in the pursuit of goals that are generally political, religious, or ideological.' Doctrinally, DoD defines insurgency as 'an organized resistance movement that uses subversion, sabotage, and armed conflict to achieve its aims. Insurgencies normally seek to overthrow the existing social order and reallocate power within the country. They may also seek to (1) Overthrow an established government without a follow-on social revolution, (2) Establish an autonomous national territory within the borders of a state, (3) Cause the withdrawal of an occupying power, (4) Extract political concessions that are unattainable through less violent means.'

An earnest probe of these definitions enables to formulate an operational definition, i.e. insurgency is an offensive armed struggle to supplant the legitimately established government and capture power. In the present context, insurgency also means running a parallel administration in the state by creating fear in the government and its people.

The term insurgency is very often accompanied by the word 'counterinsurgency' (COIN) amongst the government and its machineries. COIN is the combination of measures undertaken by a government to defeat an insurgency. Effective counterinsurgency integrates and synchronizes political, security, legal, economic, development, and psychological activities to create a holistic approach aimed at weakening the insurgents while bolstering the government's legitimacy in the eyes of the population[5].

Characteristics of Insurgent groups

Insurgents will always try to denounce the government, portraying it incapable of ensuring the welfare of the people. Secondly, insurgent groups will provide certain facilities to the common people to project that they can deliver what the government failed to do. Thirdly, insurgent groups will always try to get the support of the people, by sympathizing or through creating fear

[5] US Government, 2012; Guide to the Analysis of Insurgency, https://www.hsdl.org/?abstract&did=713599

or intimidation. Fourthly, they use guerrilla attacks or terrorism. Fifthly, certain times, these groups incite the government in such a way that it (government) commits wrong which will be exploited by the insurgent groups to gain the support of the people. Sixthly, insurgent groups will have international support in the form of funding, weapons, training and so on.

Insurgency in the Northeast: A Brief Narration

There are various groups and outfits that have dissimilar aims in different ethnic and linguistic domains, and these groups are by and large autonomous in India's Northeast. Due to differences in their missions and objectives, intergroup violence and clashes have become common. There were other factors too.

During the British rule, the reorganization of Bengal and Assam had contributed greatly in sowing the seeds of enmity among the local people as well as those from newly annexed or separated region, which were blown out in the form of social tension and conflict at a later stage. This discontentment or disharmony grows gradually on trivial issues when there are 'unseen' elements that support covertly. The separation of Assamese dominated region and its annexation with Bengal led to linguistic tension and disharmony, for example, the annexation of the Assamese heartland and making it a part of Bengal in 1826. Similarly, the separation of certain parts of Bengali populated areas and joining it with Assam in 1874, the reorganisation of Bengal in 1905, the moving in of a large number of Muslims from East Bengal to Assam in and around 1911and so on, created ethnic and language imbalance and identity crisis amongst the local people of the area. Similarly, the enactment of the Assam Official Languages Act 1960[6], and unequal distribution of resources and employment opportunities created the fear of attack on the cultural identities of the non-Assamese population. No doubt, these kinds of 'realignments' and the inadequate platforms to resolve such issues

[6] https://shodhganga.inflibnet.ac.in/bitstream/10603/116506/9/09_chapter%204.pdf

were enough to sow the seeds of feud. There were major incidents like the Shillong procession of May 21st 1960, firing at the Cotton Hostel on 4th July 1960, uncontrolled mob violence that resulted in the death of 39 persons, injuries to 487, burning, damaging and looting of 10891 houses, the language related riots of 1972, to name a few. These incidents should not be seen in isolation, but a chain of events that strengthened the intensity of hostility, violence and thus insurgency.

The rising unemployment forced a large number of youths to join insurgency – genuine or pseudo. At the same time, several local extortionist groups also mushroomed. Diverse ethnic groups, domination, exploitation, identity crisis, taking revenge, marginalization, and so on caused/encouraged inter-ethnic rivalry/insurgency in the Northeast. Consequently attacks and bloodsheds had become a routine affair in those days.

There were several ethnic groups in the Northeast and they wanted to safeguard their identity, and hence, separate land. Thus, ethnicity and insurgency are very much intertwined. Bodo people wanted to have a separate land, Karbi Anglong and North Cachar Hills wanted their separate state, Ahoms raised the issue of autonomous, Nagas wanted to have union of all the Naga dominated areas lying in different states, Mizo National Front fought for the cause of Mizos, Meities of Manipur had their own demands, Tripura National Volunteers (TNV) wanted to protect the interests of Deb Barmans, Bodo, Karbi, Dimasa and Bru fought for the interests of their respective communities, and so on. Thus, an element of ethnic issue can be observed in all insurgencies in the Northeast, in which the role of unemployed youths has been significant.

External Support

Support to the insurgent groups from India's neighbouring countries was another important factor that helped keep the insurgency alive in the Northeast region. It may be recalled that the NSCN was formed inside Myanmar and it provided arms training and other logistic support to insurgent outfits of the Northeast.

Similarly, safe havens were provided to Indian insurgents in Bangladesh (Hussain)[7]. In an interview T. Muivah said that in earlier days they had procured arms from China and Pakistan (Rediff Interview)[8]. When a section of NNC leaders signed the Shillong Accord in November 1975, Muivah and his 140 members were in China, who refused to accept the agreement[9]. These are a few examples manifesting the significant role of our neighbouring countries in supporting insurgency in Nagaland and in other North-eastern states. The insurgents got training, weapons, explosives, financial and logistical supports from them. No doubt, today our improved relationship with Bangladesh and Myanmar has enabled the closing down of several insurgent training camps in these countries. However, the possibility of movement of insurgents across the border cannot be denied, which is one of the factors in sustaining insurgency in the Northeast.

Insurgency in Nagaland: A Brief

The British annexed Assam in 1826, and in 1881 the Naga Hills were also captured and made part of British India. The first sign of Naga resistance was seen in the formation of the Naga Club in 1918, which told the Simon Commission in 1929 to leave them alone to determine for themselves as in ancient times. This shows that the Nagas from the very beginning opposed any authority ruling them. In 1946 the Naga National Council (NNC) was formed under the leadership of Angami Zapu Phizo, and this declared Nagaland an independent state on August 14, 1947. The

[7] Hussain, Wasbir, Insurgency in India's Northeast Cross-border Links and Strategic Alliances https://www.satp.org/satporgtp/publication/faultlines/volume17/wasbir.htm#_ftn35

[8] Rediff Interview, https://www.rediff.com/news/2001/jun/25inter.htm

[9] Kashyap S Gupta & Swami Praveen, 2015; Explained: Everything you need to know about Nagaland insurgency, *The Indian Express*, 4th August https://indianexpress.com/article/india/india-others/everything-you-need-to-know-about-nagaland-insurgency-and-the-efforts-to-solve/

NNC resolved to establish a 'sovereign Naga state', as they faced lots of discrimination and did not want to submit to the Indian rule.

A Nine-point agreement viz., The Hydari Agreement, was signed between the NNC and the Governor of Assam in June 1947. This dealt with the recognition of the right of the Nagas to develop themselves according to their freely expressed wishes (Luithui & Haksar, 1984, p-150)[10]. A year later, realizing that their dream of a sovereign Naga state would not get fulfilled, on 22nd November 1948, a letter was written by A. Z. Phizo, the President of NNC, from the Presidency jail, Calcutta to H.E. Shri C. Rajagopalachari, the Governor General of India, mentioning the issues faced by the Nagas. He demanded that India, being under the rule of British for more than two hundred years had experienced the bitterness of ruling by an alien nation, and now Nagaland is undergoing the same situation. Considering this fact, it would be a matter of great honour for India if she becomes a benevolent giver of freedom to Nagaland. "I always entertain the hope that one Eastern race, especially those who got back their freedom from their white master, will not attempt to dominate another people. No other nation had a better experience than India to lead the world to freedom from the course of imperialism and domination. It is for India to show the way out" (Luithui & Haksar).

Another letter by Phizo to the President of India on 1st January 1951 spoke about a plebiscite that would be held in Nagaland to know the minds of Nagas, about whether they wanted to remain with India or go for a separate Naga Sovereign State. The letter also requested the Government of India to send their observers to witness the plebiscite process. The plebiscite was held by the NNC from 16th May 1951 and continued for three months. Its outcome was that 99.9% people of Nagaland opted to stay independent by having a sovereign nation[11]. The anniversary of Naga plebiscite is

[10] Luithui, Luingam and Haksar, Nandita, 1984; Nagaland File: A Question of Human Rights, Lancer International, New Delhi.

[11] The Morung Express, 2018; Naga Plebiscite Day is 67 years Old, 16th May.

commemorated every year on 16th May by the NNC veterans and sympathisers in Nagaland.

However, the Indian government was not ready to accept the outcome of the plebiscite. The general elections conducted in 1952 were boycotted by the NNC, and they continued their fierce secessionist movement. Adopting violent path, the NNC cadres raided police outposts and villages. The government used all its machineries and adopted various tactics to weaken the movement. The movement, on the contrary, gained more strength and the antagonism went high between the Naga people and the government.

The result was that on March 22, 1956, Phizo formed the underground Naga Federal Government (NFG) and the Naga Federal Army (NFA). Subsequently, the NFA was involved in innumerable violent incidents, attacks, deaths and destruction of properties across Naga Hills, due to which the Indian Government had to send its army in April 1956 to crush the insurgency. However, the insurgency continued unabated without any kind of respite and the situation became so grave that in 1958 the Indian government had to declare the area as 'disturbed' and enact the Armed Forces (Special Powers) Act 1958 that controversially gave Indian security forces immunity in conflict-ridden areas.

In such a volatile situation, certain peace steps were initiated by some moderate Naga leaders. Subsequently, peace conferences were held between the Governor of Assam and these moderate Naga leaders. Thus, the first Naga People's Convention was held in 1957 and according to its resolution, the Naga area of the earlier Tuensang Division was taken out of the North East Frontier Agency (NEFA) and amalgamated with the then Naga Hills District of Assam. The entire newly established Naga Hills Tuensang Area (NHTA) was placed under the charge of a Commissioner, who was directly responsible to the Governor of Assam, who was the representative of the President of India. As there was encouraging signs of peace, the second Naga People's Convention was held at Ungma village from 21st May 1958. However, the deliberations found that there were two different view-points of the meeting, (1) the Naga People's Convention was only a peace body, and as such it was not competent to take any political decisions, whereas (2) the Naga People's Convention should go ahead with preparing a basis for political settlement. Thereafter, to prepare a draft on this line, a Drafting Committee was formed, which prepared the draft, and was accepted in the third Naga People's Convention held at Mokokchung in 1959. This turned out to be the Sixteen-point Agreement of 1960 between the Naga People's Convention and the Government of India (Luithui & Haksar).

After India's independence, Nagaland became the 16th state of India on 1st December 1963. However, some sections of the insurgent groups did not agree to this and demanded a sovereign Naga nation. Although a fragment of the separatist groups signed ceasefire agreements with the Indian government, these were violated by the insurgent groups. "In 1972, the Centre banned the NNC, the NFG and the NFA as 'unlawful associations' under the Unlawful Activities (Prevention) Act of 1967. Shillong Accord was signed between the Centre and a section of the NNC and the NFG on November 11, 1975. According to the terms of the Accord, the NNC-NFG accepted the Indian Constitution and agreed to come overground and surrender their weapons. However, a group of about 140 activists of the NNC, who had gone to China for training, repudiated the Shillong Accord and refused to surrender. They formed a new underground organisation called the National Socialist Council of Nagaland (NSCN) under the leadership of Thuengaling Muivah, Isak Chisi Swu and S.S. Khaplang on Myanmarese (Burmese) soil in 1980. With the passage of time, the NSCN emerged as the most radical and powerful insurgent group fighting for the Naga cause, as the NNC-NFG became less active" (Nagaland Backgrounder)[12]. However, difference of opinion amongst the NSCN led to its split into NSCN-Isak-Muivah (NSCN-IM) and NSCN-Khaplang (NSCN-K) on 30th April 1988. Attacks and killings continued to be a part of daily life in Nagaland.

Today there are several major and small separatist groups in

[12] Nagaland Backgrounder, 2001; South Asia Terrorism Portal (SATP) http://old.satp.org/satporgtp/countries/india/states/nagaland/backgrounder/index.html

Nagaland. Each runs a parallel government of sorts in the state, fights against the others, and levies taxes on state residents. The NSCN (IM) justifies their acts saying "We have the legitimate authority to tax people. It's a way for people to participate and contribute to the mass movement of the Nagas. Peace talks require money. We have coordination offices in 10 countries and thousands of armed men from Nagaland deployed there. We cannot call them back or stop sending them rations and other necessary supplies. It'll be extremely easy for us to engage in illegal activities and make money, but we don't want to do that, so we seek people's support." said Varengam Horam, who identifies himself as the minister of information and publicity for NSCN (I-M). Parallel taxation system created by the insurgent groups is well aware to the state and central governments (Santoshini, 2016)[13].

A new Naga political group viz., NSCN (Reformation) was formed on 6th April 2015 by Y. Wangtin Konyak and P. Tikhak[14] with an agenda to develop a sense of brotherhood among the Naga family and also to rebuild the trust and faith among the Naga society. The new political party would give opportunity to all the Naga people, NGO's, social organizations, intellectuals and leaders of various tribal councils to share their ideas in building a renewed Naga society. It will also make efforts to run the party without becoming a liability to the people.

On 3rd August 2015, a framework agreement was signed between T. Muivah and the Government of India setting the parameters within which a final agreement was to be worked out. Some of the conditions are – recognition of the uniqueness of Nagas by the Indian government, boundaries of the state will not be touched, no Greater Nagalim, and special arrangements will be

[13] Santoshini, Sarita; 2016; In India's Nagaland, a tale of taxes and corruption; 14th April https://www.aljazeera.com/indepth/features/2016/04/india-nagaland-drowning-taxes-corruption-160411062725238.html

[14] The Morung Express, 2015; Wangtin, Tikhak Form 'NSCN (Reformation); 6th April. http://morungexpress.com/wangtin-tikhak-form-nscn-reformation/

made for Nagas. Thereafter, in November 2017, the Centre signed a preamble with six Naga National Political Groups to continue holding discussions to find a solution to the decades old problem. However, one or the other trivial issues cropped up occasionally that resulted in stalemate and uncertainty.

The Problem Statement

The outbreak of Naga insurgency started in the 1950s with the demand for a separate nationhood, though their claim was raised initially when the Naga Hills was annexed with the British India in 1881. Even after the British left India, Nagas fought for the same with utmost love for their soil. That is why in the 1950s the NNC boycotted the general elections, the underground NFG and NFA were established, involved in large scale violent acts and fought for separation from India. However, after the late 1960s certain changes were observed in the purpose of insurgency, i.e. waning devotion for the land, coupled with vested interests and accumulation of wealth. This began when the state started to get huge funds for developmental purposes from the central government. Gradually these opportunist motives gained more significance while welfare of the people took the backseat, the government offices became center of corruption and over a period of time there emerged a 'culture of corruption'.

The NSCN, which was formed in 1980, raised the demand for the creation of 'Greater Nagaland' or 'Nagalim'. This would be a sovereign Naga territory, consisting of the Naga-dominated areas of Manipur, Assam and Arunachal Pradesh, as well as parts of Myanmar. In spite of signing the new framework agreement in 2015 by the Indian government and the NSCN (IM), doubts were raised[15] whether this agreement would bring peace to this

[15] Rajshekhar M & Chakravarty Ipsita; 2018; What does the new 'historic' Naga peace accord have that the Shillong Accord of 1975 did not?; 5th August 2015. https://scroll.in/article/746319/what-does-the-new-historic-naga-peace-accord-have-that-the-shillong-accord-of-1975-did-not

state, because of the engagement of only one organization and no mention about 'Greater Nagaland.'

Why Study Naga Insurgency?

Naga insurgency was the first blast out encounter that India witnessed after independence, and this had high impact on insurgencies in other Northeastern states. Further, it was the oldest insurgency, so gruesome and ghastly that it unparalleled to violence in other states, the government was forced to invoke the AFSPA, and also considered to be the mother of all insurgencies. Its study would help to understand the basic causes of this and other insurgencies. Finding causes and solutions of Naga insurgency would help to understand the insurgencies in other parts of Northeast and apply the solutions to those problems by changing the context. Though causes of insurgency are numerous, as mentioned earlier, this study would be focusing on the culture and corruption in the state. Secondly, the researcher wanted to study a society where three elements were present - strong family/ clan ties, corruption, and insurgency. And these were present in Nagaland. Thirdly, the researcher had already conducted a study on Nagaland insurgency in 2008, but with a different angle, i.e. the structure of insurgent groups, their modus operandi, sources of funding, their link with other insurgent groups, network with terrorists and narcotics smugglers, link with foreign countries, training camps in India and abroad, type of weapons and explosives they possess, measures taken by the state to counter insurgency, and so on. For this, the researcher sent questionnaire, got it filled up, thereafter visited Nagaland and conducted personal interviews with state police officials, Central Armed Police Force (CAPF) authorities, intelligence bureau officials, academicians, etc. So, the past experience was an advantage in conducting this study. Fourthly, the policy recommendations in the context of Naga insurgency would be useful to contain other insurgencies in India.

Why identified Culture and Corruption?

The culture of corruption prevailing in Nagaland public offices raises a question whether there is any element in Naga culture that directly or indirectly causes this menace (corruption). When corruption surpasses beyond the limit and threatens to bring down the functional capability of different organs of the government, then the insurgent groups will take advantage of such a situation.

Klitgaard (2017)[16], quoting different studies, mentioned that cultures with stronger family ties were more likely to experience public sector corruption than those with weaker family ties. In some cultures, where kinship-related obligations to use their office to favour family and friends exist, the 'essential tension' to use official power illicitly can move from a selfish temptation to a cultural mandate. Quoting Husted's study, Gonzalex-Trejo (2007)[17] mentions that culture and corruption are significantly correlated. So, it is interesting to know whether the strong family/clan ties and obligations amongst the Nagas have caused the evolution of culture of corruption in public offices in Nagaland.

Corruption evokes indignation in populations, making it a factor in social unrest and insurgency. It contributes to other international security threats, such as symbiotic relationships between states and transnational organized crime networks, facilitation of insurgent organizations, permeable international security regimes, and acute economic disruptions (Carnegie Endowment for International Peace, 2014)[18]. Teets and Chenoweth[19]

[16] Klitgaard, Robert, 2017; On Culture and Corruption; BSG Working Paper, BSG-WP-2017/020 July https://www.bsg.ox.ac.uk/sites/default/files/2018-05/BSG-WP-2017-020.pdf

[17] Gonzalex-Trejo,Eli Samuel, 2007; Corruption and Culture: A Relationship Comparison Between 1996 and 2004, Central Business Review, vol. XXVI, No. 1-2, p. 23.

[18] Carnegie Endowment for International Peace, 2014; Corruption: The Unrecognized Threat to International Security; http://carnegieendowment.org/files/corruption_and_security.pdf

[19] Teets, Jessica & Chenoweth, Erica; 2009; To Bribe or to Bomb: Do Corruption and Terrorism Go Together?; in Corruption, Global Security,

opine that corruption facilitates terrorism (insurgency). Then, has corruption got any relationship with the insurgency in Nagaland?

Hence, the questions raised in this research are – does Naga culture encourage corruption in public offices, or vice-versa? If yes, what are the cultural elements that embolden corruption? And does it lead to a culture of corruption in government offices in Nagaland? Has such corruption had any relationship with the prevailing insurgency in Nagaland?

Violent Acts

In the mid-1960, there had been many explosions on the railway tracks between Titabarh and Mariani stations of the Northeast Frontier Railway line by the NNC. The National Socialist Council of Nagalim (Isak-Muivah), had purchased weapons from Bangladesh, Bangkok, China and North Korea and smuggled in to Nagaland, and the cadre strength of insurgent groups was enhanced (Baruah, 2011)[20]. They had purchased 10,000 assault rifles, pistols, rocket-propelled grenades and ammunition (Unnithan, 2011)[21]. Recently, they attacked Indian Reserve Battalion and snatched 20 weapons in December 2016 (News18, 2016)[22].

In April 1964 a Peace Mission was set up to bring an end to violence, but the NNC/NFG/NFA continued to indulge in violence,

---

and World Order, Ed. Robert I Rotberg, Brookings Institution Press, Washington DC.

[20] Baruah Sanjib Kr; 2011; NSCN on Arms Buying Spree, Building Cadre; 18th Jan. https://www.hindustantimes.com/delhi-news/nscn-on-arms-buying-spree-building-cadre/story-2gQE76CuZ95rTSiDzjSEmJ.html

[21] Unnithan Sandeep; 2011; Chinese agents smuggle arms to revive militancy in north-eastern India, 28th May https://www.indiatoday.in/magazine/investigation/story/20110606-chinese-agents-smuggle-arms-to-spread-militancy-in-north-east-746248-2011-05-28

[22] News18; 2016; 70 NSCN-IM Cadre Attack Imphal Security Posts, Snatch 20 Weapons, 17th December https://www.news18.com/news/india/70-nscn-im-cadre-attack-imphal-security-posts-snatch-20-weapons-1324276.html

and after six rounds of talks, the Peace Mission was abandoned in 1967, and the state witnessed continued violence. In 1988, the NSCN split into NSCN (IM) and NSCN (K) after a violent clash. While the NNC began to fade away, and Phizo died in London in 1991, the NSCN (IM) became very powerful. The Government of India signed a ceasefire agreement with NSCN (IM) on July 25, 1997, which came into effect on August 1, 1997. Over 80 rounds of talks between the two sides were held subsequently (Indian Express)[23].

A charge-sheet filed by the National Investigation Agency (NIA) in May 2011 against Anthony Shimray, chief arms procurer of the Isak-Muivah faction of Nationalist Socialist Council of Nagaland (NSCN-IM), specifically mentions Norinco, one of China's largest state-owned weapons manufacturers. Bangkok-based NSCN-IM rebels had allegedly paid $100,000 to Norinco to buy 10,000 assault rifles, pistols, rocket-propelled grenades and ammunition (Unnithan, 2011). In December 2016, around 70 heavily armed NSCN(IM) cadres attacked seven posts of the Indian Reserve Battalion and snatched 20 weapons from the security personnel (News18, 2016)[24].

The central government allotted huge funds to Nagaland for developmental purposes. The central government did not seek accountability from the state for these funds. The flow of money without any oversight and accountability enabled the leaders of insurgent groups to divert money as they wished and it is alleged that the leaders who want Nagaland to be a separate nation, started to use these funds for violent purposes. It can be assumed that such flow of funds could have contributed in boosting insurgency in the state. Hence, this study would be examining the extent of

[23] Indian Express, 2015; Everything you need to know about Nagaland insurgency, 4th August http://indianexpress.com/article/india/india-others/everything-you-need-to-know-about-nagaland-insurgency-and-the-efforts-to-solve/

[24] News18; 2016; 70 NSCN-IM Cadre Attack Imphal Security Posts, Snatch 20 Weapons, 17th December https://www.news18.com/news/india/70-nscn-im-cadre-attack-imphal-security-posts-snatch-20-weapons-1324276.html

relationship between culture, corruption and insurgency in the state of Nagaland.

Review of Literature

A literature review surveys books, scholarly articles, and any other sources relevant to a particular issue, area of research, or theory, and by so doing, provides a description, summary, and critical evaluation of these works in relation to the research problem being investigated (USC libraries)[25].

In 'Introduction to Sociology', Biesanz and Biesanz[26] narrate in detail about society. The work comprises of five parts in which the first one elaborates on man and culture, especially on culture's nature, content, organization, integration and its functions. Part two deals with social structure, social organization, stratification and intergroup relations, while part three explains the role of person in culture and society, personality development, deviance, and autonomy. Part four principally describes social and cultural change, including modernization, environment, and social movements, while part five primarily explicates social institutions like family, religion, education, and trends in economic, political, social, cultural, and belief systems. Regarding culture, the authors state that it is "the learned portion of human behaviour", and language plays a significant role in any culture.

According to Bhattacharjee (2007)[27], there is no one Northeastern insurgency, but numerous, in different states with a variety of reasons, such as ethnic, linguistic, secessionism, separate state, regional autonomy, protection of cultural identities, and so on. All these have its base in ethnicity. Culturally and historically

25 USC Libraries, http://libguides.usc.edu/writingguide/literature review; http://libguides.usc.edu/writingguide/theoreticalframework

[26] Biesanz, H Mavis and Biesanz, John, 1973; Introduction to Sociology, Second edition, Prentice-Hall, Inc. Englewood Cliffs, New Jersey.

[27] Bhattacharjee JB, 2007; Roots of Insurgency in Northeast India, Akansha Publishing House, New Delhi.

these people, especially Nagas, are independent-minded and they did not like outsiders' interference in their life. There were many insurgent groups in the Northeast. The Centre has and still continues, to pump in colossal amount of money the Northeast, in the name of assistance, special package, subsidy, and relief, and today, the contractors, bureaucrats, authorities, and politicians who have a vested interest in the continuance of the violence, have become the biggest beneficiary of it. "There has been constant accusation of the politicians sponsoring, supporting and receiving kickback from certain insurgent groups" (p. 52). This kind of linkage between politicians and insurgent groups may encourage the bureaucrats and the officials in public offices to go for corrupt practices and offering some favours to the insurgents. The ideology that prevailed in the initial stages of insurgencies have gone, and now the informers, cadres, and leaders thrive on extortion, and "insurgency has emerged as the fastest means to earn easy money. The number of fake groups and cadres far exceeds the real groups, which points out as to how lucrative they have become" (p. 53).

In his book "Insurgency and Counter Insurgency", Anand (1981)[28] enumerates different features of insurgency, its elements, atmosphere that promotes its growth, approach to counter insurgency, foundationary measures, etc. For countering insurgency, it is necessary to understand its history, the structure and strength of insurgent groups, their ideologies and operational models; promote confidence building between security forces and common people; encourage development and welfare measures; rehabilitation of affected people; strengthen intelligence, disrupt functions of insurgent organizations; identify foreign support; implement policies and programmes to change the mind-set of people, and so on.

Where did the Naga tribes come from? Quoting Prof. John Hutton, Chandola (2013)[29] in "The Naga Story: First Armed

[28] Anand VK, 1981; Insurgency and Counter-Insurgency, Deep & Deep Publications, New Delhi.

[29] Chandola, Harish, 2013; The Naga Story: First Armed Struggle in India, Chicken neck, New Delhi.

Struggle in India" points out that the Naga tribes came from Borneo, slowly moved Northwest, set up habitations along the way and moved further hunting and farming, reached the region we call the Naga area around the tenth century (p.205). This work discusses Naga community, their armed movement for an independent country under the leadership of Phizo, mobilizing political consciousness, setting up of a fighting force, establishing foreign links and acquiring weapons, fighting and bloodshed, birth of the State of Nagaland, negotiations between NSCN and the Indian government, and so on. Citing example, the work mentions that the first lesson in corruption was taught to Nagas by Indian officials, and Nagaland is now one of the most corrupt states (p.219). Naga movement had in many ways impacted and encouraged insurgencies in other parts of Northeast.

The book "Unheeded Hinterland" edited by Gogoi (2016)[30] gives an account of the debates on sovereignty, self-determination and nationalist upsurges in India's Northeast. The document locates internal tensions and contradictions among different ethnic groups, as well as the complex interrelationships between the Centre and the region. The volume argues that challenges to the Indian nation-state from Assam and the Northeast primarily came out of the continuation of the same colonial legacies, a form of 'colonial constitutionalism' maintained by the Centre (p.7). The book proposes a new structure of 'Common Ethnic House' to resolve persistent inter-ethnic tensions among different communities and the impasse between the Northeast and the Centre.

"Naga Polity" by Horam (1975)[31] deals with the political institutions that existed in earlier days and attempts to elucidate how the family, village and the customary laws were associated with these institutions. Elaborate explanations has been made about the Naga family, the clan, morung, the prevelant taboos, and

[30] Gogoi, Dilip, 2016; Unheeded Hinterland: Identity and Sovereignty in Northeast India, South Asia Edition, Routledge India.

[31] Horam, Mashangthei, 1975; Naga Polity, BR Publishing Corporation, Delhi.

the conduct of the administration of the village. Elaborating on morung, the author mentions that it is the young men's dormitory where every boy has to live from the time he attains puberty till he gets married. Morung has significant role in the life of Nagas, as it is the place where the boys learn how to lead a community life, how to preserve their honour and customs, how to respect elders, how to observe the exiting taboos, and so on. In brief, the moulding of culture happens at the Morungs.

Horam (1977)[32] in another book "Social and Cultural Life of Nagas" depicts in depth, the topography of Naga dominated areas, the people, and their activities during different festivals. Family and community are given significance, and everybody has to take part in any activity taken up by a clan. Morung or bachelor's dormitory has high importance in the life of Nagas, as this is the centre where a youth is culturally moulded. The volume also deals with village administration, head hunting and the social changes that happened in the life of Nagas.

"India's North East" by Udayon Misra (2014)[33] is a collection of essays written over three decades on the socio-political scenario of Northeast, including the Naga struggle. The work revolves around several identity movements, the role played by civil society as well as the state. The essays elaborate that there have been vast changes in the Naga society from the time the Naga struggle started for self-determination with fervent nationalism, and the present context, wherein these honest ideologies have given way to unethicality, conflict, extortions in the name of 'taxes', and how people have become disappointed and disillusioned. Everything is measured in terms of money and corruption has become rampant.

Nienu (2015)[34] in "Naga Cultural Milieu" explains the Naga concept of natural environment, their origin, Naga social

[32] Horam, Mashangthei, 1977; Social and Cultural Life of Nagas, BR Publishing Corporation, Delhi.

[33] Misra, Udayon, 2014; India's North East, Oxford University Press, New Delhi.

[34] Nienu V, 2015; Naga Cultural Milieu: An Adaptation to Mountain Ecosystem, Dorylus Publishing Group (DPG), California.

structure, their cultural patterns and various aspects of their life. He believes that there are minor variations from tribe to tribe, but these variations are not very significant and they follow similar cultural practices. Nagas believed in the ideals of personal and national pride and freedom. There is a birthright connection established between the Naga people and the land they inhabit as their homeland. Their attitudes towards their landscape have been formulated over several millennia. Mountains, hills, forests, and rivers were held sacred and were respected, for they were the source of all good things and had the power to affect crops and fertility – all believed to be controlled by supernatural forces. These features of the natural world became the source of the Nagas' spiritual and emotional aspirations, and directly attached with their land. This strong bond with the land could be an important reason why Nagas stiffly opposed the annexation of Naga Hills by Assam in 1881.

All these literatures individually discuss a lot about various dimensions of Naga culture, corruption practiced in the government offices, and insurgency. However, they did not try to draw a link between culture and corruption, and corruption and insurgency in Nagaland. This study would attempt to fill this gap.

Theoretical Framework

Klitgaard (2017) and Gonzalex-Trejo (2007) opine that there is close relationship between culture and corruption. The cultural elements support the prevalence of corruption in public offices. At the same time, with regard to the relationship between corruption and insurgency/terrorism, the facilitation theory suggests that corruption in governance indirectly increases the ability of insurgent/terrorist groups to carry out attack, because such (corrupt) governments are unable or unwilling to enforce the rule of law. This leads to the creation of a criminal infrastructure that the insurgent/ terrorist groups use for funding, weapons, transport, and forged documents, thereby strengthening insurgent/terrorist organizations. Thus corruption and insurgency/terrorism coexist in a mutually reinforcing relationship (Teets and Chenoweth, 2009). Thus, facilitation theory is applicable in both the instances, i.e. to study the relationship between culture and corruption, and corruption and insurgency in the context of Nagaland.

SWOT Analysis

SWOT stands for Strengths, Weaknesses, Opportunities, and Threats. This approach can suitably be used for planning counterterrorism operations in an insurgency-infested situation, as well as for taking preemptive measures against insurgent attacks on humans or infrastructure, as a short-term measure. This method can also be used for studying the situations prevelant during the insurgent attacks, learning lessons from it, preparing plans to thwart further attacks – the exisiting situation, identifying vulnerabilities, and plugging those vulnerabilities.

Before carrying out an attack, the insurgents decide on a particular modus operandi considering the benefit, loss, vulnerability, convenience, accessibility, etc. and when they find that a particular target and modus operandi will lead to maximum benefit (casualty, destruction, publicity, etc.), the attack is carried out. For taking this decision they study the prevailing circumstances, like presence and alertness of security agencies, facilities of hide outs, transportation of weapon/explosive secretly, and consequences like maximum casualty and destruction. After surveying all these factors, when they find that the attack can be carried out and it would give their expected results, they prepare the plan and execute it. On the other hand, had security agencies conducted such a risk and vulnerability analysis, they would have been able to identify the existing vulnerabilities, which further could have enabled them to plug the loopholes and strengthen those areas, which would have discouraged the terror perpetrators to carry out the attack. The important aspect of this method is to identify the Risk that the target (human/infrastructure) faces, and this can be done with a simple formula R= T x V x C, wherein

R = Risk
T = Threat (target will be selected by a threat actor depending on its importance, likelihood of an attack, probability)

V = Vulnerability (exposure, access control)
C = Consequence (expected Impact of attack)

This will help to identify the causes of attack that happened earlier, and to propose measures to prevent future attacks.

Objectives

The general objective is to find out the relationship between culture, corruption and insurgency in Nagaland during the second half of Twentieth century (1950 – 1999) and to recommend policy measures to contain the same. The specific objectives are:

- To examine Naga culture and how certain aspects encourage corruption in Nagaland public offices.
- To understand the extent of corruption prevalent in different fields in Nagaland, with the help of reports of Comptroller & Auditor General (CAG), studies and media reports.
- To study whether a portion of the Central Government funding to Nagaland had been diverted to insurgent groups or not.
- To analyze whether corruption in public offices facilitated the insurgent groups to strengthen their activities in the state of Nagaland.
- To examine the connectedness of the government with the common people.
- To suggest measures to contain insurgency.

Research Question

Research question is an answerable inquiry into a specific issue. It is the initial step in a research project, after having an idea of what has to be studied (study.com)[35].

The pivot question of this study – *What is the relationship between culture, corruption and insurgency in Nagaland?* Many sub-questions are formulated to answer this principal question.

[35] study.com, https://study.com/academy/lesson/writing-research-questions-purpose-examples.html

Hypothesis

Hypothesis is a proposition or a set of proposition set forth as an explanation for the occurrence of some specified group of phenomena either asserted merely as a provisional conjecture to guide some investigation or accepted as highly probable in the light of established facts (Kothari, 2004)[36].

(Chapter II) **Null Hypothesis**: *Cultural factors do not promote corruption in public offices in Nagaland.*

Alternative Hypothesis: *Cultural factors do promote corruption in public offices in Nagaland.*

(Chapter III) **Null Hypothesis**: *Corruption in public offices has no relationship with the domestic insurgency in Nagaland.*

Alternative Hypothesis: *Corruption in public offices has relationship with the domestic insurgency in Nagaland.*

Scope of the Study

This study would identify the relationship between culture, corruption and insurgency in Nagaland in the second half of twentieth century, i.e. 1950 to 1999. For this purpose, whether the culture has any role in promoting corruption in public offices, has been examined. Funding to the state government and its utilization by different stakeholders including insurgent groups, process through which funds are being generated by insurgent groups, procuring manpower, weapons, etc. are also analysed.

In almost all countries where insurgency prevails, it is seen that corruption is a precursor in that society, and this is principally due to weakness in governance. Has corruption in public offices in Nagaland related in any way with their culture? Did the prevalence of corruption facilitate insurgency in the state? Have the insurgent groups exploited the weakness of corruption, facilitated further

[36] Kothari C R; 2004; Research Methodology; New Age International (P) Ltd., Publishers, New Delhi

vulnerability in the governance system, and strengthen their organization and activities? This study has also suggested policy recommendations for containing insurgency.

Research Methodology

Research methodology refers to a systematic method of enunciating the problem, formulating a hypothesis, collecting the facts or data, analysing the facts and reaching certain conclusions either in the form of solutions(s) towards the concerned problem or in certain generalisations for some theoretical formulation (Kothari; 2004).

This is an exploratory study attempting to find out whether there is any relationship between culture, corruption and insurgency in Nagaland, and if yes, *why?* Correlation is made to find out the relationship between two variables, i.e. *culture* & *corruption*, and, *corruption* & *insurgency* in the state. The study has used both, primary data as well as secondary data.

The study has broadly three purposes, (1) to examine the link between culture and corruption in Naga public life, (2) has corruption facilitated insurgency?, and (3) to suggest policy measures to contain insurgency. Here an important issue is how to understand the link between culture and corruption, because no study has been done in the Indian context to examine the relationship between these two variables. The study topic is so relevant and sensitive that everybody faces the problem, but hardly likes to have an open discussion. So, it was impossible for me to select the respondents from all walks of life. One of my friends in Kohima persuaded me not to go there personally, or to change the subject matter of the research. Further, though sought, I could not get support to conduct the study amongst the police personnel working on the ground. Moreover, extensive field work was not feasible in this pursuit due to shortage of time. However, the researcher, from his policing background could sense that there are some latent causational factors that give impulse to corruption and insurgency, in addition to the external factors that were visible. To understand this, a systematic study is the only way. Taking in to account all these situations and limitations, it was decided to use whatever primary and secondary data I could collect and do the analysis, so that the study could achieve its highest authenticity.

In the **first part of the methodology**, during the field work in Nagaland, the respondents were selected using purposive sampling method. This technique was used keeping in mind different factors, like the complexity of the study topic, hesitation of the people to speak out due to its sensitivity, universe of study and the respondents. Considering the nature of the topic, there was no good response from the authorities of other departments. It was purposively decided to have the respondents from the academic field as it represented students from different clans, faculties, and employees. The sample has the heterogeneous nature. Permission was sought from the Nagaland University authorities, and one of my friends helped me to meet professors, students and employees, explained my intention, which enabled me to manually deliver the questionnaire schedule to a large extent. In total 142 respondents were given the questionnaire. Though the method used was purposive sampling, the sample included respondents between the age of 21 and 60, males, females, married, unmarried, employed, academicians, and students from different Naga tribes. Systematic effort was made to ensure that the sample attained near accuracy of random sampling. The questionnaire schedule was prepared with 5-point Likert scale answers, i.e. Strongly Disagree, Disagree, Can't say, Agree, and Strongly Agree. A small number of Naga students from Nagaland studying in the North East Hills University (NEHU), Shillong also took part in the session. The data thus collected was analysed using SPSS and its Mean, Standard deviation, Skewness, Kurtosis, Chi square, and P-value were found out. Additionally, dialogue was held with senior police officers, former IB official, etc. in Nagaland. They were not ready to fill up the questionnaire schedule, but held discussions under the condition that it will neither be recorded nor would their identity be disclosed. In an insurgency-infested environment, their hesitations and apprehensions have to be respected. The brief of their discussions were added at appropriate places.

In the **second part of the methodology,** secondary data was collected from pertinent books, journals, research reports, media and other publications. Websites dealing with corruption, insurgency in India and Nagaland were looked through. Websites of the IIAS, CIA World factbook, South Asia world site, India Monitor, Himalayan Affairs, U.S. Department of Justice, and FBI terrorism reports, and consortium for the START at the University of Maryland were searched. E-Journal Finder was used for referring academic journals. Key terms and subordinate terms from titles and abstracts were identified and searched. Databases like Education Resources Information Center (ERIC), PsycINFO, and Sociological abstracts were useful for this study. Scanning Table of Contents has also helped to locate the necessary topics and collect required information. Further, analysis of directives of the UN Convention Against Corruption (UNCAC), the Vohra Committee Report 1993, reports of Transparency International India, etc. provided valuable information for this study.

As there was large volume of literature, purposive sampling was used by identifying the works that dealt with the three factors (culture, corruption, and insurgency) in Nagaland and 41 pieces of literature were selected. From these sample literatures (41), statements, themes, opinions, discussions and speeches, that directly or indirectly implied that there was corruption in Nagaland and that it was linked with the culture, were identified. From these, specific variables (24) were selected that have got similar meanings (Concept categorization). Content analysis method helped to quantify it for further analysis (Chapter 2, Table 2.26). Content analysis[37] is a research tool used to determine the presence of certain words or concepts within texts or sets of texts. Researchers quantify and analyse the presence, meanings and relationships of such words and concepts, then make inferences about the messages within the texts. Texts can be defined broadly as books, book chapters, essays, interviews, discussions, newspaper headlines and articles, historical documents, speeches, conversations, advertising, theater, informal conversation, or really any occurrence of communicative language. There are

[37] An Introduction to Content Analysis http://www.umsl.edu/~wilmarthp/mrpc-web-resources/content-analysis.pdf

generally two categories of content analysis - Conceptual analysis and Relational analysis. Conceptual analysis can be thought of as establishing the existence and frequency of concepts – most often represented by words of phrases in a text. Relational analysis, like conceptual analysis, begins with the act of identifying concepts present in a given text or set of texts, and further explores the relationships between the concepts identified. In other words, the focus of relational analysis is to look for semantic, or meaningful, relationships. Individual concepts, in and of themselves, are viewed as having no inherent meaning. Rather, meaning is a product of the relationships among concepts in a text. Here, Relational analysis is used. Thereafter, frequency of these variables is explored (Chapter 2, Table 2.27).

By using Pearson's correlation tool, correlation between variables identified. With an aim to further validate the correlation, Factor Analysis method was also used that marked out six components. Further, the researcher felt necessary to explore whether the findings have got any relationship with Hofstede's cultural dimension of Power Distance. By using Thematic approach, the above mentioned statements, themes, opinions, discussions, speeches that gave similar meanings, were used to formulate certain themes that showed the relationship between culture and corruption. These themes have been put into five inter-linked categories. After formulating these themes, it was found that these (themes) are related to Hofstede's cultural dimension of Power Distance. This relationship is important because his theory has made 'the most well-known, referenced, and adopted cultural value' classifications. Additionally, this is very relevant to the present study as this tries to explore the relationship between culture and corruption. (Here it is worth mentioning that Hofstede had used massive primary data to prove this theory). Drawing the model from Hofstede's culture theory, Babatunde Akanji (2017)[38]

[38] Babatunde Akanji, 2017; The Relationship Between Culture and Corruption in Nigeria – Prospecting Culture Change in Dealing with this 'Big Black Hole', The Romanian Economic Journal, Year XX no. 63, March.

conducted a qualitative study to explore the views of Nigerians on the extent to which cultural factors impacted corruption in their country. The study did prove the relationship between culture and corruption. As mentioned above, the formulation of themes and its relationship with Hofstede's culture theory is explained in Chapter 2. The themes thus identified are: (1) Prevalence of culture of corruption in government offices, (2) Internalization of norms and values and corruption in public offices, (3) Custom of giving high respect to the people who accumulate wealth by any means, (4) Preference for jobs that enable to amass extra illegal money, and (5) The Moral Economy of Resentment (Chapter 2, Table 2.36). This effort further enabled the exploration of the relationship between culture and corruption.

To understand the relationship between corruption and insurgency (Chapter 3), incidents of corruption in public offices in different modes, that supported insurgency, have been examined. Here also, (as in Chapter 2, in addition to primary data), statements/opinions/ discussions/speeches were selected and based on it, a Theme was formulated to show the relationship between corruption and insurgency. Similar method was used in Chapter 4 also, which dealt with the relationship between the government and people.

Research Design

Research design is the conceptual structure within which research is conducted. The decision regarding what, where, when, how much and by what means concerning an inquiry (Kamuzora, 2008)[39]. The function of research design is to primarily provide a paradigm where relevant evidence can be collected with minimum

---

Rodrigo Santiago Juaçaba, 2018; The Contingency Effect of National Culture on Corruption; Master's dissertation submitted to the Department of Geography at the Norwegian University of Science and Technology.

[39] Kamuzora A; 2008; Research Methods for Business and Social Studies, Morogoro Mzumbe Book Project.

expenditure of time, efforts and money (Kothari; 2004). This study is principally exploratory, aiming to find out the relationship between culture, corruption and insurgency in Nagaland, and analytical to understand *how* and *why* the relationship exists. The study focused on five decades, i.e. between 1950 and 1999.

Research Area

Area of study is Nagaland. This state has been selected due to multiple reasons, like (1) Naga insurgency is the mother of all insurgencies and its study will help to understand the other insurgencies, (2) wanted to study a society where three elements were present - strong family/clan ties, corruption, and insurgency, (3) study a topic that was relatively unexplored, (4) though corruption is prevailing in other states, no there are no insurgencies there, (5) there could be a hidden agenda between the government and the insurgent groups, and the government has to 'buy' peace, and (6) the policy recommendations in the context of Naga insurgency would be useful to contain other insurgencies in India.

Research Output and Policy Relevance

Corruption and insurgency are very serious problems faced by the state of Nagaland. This study has identified the relationship between culture and corruption in public offices in Nagaland, and how corruption facilitated insurgency. Certain methods have been put forward for the Law Enforcement Agencies, which could help containing insurgency. Considering the SWOT approach certain suggestions have been made for the policy makers that can be used for formulating policies for countering insurgency.

Chapterization

The first chapter 'Introduction' briefly discusses insurgency in the Northeast and Nagaland – states the problem statement, review of literature, objectives of the study, hypothesis, and research methodology. Being a pioneer study of this nature in India, the researcher has used both - analysis of the secondary data as well as primary data to justify the findings.

Second chapter deals with the relationship between culture and corruption in Naga public life. Detailed analysis of primary data was done to find out this relationship. Similarly, secondary data was used to show how specific elements of Naga culture – like strong family/clan bonds, custom prevailed in the clan to support their own members working in government offices, even if the latter were involved in irregularities/corruption; obligation of the government officials to help their own family/clan members in spite of misusing official powers; learning from the behaviour of politicians, etc. were studied.

The third chapter examines the relationship between corruption and insurgency in Nagaland. Here also, primary and secondary data were used to study the linkage. Corruption in public offices, sharing of funds by the politicians and officials, illegal tax collection, 'cuts' from the public funds to the insurgents, and so forth are also discussed.

The fourth chapter studies the connectedness between the government and people of Nagaland. Examination of both the primary and secondary data brought out the sorry state of relationship between the government and people, their dissatisfaction due to the prevailing corruption at different levels, lack of development and welfare measures, threat of insurgency, measures to minimize corruption and insurgency etc. were dealt with.

The fifth chapter deals with the theoretical perspectives of counterinsurgency (COIN) in the US and India. The way in which SWOT analysis can be used for preparing COIN plans in India has also been dealt with.

The sixth chapter is Policy Recommendations, which has 3 Sections: Section-I deals with the security preparedness needed in an insurgency infested area; Section-II elaborates on raising of a new Counter Insurgency Intelligence Unit and an Assault Unit in all districts, its structure and functions; and Section-III describes the model of a counterinsurgency operation that has to be carried out in Nagaland.

Finally there is the Conclusion, References and Appendix.

CHAPTER II

Culture and Corruption in Naga Public Life*

What is culture? Taylor[1] (1871) defined culture as "that complex whole which includes knowledge, belief, art, morals, law, custom, and any other capabilities and habits acquired by man as a member of society". This definition gives an understanding that the life we live and the actions we do has relationship with our own or others culture, directly or indirectly. It can be the society we live, language we speak, food, customs, behavioural pattern, personality, dress, jewelry, education, interpersonal relationships, and many more. When imitating an alien culture wholly or partially, we are trying to become part of that culture. In our own society, when we try to imbibe certain traits of another person, be it good or bad, our effort is to become a person similar to the other. When the entire or majority of the society adopts this trait, it becomes the culture of the society. It can be related to religion, spirituality, honesty, truth, values, morality, materialism, deception, manipulation, crime, taboos, corruption, violence or any attribute or distinctive characteristic. Thus, culture is what we learned and the way in which we live.

Biesanz and Biesanz[2] (1973) distinguish culture in two forms, i.e. general and specific. "In the general sense, culture is

*The term 'public life' has different meaning. Here this term is used to denote 'the work that you do especially for the government', as specified by Longman, https://www.ldoceonline.com/dictionary/public-life

[1] Taylor, Edward, Burnett, 1871; Primitive Culture: Researches into the Development of Mythology, Philosophy, Religion, Art, and Custom, Vol. 1, Dover Publications, Inc., Mineola, New York.

[2] Biesanz, Mavis Hiltunen and Biesanz, John, 1973; Introduction to Sociology, Second edition, Prentice-Hall Inc., New Jersey, p-54.

the *learned* portion of human behaviour, the patterned ways of thinking, feeling, and doing that man himself has developed and made part of his environment. Culture adapts man to his physical environment, his biological nature, and his group life. In the specific sense, a culture is the distinctive way of life of a society; it is that combination of behaviour and beliefs that makes one society different from another. It is learned and shared by members of the group, and presented to the growing child as the social heritage of past generations".

Hofstede[3] (2001) defines culture as "the collective programming of the mind which distinguishes the members of one group or category of people from another".

Culture, according to Geertz[4] (p. 89), is "an historically transmitted pattern of meanings embodied in symbols, a system of inherited conceptions expressed in symbolic forms by means of which men communicate, perpetuate, and develop their knowledge about and attitudes toward life". Quoting Kluckhohn, Geertz (p. 4-5) mentions culture as: (1) "the total way of life of a people"; (2) "the social legacy the individual acquires from his group" ; (3) "a way of thinking, feeling, and believing"; (4) "an abstraction from behavior" ; (5) the way in which a group of people in fact behave; (6) a "store-house of pooled learning" ; (7) "a set of standardized orientations to recurrent problems"; (8) "learned behavior"; (9) a mechanism for the normative regulation of behavior; (10) "a set of techniques for adjusting both to the external environment and to other men"; (11) "a precipitate of history".

A study was conducted by Babatunde[5] (2017) on the interface between the national culture and the realities of corruption in

[3] Hofstede, G., 2001; *Culture's Consequences: Comparing Values, Behaviours, Institutions and Organisations across Nations*, Sage, London, p.9.

[4] Geertz, Clifford, 1973; *The Interpretation of Cultures: Selected Essays*. New York: Basic Books, Inc., Publishers.

[5] Babatunde Akanji, 2017; The Relationship Between Culture and Corruption in Nigeria – Prospecting Culture Change in Dealing with this 'Big Black Hole', The Romanian Economic Journal, Year XX no. 63, March.

Nigeria. Drawing from Hofstede's culture theory, a qualitative design was used as a framework to explore views of 40 Nigerians on the extent to which social norms, traditions, values, and personal orientations interplay with the magnitude of corruption in the country. The findings provided empirical support for uncertainty avoidance values, patriarchy, and collectivist practices as influencing levels of corruption. Further results revealed the need for a pragmatic approach that places more emphasis on functional education that can raise cultural consciousness which will promote accountability, transparency and moral adherence to anti-corruption values. By implication, the findings offers valuable insights that unveils corruption in Nigeria as more cultural than political.

In a study by Rodrigo[6] (2018) on two companies, one each in Brazil and Norway, it was found that national culture played an important contextual role in causing corruption. By challenging the notion of a universal solution for corruption, this study suggests that national culture must be taken into account by policymakers in order to effectively combat it.

Thus, culture is the integral part of an individual's imbibed belief system, behaviour, knowledge, ceremonies, rituals, customs, codes, morals, habits and capabilities acquired as a member of a society. The internalization of social norms has significant role in motivating a person to behave in a particular way. In entirety this helps moulding the personality of an individual. Thus, culture is what we learned, the way in which we behave and live. In the present context, the characteristics of corruption prevailing in the society are imbibed by the younger generation that gave birth to a culture of corruption, and hence, they do not look at it as a 'sickness' of the society.

[6] Rodrigo Santiago Juaçaba, 2018; The Contingency Effect of National Culture on Corruption; Master's dissertation submitted to the Department of Geography at the Norwegian University of Science and Technology.

NAGA History

The first Anglo-Burmese battle was fought between 1824-26, and it came to an end with the signing of the Treaty of Yandabo in February 1826[7]. This led the King of Ava to hand over Assam and the neighbouring kingdom like Cachar, Jaintia and Manipur to the British. This treaty had profoundly affected specifically Nagas as it carved up Naga territory and placed them in Burma and India. Thereafter, 1832 witnessed the advent of the British in Naga Hills, as they (British) wanted to construct a road from Manipur to Assam which had to pass through the Naga Hills. This was the first time that the Nagas came in direct contact with the British and both had bitter experiences from each other. As the British wanted to prevent the raiding of the plains by the Nagas, after implementing different policies and meeting failures, the Naga Hills District was created in 1866, and the Naga Hills was brought under the British administration in 1881 by annexing it with Assam[8].

The history of Nagas shows that they had several fights internally and externally – between different clans, raiding of plains, with the Ahom community. They had their first hostility and fight with Sukhapha – the founder of the Ahom kingdom in the early 13th century, in which several Nagas were killed. The Nagas carried this revenge in their mind for more than two centuries, and in a retaliatory action, Nagas carried out a raid during the reign of Sushenpha (Ahom) in 1487 and killed a large number of Ahoms. This hostility between Nagas and Ahoms continued till 16th century and in the mid of 17th century, the relationship was improved and there was exchange of gifts. Thereafter, fresh enmity

[7] Chasie, Charles, 2005; Nagaland in Transition; Indian International Centre, Quarterly journal, Vol. 32, No. 2/3. https://www.jstor.org/stable/23006032?seq=1#metadata_info_tab_contents

[8] Ketholesie, 2015; British Policy Towards Annexation of the Naga Hills; International Journal of Engineering, Management, Humanities and Social Sciences Paradigms (IJEMHS), Volume 13, Issue 01. http://www.ijemhs.com/Published%20Paper/Volume%2013/Issue%2001/IJES%2011/IJEMHSJune2015_55_57_Keth.pdf

and attacks broke out in 1807, number of lives were lost on both sides, and a peace treaty was signed[9] (Horam).

Though the Nagas were defeated on certain occasions, they were not ready to accept the conqueror as their ruler and were not prepared to remain subdued. They took revenge whenever they got an opportunity as they considered themselves superior to others and wanted to hold their honour and prestige high. They were ready to die for their self respect.

Same was their approach towards the British. The Nagas conducted many raids on the latter that caused death of many, including several officers. The frequent Naga raids forced the British to enact a regulation viz., 'Inner Line Regulation of 1873', under which permission was needed to be procured from the authority for an outsider to go beyond a certain limit in Naga hills.

In 1945, the Naga Hills District Tribunal Council was formed for the unification of Nagas, which was later on renamed as Naga National Council (NNC) in 1946 that aimed to achieve local autonomy for the Hills. By 1947 demand by the NNC to separate Naga Hills from India became stronger, and a delegation visited Delhi to press for their demand. Subsequently, there was an agreement between NNC and Sir Akbar Hydari, the then Governor of Assam, which was known as Hydari Agreement.

Esteem of Nagas

Maslow's esteem needs are more focused on external measures of esteem, such as respect, status, recognition, accomplishment, and prestige (positive psychology)[10]. Every individual seeks recognition, and to achieve this people engage in different type of activities, as recognition gives satisfaction. Getting recognition after certain work boosts our morale that motivates to conduct further tasks. This is a psychological factor that acts as energy

[9] Horam, Mashangthei, 1975; Naga Polity, BR Publishing Corporation, Delhi, p. 56.

[10] Maslow; Positive Psychology, https://positivepsychology.com/self-esteem/

that proves value to life. Nagas are highly particular about their self esteem and the recognition that they get from their family and society. They are ready to go to any extent to oppose any action by other that could adversely affect their prestige and self respect. It may be remembered that recognition and self respect are highly interdependent. One of the reasons for the emergence of the custom of headhunting was that it gave recognition and self respect to the head-hunter. By accomplishing this act, he proved his mettle for which he was praised, recognized and treated as a hero by his friends and relatives, thereby accorded him high status in the society. The head-hunting was also believed to bring prosperity, good crop and good luck to his clan.

Another factor that gives high esteem to Nagas is their freedom and right. Any kind of interference in it by anybody is stiffly resisted as this is seen as an attack on their personal life. Naga is "one in which there was an unequalled thirst for the ideals of personal and national pride and freedom". They are "a uniquely proud and self-sustained group of people" (Nienu, 2015)[11]. This was the principal reason behind the opposition against annexing of Naga Hills with Assam by the British in 1881. This further gave rise to the formation of Naga Club in 1918, opposition to the visit of the Simon Commission in 1929, establishment of NNC in 1946 raising the demand for Greater Nagalim. They are a people who are mentally and bodily highly attached to their soil and environment and gives high regards to it because that is in their blood. All these characteristics gave them enough courage and perseverance to fight against any external threats, be it from other clan, village, authority or government. Fighting on flimsy ground, taking revenge, and going for raids were routine affairs and peace was very rare among Nagas in the pre-colonial and initial days of colonial days. This characteristics in their personality is one of the reasons for their opposition against the British as well as India's rule over them.

Quoting Ptolemy's Eleventh Map of Asia, and Stevenson,

[11] Nienu, V, 2015; Naga Cultural Milieu: An Adaptation to Mountain Ecosystem, Dorylus Publishing Group, California, p-xviii, xx.

Nienu further mentions that the territory where Nagas lived was "an unprotected country," meaning "an independent country", and not under the control of any nation or power that existed in those times (p-92). Nagas were not ready to compromise their freedom and wanted to keep hold of their right to continue with the belief, customs and rituals of their religion. In old days, Nagas were fierce fighters and every youngster aspired to be a good warrior. The head-hunting custom they followed itself shows their firm faith in their superiority over others and submitting to none. It was because the Nagas were not ready to work under the British that the latter had to bring in Assamese and Bengalis for doing their work.

Before the advent of the British, the fighting was mainly between different tribes, and head-hunting was common. However, the hunting was stopped by the British by implementing new laws. Once this menace was stopped, they started to realize many similarities between different Naga tribes, which convinced them to come together and to have a peaceful life. This inter-tribe ties helped to have strong unity among them which turned out to be a powerful tool in the origin and progress of Naga movement demanding Greater Nagalim. Another important element that gave soaring strength and momentum to the movement was the mass support. The Nagas, once realized the common similarities between different tribes, there was the emergence of brotherhood among them which tied them to a single thread. For this, the idea mooted by Phizo was that the movement needed to have "a son from each family" which "made each family supposedly pro-underground" (Horam 1977, p-101)[12]. It is simple to understand that when the son is part of an organization, his family members will have sympathy and an unseen attachment towards that group, and support it. But, after two decades of its operations, the genuine love for the motherland has lessened, the principles they carried in the initial stage started to fade, and the organization got involved in many illegal activities, were the hard realities. Political

[12] Horam, Mashangthei, 1977; Social and Cultural Life of Nagas, BR Publishing Corporation, Delhi, p.101.

persuasions, economic greed and gratification, and different other vested interests caused such a situation.

Cultural causes of Insurgency in Nagaland

There are different causes of insurgency in different states in the North east. Assam, Nagaland, Mizoram, Manipur, Meghalaya, Tripura has its own causes for insurgency. While its causes are different, no doubt, insurgency in one state has influenced this menace in another state. Since Naga insurgency was the first in the Northeast, it had certainly influenced the insurgencies in other states of this region. At the same time, cultural factors, policies of the British, attitude of the Indian as well as the state governments towards the tribals of the hills in the post independent period, all have contributed in one way or the other in precipitating and enlarging insurgency in these states.

The land Nagas inherited from their forefathers is highly beloved to them and they are undetachably attached to it as it is their livelihood. They are ready to sacrifice their lives for this land as they see their as well as their forefathers' lives in it, and this land is a significant part of their culture. Any kind of encroachment is opposed fiercely and many times resulted into bloodletting. The strong attachment to the land is one of the factors that encouraged enmity and head-hunting till colonial rule.

Before the British annexation, Nagas were not under anybody. British annexed Naga Hills with Assam, and later on the NNC signed a 9-point Hydari Agreement. The accord was signed between the Governor of Assam, Akbar Hydari, being the representative of the Indian government and the NNC. It is still a matter of debate - had the NNC not signed the agreement, India would have to struggle to show any linkage of Naga Hills with India. On the other hand, the NNC was not having any other alternative at that point of time. Before moving further, let us have a look at the 9-point agreement.

Naga-Akbar Hydari Accord (Nine Point Agreement) (Kohima, 26-28 June 1947):

That the right of the Nagas to develop themselves according to their freely expressed wishes is recognized.

1. Judicial – All cases whether civil or criminal arising between Nagas in the Naga Hills will be disposed of by duly constituted Naga Courts according to Naga customary law or such law as may be introduced with the consent of duly recognized Naga representative organizations: save that where a sentence of transportation or death has been passed there will be a right of appeal to the Governor. In cases arising between Nagas and non-Nagas in (a) Kohima and Mokokchung town areas, and (b) in the neighbouring plains districts, the judge if not a Naga will be assisted by a Naga assessor.
2. Executive – The general principle is accepted that what the Naga Council is prepared to pay for, the Naga Council should control. This principle will apply equally to the work done as well as the staff employed. While the District Officer will be appointed at the discretion of the Governor, Subdivisions of the Naga Hills should be administered by a Subdivisional Council with a full time executive President paid by Naga Council who would be responsible to the District Officer for all matters falling within the latter's responsibility, and to the Naga Council for all matters falling within their responsibility. In regard to:
   (a) Agriculture – the Naga Council will exercise all the powers now vested in the District Officer.
   (b) C.W.D. – The Naga Council would take over full control.
   (c) Education and Forest Department – The Naga Council is prepared to pay for all the services and staff.
3. Legislative – That no laws passed by the Provincial or Central Legislature which would materially affect the terms of this agreement or the religious practices of the Nagas shall have legal force in the Naga Hills without the consent of the Naga Council. In cases of dispute as to whether any law did so affect

this agreement the matter would be referred by the Naga Council to the Governor who would then direct that the law in question should not have legal force in the Naga Hills pending the decision of the Central Government.

4. Land – That land with all its resources in the Naga Hills should not be alienated to a nonNaga without the consent of the Naga Council.
5. Taxation – That the Naga Council will be responsible for the imposition, collection, and expenditure of land revenue and house tax and of such other taxes as may be imposed by the Naga Council.
6. Boundaries – That present administrative divisions should be modified so as (1) to bring back into the Naga Hills District all the forests transferred to the Sibsagar and Nowgong Districts in the past, and (2) to bring under one unified administrative unit as far as possible all Nagas. All the areas so included would be within the scope of the present proposed agreement. No areas should be transferred out of the Naga Hills without the consent of the Naga Council.
7. Arms Act – The Deputy Commissioner will act on the advice of the Naga Council in accordance with the provisions of the Arms Act.
8. Regulations – The Chin Hills regulations and the Bengal Eastern Frontier Regulations will remain in force.
9. Period of Agreement – The Governor of Assam as the Agent of the Government of the Indian Union will have a special responsibility for a period of 10 years to ensure the observance of the agreement, at the end of this period the Naga Council will be asked whether they require the above agreement to be extended for a further period or a new agreement regarding the future of Naga people arrived at.

There was a great misunderstanding about 'clause nine' of the agreement between the NNC and the Government of India on account of ambiguity in wording and interpretation of the clause. Nothing in the Hydari agreement suggested that the Naga participation in India was temporary, though the NNC interpreted and insisted that it was provisional. The government interpreted the agreement in the light that Nagas had the freedom only to suggest revision of the administrative pattern after ten years, which was unacceptable to the NNC (Kotwal, 2000)[13]. Both the Indian government as well as the NNC stuck to their own interpretation and the issue has been dragging on till now.

India could not agree the demand of Nagas simply because Naga Hills were a part of Assam, and Assam was and is a part of India. Further, had India agreed to the demands of the NNC, it would have led to the disintegration of the nation as a whole in general, and Northeast in particular. Nagas inhabit in all neighbouring states of Nagaland, such as Arunachal Pradesh, Assam, Manipur and certain parts of erstwhile Burma. Approval of the demand by India would encourage Nagas in these states also to raise such demand, which would lead to breaking of all these states. Moreover, in such a situation Pakistan and China would have attacked Nagaland and taken it into their control. This would be disastrous to India as well as to the Nagas. Ensuring security and welfare of Nagas is the prime responsibility of India. It needs to be remembered that from the time Nagas revolted against India, China and Pakistan had been extending all supports to the insurgency. So, they would not forgo any opportunity to disintegrate India. Further, if the demand is endorsed, Nagas in Burma will also raise the claim to join 'Nagalim', which would lead to further conflicts and violence. This will have serious implications on Indo-Burma relations as well as on India's national security.

On the other hand, Nagas always maintained that they constituted a separate and independent nation. In this relevance, Udayon Misra (1978)[14] mentions, "Throughout their nearly 30 years of struggle against the Government of India, the Naga

[13] Kotwal, Dinesh, 2000; The Naga Insurgency: The Past And The Future; Strategic Analysis, Volume 24, Issue-4, Taylor & Francis Online. https://www.tandfonline.com/doi/abs/10.1080/09700160008455245

[14] Misra, Udayon, 1978; The Naga National Question, Economic and Political Weekly, Vol. 13, No. 14, 8th April, https://www.jstor.org/stable/4366506?seq=1#metadata_info_tab_contents

National Council (NNC), the political wing of the underground Naga Federal Government (NFG), has consistently maintained that the Nagas constituted an independent nation. The NNC claims that, except for a century of British rule, the Nagas had never been subjugated and ruled by any other people and had never been part of what today constitutes the Indian nation". Moreover, it needs to be remembered that the British had never exercised their jurisdiction over all the Naga tribes. Most of the Northeastern Naga-inhabited areas were left completely untouched till 1947 (Yonuo Asoso, 1948)[15].

Here, a noteworthy point is that even during Indian struggle for independence, its leaders did not make any effort to involve the Hill people in this movement. Neither before 1881 Naga Hills were a part of India, nor during freedom struggle were they convinced to take part in it. Then certainly they will not have any emotional attachment with India. But, after the British left, Assam became a part of India alongwith Naga Hills. This move agitated the Nagas because up till that time they were opposing the British rule, and thereafter they had to resist a new rule, i.e. India. They found the British occupation unjustified earlier, and now the Indian rule unfounded. Hence, they started violent protests against India killing government representatives, arson, destruction of properties and so on with the covert support of China, Pakistan and Burma, which forced India to send its army to establish order, and later on the imposition of controversial AFSPA.

Imposition of AFSPA in Nagaland

The NNC declared Naga Hills as an independent nation on 14th August 1947 and boycotted India's independence on the next day. In 1951, the NNC conducted a plebiscite, which showed 99% people wanted Nagaland to be an independent nation, though Indian government did not agree with this. The same year, India conducted its first general elections, which were also boycotted by the NNC. These discontentment and opposition sent a signal

[15] Yonuo Asoso, 1948; The Rising Nagas, Manas Publications, Delhi.

to the Indian government about the uphill task ahead. With the formation of Naga Federal Government (NFG) and Naga Federal Army (NFA) in 1952 by Z A Phizo, attacks on villages and government officials, killings and destruction of properties became routine affairs in Naga Hills. It needs mention here that the insurgent group got full-fledged support from Burma, in addition to China and Pakistan. To counter this situation, the government took various stringent steps like opening police outposts in Naga Hills, intensified actions against NNC members, imposed Assam Disturbed Areas Act 1955, deployed army units in important places, and so on. Insurgencies with various demands have already emerged in other Northeastern states. When the government found that these actions were not able to contain the insurgencies in the Naga hills and its neighbouring states, these areas were declared as 'Disturbed Areas' and Armed Forces Special Powers Act (AFSPA), 1958 was enacted and imposed in such parts. This act gave enormous powers to armed forces such as carry out search operations and arrests without warrant, fire upon or otherwise use force even to the causing of death, destroy any arms dump or shelter, or any forceful action as deems suitable, but with caution and certain conditions. Needless to mention, these conditions were never followed, and the army and para military personnel acted according to their own whims, tyranny and killings of innocent people became routine affair without any redressing mechanism and accountability. Large scale violence continued in the whole of Naga Hills (known as Nagaland) which was part of Assam, and AFSPA was in force in the entire area.

For the suppression of subversive activities, maintenance of essential supplies and services and control of military requirements, the President of India issued the Nagaland Security Regulation, 1962 on April 11, 1962. Thereafter, the State of Nagaland came in to existence on 1st December 1963. However, the underground activities by the insurgents continued unabated. There had been several peace accords between the government and the insurgent groups. But, the AFSPA once imposed in 1958 has never been repealed in Nagaland and continuously got extended. As of late, the Centre extended the tag of 'disturbed area' and thus AFSPA in

Nagaland with effect from 30th June 2019 for next six months, and thereafter on 30th December 2019 declared the whole of Nagaland as a "disturbed" area under the Armed Forces (Special Powers) Act, 1958, for a further period of six months.

Culture and Corruption in Nagaland

Culture

'Naga' is a broad term and under its ambit comes different Naga tribes. It is estimated that there are 35 major Naga tribes spread across Arunachal Pradesh, Assam, Manipur, Nagaland and Myanmar. It is by amalgamating all these Naga dominated areas into one that they consider to establish 'Greater Nagalim'. As per the Department of Personnel and Administrative Reforms, there are 14 officially recognized Naga Tribes in Nagaland[16] viz., Angami, Ao, Chakhesang, Chang, Khiamniungan, Konyak, Lotha, Phom, Pochury, Rengma, Sangtam, Sumi, Yimchungru, and Zeliang. Each Naga tribe has its cultural identities that they inherited from their ancestors. According to Chasie (2005)[17], each Naga tribe has its own language, and sometimes several dialects within the language. But they all belong to the Tibeto-Burman family. Horam (1975, p.28) mentions that the Nagas belong to the 'Indo-Mongoloid' tribes, viz., the Himalayan tribes. There are all possibilities that once up on a time Nagas were a wandering community, who later on settled down permanently.

Nagas believe in strong ties among members of their family which is essential for building a strong society. They have the patrilineal system, whereby the clan identity is found through males. Before British annexed Naga Hills with Assam, each Naga village was independent, and its administration was carried out

[16] List of recognized Naga tribes in Nagaland, https://dpar.nagaland.gov.in/list-of-recognized-nagascheduled-tribes-certificate/

[17] Chasie, Charles, 2005; Nagaland in Transition; Indian International Centre, Quarterly journal, Vol. 32, No. 2/3. https://www.jstor.org/stable/23006032?seq=1#metadata_info_tab_contents

by a council headed by one or two headmen who were respected and had influence in the society. There was no centralized system. Being an independent entity, each village had its own separate norms and customary laws which were self sufficient to control the behaviour of the people. There was democracy in true sense. According to Nienu (2015, p.114), the types of village government included theocratic set ups (Konyaks), autocratic chieftains (Semas) and democracies ranging from the well organized system of the Aos to the purest form of democracy (all other tribes).

The centre of Naga life and culture used to revolve around his family, the clan, land and the village, and he does not like these to be meddled by an outsider. Land is regarded as his life-giver. Verrier (1961)[18] touches the heart of a Naga when he says that the basic interest of every Naga is in his family, the clan, the *khel,* the village. This is what he regards as his culture which must not be interfered with. He is passionately attached to his land, his system of land-tenure, the arrangements for the government of his village, the organization of cultivation, the administration of tribal justice through the village and tribal courts. There were two important institutions that every Naga village subscribes to – Ariju (Morung) and Peli Krotho. Ariju is the nerve center of the Naga village, a multipurpose organisation. It is the seat of the village government, a military complex, a learning center, a community center, and a sacred place for conducting certain rituals for the community (Nienu, 2015, p.121). Peli Krotho is a form of the Naga agrarian labour exchange system, a collaboration of groups of people working together in each other's fields on a rotation basis, to produce better effect (p. 125). Each household help the other in their fields and in other areas whenever help is needed. The beneficiary reciprocates to the former when work is being done in his field. In this way, turn by turn, everybody helps each other to complete the agricultural works. In addition to work in fields, when a house is in need of additional hands to accomplish certain work, members of Peli Krotho come forward to extend help. Most

[18] Verrier Elwin, 1961; Nagaland, Research Department, Adviser's Secretariat, Shillong.

of the Naga tribes had separate houses used as Ariju (Morung), and those did not have, used the house of the village chief. While Ariju can be considered as the epicentre of Naga culture, Peli Krotho is principally focussing on helping each other in economic activities and other social purposes.

In olden days, Nagas emphasized on accumulating wealth and becoming rich through honest and legal ways. Nagas did not give respect to an individual who has hoarded wealth through dishonest or illegal means. As everybody was very much concerned about their prestige in the society, hardly anybody engaged in any kind of untruthful activity. At the ssame time, the possession of each individual is known to everybody as they emphasized transparency. Hence, virtues like truthfulness, loyalty, respect to elders and cooperation were given importance in rearing a child by the Nagas. Hills, forests and rivers were revered and they strongly believed in supernatural powers.

Christianity, western education, moving outside of their villages, witnessing and adopting new customs, have knowingly and unknowingly brought several changes in their culture. While the young people seem more fascinated towards such 'changes' in the modern times, the elders look at it with certain level of suspicion, frowningly and awfully. However, they are incapable of preventing such changes. At the same time, a good number of youngsters who are not happy with the eroding of their traditional customs and habits, are serious in devising ways and means to revive and preserve the customs of those good old days. They want to preserve their legends, stories, customs, festivals, songs, habits, rituals, interpersonal relationships, social and economic interactions and interpretations, and so on. On the other hand, it is also a fact that everything in its entirety cannot be preserved because change is the rule of nature. So, what the human can do is to make maximum efforts in the areas that are possible and mentally prepare to accept the changes that are happening, according to nature's law.

Having said this, today the reality is that there has been a sea-change in the Naga society. The concern for the community existed earlier has given way to individualism, and everyone is interested to accumulate wealth for themselves. The Naga struggle that started with ethics and ideology have given way to vested interests, internecine conflict, and in the name of 'taxes' extortion is happening in a massive way. To put in Temsula Ao's[19] words, "It was as though a great cataclysmic upheaval threw up many realities for the Nagas within which they are still struggling to settle for a legitimate identity.... Nagaland's story of the struggle for self-determination started with high idealism and romantic notions of fervent nationalism, but it somehow got re-written into one of disappointment and disillusionment because it became the very thing it sought to overcome" (p. x). The Naga society which was once considered to be simple and humble by the people has not remained the same today and struggling in the inequalities.

Corruption

Corruption has become a menace in the government offices in Nagaland. As common people have to interact with public offices in their day to day life, they have no option but to fall prey to it. There are various causes for the spread of corruption. The first and foremost is the approach of people towards this evil. In the words of Ezung (2012)[20], the most important factor causing corruption is found to be "the attitude of the people". And the attitude is an important part of the culture. Thus, the culture is evolved in such a way that corruption has been accepted as a way of life. Ezung's study of corruption in Nagaland found that "misutilization or misappropriation of government funds, bribery and nepotism, abuse of power and corrupt activities of the public in the state was very high and continues unabated. Corruption was also found to be curtailing the developmental fund from the actual amount sanctioned, increasing inequality in society and employing

[19] Temsula Ao, 2006; These Hills Called Home: Stories from the War Zone, Zubaan, New Delhi, p. x.

[20] Ezung, Zarenthung T, 2012; Corruption and its Impact on Development: A Case study of Nagaland, International Journal of Rural Studies (IJRS), vol. 19, no. 1, April.

unskilled and inefficient manpower" (p.1). Some of the causes of corruption in Nagaland identified by Ezung were complacent attitude of the people, donation culture, expectation for jobs, election system, black sheep among freedom fighters, collection of donations by the NGOs, unprincipled nongovernmental organization leaders, expectation to get the work done faster, practice of sanctifying corrupt officials by his community, and so on (p. 2-3).

Quoting the Governor of Nagaland, Wouters[21] (p. 170) mentions, "Nagaland is rich, but because of corruption the people are poor". Wouters adds, "In Nagaland corruption is not the exception but the very norm of government and governance. It does not just exist, but thrives".

According to Purkayastha (2007)[22], "Some of the local politicians have developed a vested interest in the violence to continue so that there is continuous inflow of funds to the states in the name of controlling the insurgency" (p. 52). This shows the interest of those in power to keep the insurgency 'alive' and how it is linked with corruption.

The Morung Express conducted an opinion survey (2011)[23] on the level of corruption in Nagaland by asking a question, "Do you believe that Nagaland is the 'corruption capital' of India?" The replies received are put below in a concise way:

(a) When the level of corruption in Nagaland is compared, it may not be as big as observed in other states. But, if the exact amount Nagaland receives from Delhi and spending for the actual purpose is analyzed, then certainly it could see that this is the most corrupt state,

[21] Wouters, Jelle JP, 2018; In the Shadows of Naga Insurgency, Oxford University Press, New Delhi.

[22] Purkayastha, Rakhal, 2007; 3rd Presentation, *in* Roots of Insurgency in Northeast India, Ed. Bhattacharjee JB, Akansha Publishing House, New Delhi.

[23] The Morung Express, 2011; Do you believe that Nagaland is the 'corruption capital' of India?, 7th November http://morungexpress.com/do-you-believe-nagaland-corruption-capital-india

(b) There is organized looting of public money by the ministers, MLAs and government servants,

(c) In other states people used to raise voice against rampant corruption, whereas in Nagaland the corrupt have immense power, get high 'respect' wherever they go, people simply could not dare them, and the corrupt just get away with it. All these led to the loosing of real Naga identity.

"The whole region of Nagaland is plagued by corruption. Corruption is a way of life and has become rampant in the State. Corrupt activities in the level of service delivery systems, the level of embezzlement of public funds, increment of bribery in tender issues, favoritism, and electoral fraud and so on can prove that corruption is rampant in the State. Ample opportunities are available for corruption and corrupt offenders are unlikely to be caught and punished. Since corruption has found its way to every cell of our government at a very rapid pace, only politicians and bureaucrats know where this huge amount of money came from and how it will be repaid" (Northeast Window)[24].

Nagas worship 'wealth' as their god and believe that economic development (growth) is the solution to all problems. Success is counted in terms of high salaried job. Involvement in corruption and destruction of nature is their hobby (Matters India)[25].

The latest big disclosure of corruption in Nagaland was the exposure of MKR Pillai, a Nagaland cop turned Kerala billionaire who built Rs 4000 crore worth business empire with his Sreevalsam Business group that was involved in multi business operations like real estate, hotels, jewellery, shopping malls, school and private money lending (Jeemon Jacob, 2017)[26].

[24] Northeast Window, 2018; Dynamics of Political Corruption in Nagaland, 10th February http://www.thenortheastwindow.com/2018/02/dynamics-political-corruption-nagaland/

[25] Matters India, 2014; Present Situation of Nagaland, 15th December http://mattersindia.com/2014/12/present-situation-of-nagaland/

[26] Jeemon Jacob, 2017; The story of Nagaland cop who turned

In 2015, Nagaland Vigilance Commission has established misappropriation of funds amounting to Rs 12.79 crore, meant for disabled children by the officials of the state's School Education department (Economic Times, 2015)[27].

According to Nagaland Congress President, K Therie (2018), "80 per cent or more voters in Nagaland consider corruption as a normal system" (PTI)[28]. This shows the link between culture and corruption.

The Nagaland Governor P B Acharya[29], on the occasion of observing vigilance awareness week on the theme 'eradicate corruption- build a new India', called for increased transparency, fairness, equity, competitiveness and leveraging of technology in all areas of functioning by the government. Acharya explained that corruption in governance took different forms like bribery, extortion, blackmail, fraud, embezzlement, misappropriation of public goods, nepotism and cronyism. Corruption had progressively increased and was now rampant in the society, besides becoming a way of life. Society itself had accepted and embraced corruption as no one questioned those who live beyond their means (UNI, 2018).

Similarly, Nagaland State Vigilance Commissioner (SVC)

Kerala billionaire, India Today,14th June https://www.indiatoday.in/india/kerala/story/nagaland-cop-turned-kerala-billionaire-mkr-pillai-sreevalsam-business-group-982715-2017-06-14

[27] Economic Times, 2015; Misappropriation of funds worth Rs 12.79 crore for disabled children in Nagaland, 19th February https://economictimes.indiatimes.com/news/politics-and-nation/misappropriation-of-funds-worth-rs-12-79-crore-for-disabled-children-in-nagaland/articleshow/46299832.cms? from=mdr

[28] PTI, 2018; Nagaland Congress mocks PM promise of corruption-free govt; in company with 'most corrupt leaders'; PTI@moneycontrolcom https://www.moneycontrol.com/news/india/nagaland-congress-mocks-pm-promise-of-corruption-free-govt-in-company-with-most-corrupt-leaders-2515149.html

[29] UNI, 2018; Nagaland Governor calls people to fight corruption, 29th October, http://www.uniindia.com/nagaland-governor-calls-people-to-fight-corruption/east/news/ 1391805.html

Mayang Lima[30] said that corruption did lot of damage to society by destabilising communities, hindering economic growth and destroying ethics of democracy and political development (Nagaland Post, 2018). The concern and disquietness expressed by the Governor and the SVC truly indicates the extent to which corruption has become widespread in Nagaland, admitting that this menace had become a part of their culture and people had accepted it. To put it in another way, such a statement from the head of the state and SVC points to the culture of corruption prevailing in Nagaland.

The same views echoed by the former Chief Minister and Governor of Nagaland Dr. SC Jamir[31], when he lamented that lack of governance and fragmentation of groups have "broken" the "strong walls built by leaders of yesterday" leaving the people in a "political quagmire." Addressing the 38th Foundation Day cum Day of Prayer at Discipleship Bible College, Dimapur as the Guest of Honour, Dr. Jamir said that owing to mismanagement at all levels, all developments were at standstill thereby landing the state in economic doldrums, and that the "monster of corruption" had devoured the society (The Morung Express, 2019).

There can be lot many reasons for evolving such a culture that directly or indirectly encouraged people to involve in corruption. One of them is the behaviour of their own political leaders. The people in Nagaland has been witnessing defection, horse trading, changing parties, joining hands with enemies, and different manipulations for the actors' personal conveniences and economic benefits. Witnessing such immoral and unethical happenings over a period of time, people imbibed these ideas and accepted that it was 'permissible' for them too to engage in corrupt practices

30 Nagaland Post, 2019; Corruption has hampered overall growth: SVC, 29th October http://www.nagalandpost.com/corruption-has-hampered-overall-growth-svc/184184.html

31 The Morung Express, 2019; Walls of Nagaland are broken: Dr SC Jamir, 20th August http://morungexpress.com/walls-nagaland-are-broken-dr-sc-jamir

for their own gains. In the words of Chandrika[32] (2004), "for the politicians of Nagaland the personal gain and prestige were greater than their party's principles, ideologies, discipline, and loyalties... Politicians talked a lot about people's welfare and assured people of giving good as well as stable government... the growing lust for power among the Naga politicians and their inclination towards obtaining maximum wealth and high prestige shattered people's democratic faith" (p. 159-60). Whichever way the politicians had twisted and turned the law for their personal gains, amassed wealth and thereby social status, it is possible that gradually it became a part of their culture. Simultaneously, as people saw it, the same culture was imbibed by many and it further strengthened the culture of corruption.

Quoting Ntsalumo Kayoing, Chandrika (2004) further mentions, "political powers and ministerial offices were abused and completely misused for the personal pleasure and material gains by the politicians of Nagaland and the state bureaucrats at the expense of the common public of the Nagas" (p. 161). One after the other Nagaland got corrupt government through their corrupt leaders. The money pumped in by the Central government in the name of containing insurgency without accountability gave further boost to corruption in the state. Chandrika supplements, "The flow of easy money in Nagaland brought more and more corruption. The Nagas began to fall easy prey to money" (p. 161). Along with politicians and bureaucrats, government officials and NGOs, who were supposed to prevent corruption, rather became a part of it that evolved a corrupt culture.

According to Chandrika, "People have also become greedy, corrupt, selfish and short-sighted. Their demands during elections are 'pork, supply orders, government jobs', and this tendency has given birth 'to corruption, frustration, and social turmoil'... "the political drama being staged currently in Nagaland is unfortunate, the reflection of the malignancy of the attitudes, values and trends of the Naga society".

[32] Chandrika Singh, 2004; Naga Politics: A Critical Account, Mittal Publications, New Delhi.

It is not that the Nagas are unaware that corruption is bad, still they use all unfair means to accomplish their desires. For this, they cannot be blamed because every field is absolutely corrupt and they are fully conscious that any preventive mechanism in the state is designed in such a way that it can be manipulated by the authorities at their will.

Literature on Naga culture are plenty (Horam[33] 1975 & 1977[34], Robert Tiba[35] 2013, Nienu[36] 2015, Chandola[37] 2013, Temjensosang[38] 2013, Gogoi[39] 2016, Misra[40] 2014, Bhattacharjee[41] 2007, Anand[42] 1981, Luithui & Haksar[43] 1984, Mate[44] 2014). Discourse of these literature are on different dimensions of Naga cultures like family bond, customs, behaviour, festivals, songs, dance, work, food, gods, land, laws, codes, corruption, way of life and so on. But they

[33] Horam Mashangthei, 1975; Naga Polity, BR Publishing Corporation, Delhi.

[34] Horam Mashangthei, 1977; Social and Cultural Life of Nagas, BR Publishing Corporation, Delhi.

[35] Robert Tiba (Robert Tiba foundation), 2013; History and Culture of the Maram Nagas, Akansha Publishing House, New Delhi.

[36] Nienu V, 2015; Naga Cultural Milieu, Dorylus Publishing Group, California.

[37] Chandola Harish, 2013; The Naga Story: First Armed Struggle in India, Chicken neck, New Delhi.

[38] Temjensosang, 2013; Self-Governing Institutions of Nagas, Akansha Publishing House, New Delhi.

[39] Gogoi Dilip, 2016; Unheeded Hinterland, Routledge, New York

[40] Misra Udayon, 2014; India's North-East, Oxford University Press, New Delhi.

[41] Bhattacharjee JB, 2007; Roots of Insurgency in Northeast India, Akansha Publishing House, New Delhi.

[42] Anand VK, 1981; Insurgency and Counter Insurgency, Deep & Deep Publications, New Delhi.

[43] Luithui Luingam & Haksar Nandita, 1984; Nagaland File, Lancer International, New Delhi.

[44] Mate, S Haukhanlian, 2014; Traditional Administrative System and Customary Laws of the Thangkhals, Akansha Publishing House, New Delhi.

primarily do not discuss whether the cultural elements have got any link with corruption in the Naga public life.

In this context, the **Hypothesis** of this chapter is:

Null Hypothesis: *Cultural factors do not promote corruption in public offices in Nagaland.*

Alternative Hypothesis: *Cultural factors do promote corruption in public offices in Nagaland.*

To prove the hypothesis, let us examine whether there is any relationship between culture and corruption in public offices in the state.

The Relationship between Culture and Corruption in Naga Public Life

As mentioned in the first chapter, this study principally used primary as well as secondary data to identify whether there is any link between culture, corruption, and insurgency. This chapter first deals with the primary data (field work), and thereafter secondary data (literature) to find the relationship between culture and corruption in Nagaland. Chapter 3 deals with the relationship between corruption and insurgency. Here, the researcher wants to emphasize that the findings of this study cannot be used to make any generalizations due to the diminutive size of the sample data, covering only one area of the society, i.e. academic, and various other limitations.

Primary Data Analysis

The field work started with identifying the data collection method, giving a serious thought on the complexity of the topic, (un)willingness of the respondents from various departments to cooperate, constraints of time and resources, and other limitations. Then it was decided to use purposive sampling method. This is a type of nonprobability sampling in which researchers rely on their own judgment when choosing members of the population to participate in their study. Subjective methods are used to decide which elements should be included in the sample[45]. Keeping in mind several aspects of research methodology, systematic efforts were made to ensure that the sample attain the nearest accuracy of random sampling. Questionnaire schedule was prepared with 5-point Likert scale answers (i.e. 'Strongly Disagree' - SD, 'Disagree' - D, 'Can't Say' - CS, 'Agree' - A, and 'Strongly Agree' – SA. The value given to SD is 1, D – 2, CS – 3, A – 4, & SA – 5 in order to explain the reliability of the data). The questionnaire was administered to 142 respondents, who were from Nagaland University and Shillong (NEHU University campus). The data thus collected was analysed and interpreted using SPSS, in which principally Mean, Standard deviation, Skewness, Kurtosis, Chi square and P-value were found out.

Before going to its analysis, let us examine the background of the respondents such as place, age, gender, marital status, and occupation.

Place

Table 2.1

Place	*No. of respondents*	*Percentage*
Kohima (NU)	136	96
Shillong (NEHU)	6	4
Total	142	100

As elucidated in the table, 96% of the respondents are from Kohima (that include Masters' students and academicians of Nagaland University, and government employees), and 4% of the respondents are students basically from Nagaland and presently doing their Masters course at the North East Hills University (NEHU campus), Shillong.

45 Paul J. Lavrakas, 2008; Encyclopedia of Survey Research Methods, Sage. https://methods.sagepub.com/Reference/encyclopedia-of-survey-research-methods

Age group

As shown in table 2.13, majority (86%) of the respondents are in the age group of 21 and 30 years, which is followed by 11% (31 to 40 years), 1% in the age bracket of 41 to 50 years, and 2% between 51 and 60 years.

Table 2.2

Age group	*No. of respondents*	*Percentage*
21 to 30 years	122	86
31 to 40 years	16	11
41 to 50 years	1	1
51 to 60 years	3	2

Gender

Table 2.3

Gender	*No. of respondents*	*Percentage*
Female	115	81
Male	27	19

Table 2.14 shows that majority of the respondents (81%) are females and 19% males.

Marital status

It is found that 94% of the respondents are unmarried, 5% married and 1% divorced.

Table 2.4

Marital status	*No. of respondents*	*Percentage*
Unmarried	133	94
Married	8	5
Divorced	1	1

Occupation

Majority (79%) of the respondents are Masters' students, followed by government employees (13%) and academicians (8%). The reason behind choosing students in large number is that they are very much conscious about the happenings in their society and craving for serious change. Young minds are full of enthusiasm, innovative ideas, freely express their thoughts and they can lead the way to bring improvement in the culture and community, and embolden changes in the society.

Table 2.5

Occupation	*No. of respondents*	*Percentage*
Academicians	12	8
Government employees	18	13
Students	112	79

(a) When views of the respondents were sought on the statement, "People have accepted corruption as a way of life", 1% of the respondents 'Strongly disagreed' and 10% 'Disagreed' with the submission. Seven percent neither agreed nor disagreed, 64% 'agreed' and 18% 'Strongly agreed' with the statement. Thus, 82% are on the agreeing side with the statement.

Table 2.6

Answers	*No. of respondents*	*Percentage*
Strongly Disagree	1	1
Disagree	14	10
Can't say	10	7
Agree	91	64
Strongly Agree	26	18

Table 2.7

Variable 7	*1 SD*	*2 D*	*3 CS*	*4 A*	*5 SA*	$\bar{X}$ *mean*	*St. Dev*	*Skew*	*Kurt*	X^2 *Chi*	*P-value*
People have accepted corruption as a way of life	1	14	10	91	26	3.894	.839	-1.110	1.338	183.845	.000

It is observed that the mean value of responses is 3.895 which is more than the standard average, i.e. 3 at five point scale (Mean less than 3 shows that the respondents are strongly on disagreeing side, while greater than 3 indicate that they are on the agreeing side). The value of standard deviation is .839, which depicts less variation in the reply of the respondents. Generally, the mean would be greater than standard deviation and it indicates that more of the data is clustered about the mean, and that the data is reliable and secured. The skewness is -1.110 which points out that variation in the mean opinion is more inclined towards the higher side of mean score. The value of Kurtosis is 1.338 which is more than zero and it depicts that the distribution of opinion of respondents is laptykurtic, i.e. concentrated. (Kurtosis defines how heavily the tails of a distribution differ from the tails of a normal distribution, the acceptable limits lies between -1 and +1). The null hypothesis that people have not accepted corruption as a way of life is rejected as the value of Chi square is 183.845 and its P value is <0.0. Thus, it can be concluded that people have accepted corruption as a way of life. Here it needs to be mentioned that .000 must be taken as $p <$ .001, i.e null hypothesis is rejected (test is statistically significant). It has to be stated here that the corrupt would have the tendency to spend and gain.

While discussing this matter, a senior police officer lamented, "*People have accepted corruption as a way of life. Earlier Nagas were humble and honest. After the Statehood, in the initial stage, the state used to surrender the unused money. Later on, instead of surrendering, the politicians and government officials decided to 'utilize' the money and started 'preparing documents' accordingly. Gradually, more demands were put forward and more money was poured in, and division of money between politicians, bureaucrats, officials, contractors, insurgents and others in the hierarchical chain systematically happened. In the beginning there was some kind of hesitation and guilty conscious among them, but the passage of time taught them that they were masters of the money and they could manipulate it the way they wanted. Gradually, they felt 'authority and right' over such money, this attitude got embedded in their characters, became a part of their culture, and could not think of doing anything without getting something in return."*

This can be the case of urbanites, but what about the villagers? Have they also accepted corruption as a way of life? To this, a former IB official said, "*In the initial stage, no, but now the situation has changed. They know the quantum of money the politicians are getting. So, the people started to demand money from the politicians for each vote during elections, and the politicians fulfilled their demands. It is unimaginable the money being spent by them. When a candidate spends such huge money and wins the election he will be anxious to collect the money that was spent, as well as to accumulate further more for spending for the next election, and thus cling to power.*" It may be recalled that similar views were echoed by Chandrika Singh (2004), who said that there was a price for the votes – money, pork, liquor, jobs, etc. are the demands of the villagers.

(b) To examine whether the government employees favoured their family/clan members in official dealings, the respondents were asked to give their view on the statement, "Government officials/employees misuse their power to illegally favour their family/clan members". Twenty nine percent of the respondents 'Strongly agreed', while 62% 'Agreed' with this affirmation. Six percent were neutral, only 3% 'Disagreed', and nobody 'Strongly disagreed'. Thus, a major portion (91%) of the respondents believed that the public servants misused their power and illegally favoured their family/community members. It is a fact that Nagas have strong intra family/clan ties and they have internalized such values, and there is social pressures to implement such values. Thus, the internalization of such values and social pressures may be playing important role in giving priority to their near and dear ones. In the context of such strong family/clan bond, is it that they do not consider misusing official power as wrong?

Table 2.8

Answers	*No. of respondents*	*Percentage*
Strongly Disagree	-	-
Disagree	4	3
Can't say	8	6
Agree	89	62
Strongly Agree	41	29

Table 2.9

Variable 5	*1 SD*	*2 D*	*3 CS*	*4 A*	*5 SA*	$\overline{X}$ *mean*	*St. Dev*	*Skew*	*Kurt*	X^2 *Chi*	*P-value*
Government officials/employees misuse their power to illegally favour their family/clan members	-	4	8	89	41	4.176	.6555	-.811	1.902	130.732	.000

It is observed that the mean value of responses is 4.176 which is on the higher side of the standard average. The value of standard deviation is .6555 (variation is small), and skewness is -.811 which indicates that variation in the mean opinion is inclined towards the higher side. The value of Kurtosis is 1.902 which is higher than zero and it illustrates that the distribution of opinion of respondents is leptokurtic , i.e. concentrated. As the P-value is .000, the null hypothesis that the government officials/employees do not misuse their power to illegally favour their family/clan members is rejected. This shows that government officials/employees misuse their power to illegally favour their family/clan members. The principal reason could be that they give more importance to the family/clan ties, and all other factors are secondary.

(c) To substantiate further, another narration offered was, "A government official not doing illegal favours to his family/ clan would lose his prestige in his clan". While 25% respondents 'Strongly agreed,' 50% 'Agreed' with this declaration. Percentage of the respondents who said 'Can't say' was 8%, whereas 13% 'Disagreed', and 4% 'Strongly disagreed'. The point to be noted here is that a sizable part of the respondents (75%) have accepted this postulation.

Table 2.10

Answers	*No. of respondents*	*Percentage*
Strongly Disagree	6	4
Disagree	18	13
Can't say	12	8
Agree	71	50
Strongly Agree	35	25

Table 2.11

Variable 6	*1 SD*	*2 D*	*3 CS*	*4 A*	*5 SA*	$\bar{X}$ *mean*	*St. Dev*	*Skew*	*Kurt*	X^2 *Chi*	*P-value*
A government official not doing illegal favours to his family/clan would lose his prestige in his clan	6	18	12	71	35	3.781	1.085	-.970	.249	96.380	.000

It is observed that the mean value of responses is 3.781 which is higher than the standard average, i.e. three at five point scale. The value of standard deviation is 1.085 and skewness is -.970 which indicates that variation in the mean opinion is on the higher side. The value of Kurtosis is .249 which is higher than zero and it illustrates that the distribution of opinion of respondents is leptokurtic , i.e. concentrated. As the P-value is .000, the null hypothesis that the government official not doing illegal favours to his family/clan would not lose his prestige in his clan is rejected, and instead, the hypothesis that the government official not doing illegal favours to his family/clan would lose his prestige in his clan is accepted.

In the result of the previous statement (b), it is seen that 91% of the respondents agree on the misuse of official power to favour family/clan, whereas here 75% believe that an official not doing illegal favour to his family/clan loses his prestige amongst them. It is to be believed that the intra family/clan ties play a significant role in the life of Nagas, and to embolden it they may be giving less attention to their other activities. Still emerges a question – To whom the government employes are more loyal, towards the state, or the kinship and social bond? If it is the latter, why so? There can be several reasons, like the custom, imitation of others who are corrupt, big bribe, least risk of being caught, and several escape routes if caught. Moreover, the prevailing environment, and the proportion of people who follow corrupt ways may have its impact on human behaviour. In nutshell, it can be said that the traditional practice, way of functioning of the government machineries, opportunities, and the risk/reward estimation have significant role in influencing an individual whether to be corrupt or not. At the same time, is it not that this kind of loyalty seen in other societies?

Seleim and Bontis (2009)[46] found similar allegiance in other

[46] Ahmed Seleim & Nick Bontis, 2009; The relationship between culture and corruption: A cross-national study, Journal of Intellectual Capital, Vol. 10 No. 1, pp. 165-184, Emerald Group Publishing Limited. https://www.emerald.com/insight/content/doi/10.1108/14691930910922978/full/html)

societies too. They state that individual collectivism refers to the strength of ties within small groups such as family and close friends. In such societies, family members and close friends have strong expectations from each other. Quoting Getz, Volkema (2001) and Gomez-Mejia et al, (1998), Seleim and Bontis add that in collectivist cultures, networks of friends and families are more oriented towards creating strong relationships that facilitate illegal transactions. Therefore, family connections might encourage corruption.

(d) Has the respect the riches get anything to do with their approach towards corruption? To verify this, the respondents were administered the statement, "Those who accumulate wealth through any means are given high respect in the society". This assertion was 'Strongly agreed' by 30 % respondents and 'Agreed' by 55% respondents. Six percent chose 'Can't say' option, 9% 'Disagreed', while nobody 'Strongly disagreed' with the version.

Table 2.12

Answers	*No. of respondents*	*Percentage*
Strongly Disagree	1	1
Disagree	12	8
Can't say	9	6
Agree	78	55
Strongly Agree	42	30

Table 2.13

Variable 2	*1 SD*	*2 D*	*3 CS*	*4 A*	*5 SA*	$\bar{X}$ *mean*	*St. Dev*	*Skew*	*Kurt*	X^2 *Chi*	*P-value*
Those who accumulate wealth through any means are given high respect in society	1	12	9	78	42	4.042	.874	-1.116	1.249	142.296	.000

The mean value of responses is 4.042 which is higher than the standard average, i.e. three at five point scale. The value of standard deviation is .874 (small variation), and skewness is -1.116 which indicates that variation in the mean opinion is on the higher side. The value of Kurtosis is 1.249 which is higher than zero and it illustrates that the distribution of opinion of respondents is leptokurtic , i.e. concentrated. The null hypothesis that those who accumulate wealth through any means are not given high respect in society is rejected as the P-value of chi cquare is .000, and instead, the hypothesis that those who accumulate wealth through any means are given high respect in the society is accepted.

Here a big question – Is it genuine respect, or overpraise or hype for personal gains? A large number of respondents (85%) strongly agree/agree that those who accumulate wealth by any means are accorded high respect in the society. One of the easy ways to amass wealth beyond legitimate earning is corruption. Here, according to the respondents, 'high' respect is given to people who accumulate wealth, whatever be the means adopted by them. However, this cannot be the genuine respect in a society that was traditionally honest. The respect that is 'shown' to them are only flattery due to three reasons, (1) to gain some material benefits, (2) the fear that the disrespect shown tō them would invite troubles as the riches are powerful too, and (3) believing in 'end justifies the means'. In fact, they "are generally viewed as dishonest and untrustworthy. They are not seen as sacrificial and selfless leaders, but increasingly as selfish individuals whose philosophies of leadership and wealth are inconsistent with traditional Naga values and practices"[47]. Here it is also seen the consequence of high power distance existing in the society. Further, in several societies, the wealth is given high esteem and considered to be an important element for 'success' in life. The 'end justifies the means', and for achieving this 'end' the environment would have taught them to internalize such norms

[47] Venüsa Tinyi and Chothazo Nienu, 2018 ; Making Sense of Corruption in Nagaland: A Culturalist Interpretation, in Jelle J P Wouters and Zhoto Tunyi (Ed.) Democracy in Nagaland: Tribes, Traditions, and Tensions, Highlander Books, (p. 176), http://www.highlanderbooks.org

that permit to keep aside ethics and rules, and follow the majority. So, it may be possible that in the recent times the culture (or the individual approach) that supports 'accumulating wealth and achieving success' is a factor that encourages corruption in public offices.

(e) Another statement made was "Corruption is practiced in government offices in Nagaland", to which 46% respondents replied that they 'Strongly agreed' with the statement. While 51% of the respondents said that they 'Agreed' with this statement, 3% said that they 'Can't say' anything about this statement. There was nobody who 'Disagreed' or 'Strongly Disagreed' with this statement. Here it can be observed that 97% of the respondents were in favour of the statement, whereas 3% were neutral in their opinion. At the same time, it was worth mentioning that no respondent was against the statement.

Table 2.14

Answers	*No. of respondents*	*Percentage*
Strongly Disagree	-	-
Disagree	-	-
Can't say	4	3
Agree	72	51
Strongly Agree	66	46

Table 2.15

Variable 1	*1 SD*	*2 D*	*3 CS*	*4 A*	*5 SA*	$\overline{X}$ *mean*	*St. Dev*	*Skew*	*Kurt*	X^2 *Chi*	*P-Value*
Corruption is practiced in government offices in Nagaland	-	-	4	72	66	4.436	.551	-.259	.965	59.887	.000

The respondents' opinion about the statement 'Corruption is practiced in government offices in Nagaland' shows that the mean value of the opinion 4.436 is higher than the standard average, i.e. 3 at 5-point scale. The variation in the opinion is .551, which depicts less variation in the reply of the respondents. The skewness is recorded at -.250, which indicates that majority responses are inclined towards the higher side of mean score. The value of Kurtosis is .965 which depicts that the distribution of opinion of respondents is laptykurtic, i.e. concentrated. The null hypothesis that corruption is not practised in the government offices is rejected as chi square =59.887 and its p value is <0.0. Thus, it can be concluded that corruption is practised in the public offices in Nagaland.

(f) To another related statement "There is 'culture of corruption' in government offices in Nagaland", nobody 'strongly disagreed', while 2% 'disagreed'. 10% of the respondents replied 'can't say', whereas 63% 'agreed' and 25% 'strongly agreed' to this statement. So, if we look at the agreeing side, it is noticed that a majority (88%) of the respondents assented with the postulation, while only 2% differed. If we look at the results of this and the previous statement, a difference of 9% respondents (97-88=9) on the compliance side is observed, in which at its lower level is 88%, which is certainly a major chunk of the respondents.

Table 2.16

Answers	*No. of respondents*	*Percentage*
Strongly Disagree	-	-
Disagree	3	2
Can't say	14	10
Agree	89	63
Strongly Agree	36	25

The responses to the statement, "there is culture of corruption in government offices in Nagaland" has the mean value of 4.112, which is more than the standard average, i.e. three at five point scale. The value of standard deviation is .653 and skewness is -.582, which indicates that variation in the mean opinion is inclined towards higher side of the mean. The value of Kurtosis is 1.140 which is more than zero and it depicts that the distribution of

Table 2.17

Variable 8	*1 SD*	*2 D*	*3 CS*	*4 A*	*5 SA*	*$\overline{X}$ mean*	*St. Dev*	*Skew*	*Kurt*	*X^2 Chi*	*P. Value*
There is culture of corruption in government offices in Nagaland	-	3	14	89	36	4.112	.653	-.582	1.140	123.408	.000

opinion of respondents is leptokurtic or concentrated. Chi square is 1.140 and its P value is .000, and hence, the null hypothesis that there is no culture of corruption in government offices in Nagaland is rejected, and the alternative hypothesis that there is culture of corruption in government offices in Nagaland is accepted.

During the field work, one of the senior professors said, "*the 'culture of corruption' in government offices has strong link with the 'Culture of Silence' that encourages corruption in different forms, and this is primarily due to the element of 'fear'. According to her, the culture of silence emenates owing to two reasons, (1) fear of the powerful, and (2) the community dictum. In the first situation, there is an element of fear in the minds of common people towards the powerful. They knew that the powerful could do anything with their money and political power. They have seen or heard from others how these 'elites' exercised their power that created fear in the minds of common people. As such, Nagas were humble and simple, but this kind of situation forced them to be submissive to those who are authoritative. In the second situation, there is community dictum to support people of their clan even if they did wrongs, and this custom is practised amongst Nagas. Hence, people blindly follow this dictum even if they find that the person whom they are supporting is wrong. Another factor supports this phenomena is the strong clan ties, which is given high significance, and thereby simply agreeing without questioning.*"

When this point was discussed with a senior police officer,

he said, "*Since the intra-clan ties are strong, members of that clan/tribe should not raise voice against anybody in the same clan who is involved in any illegal act or crime. If such person has accumulated huge money (illegally), he gets high respect in his clan. Everybody disregards his wrong doings and looks only at his money, power and influence. Another facet of culture of corruption is that anybody donating huge funds are invited as chief guest of any function.*"

Offering a cultural reason for such culture of silence and corruption, Venusa and Chotazo[48] mention, "Within Naga culture, any talk that might embarrass or shame other persons was shunned or discouraged." Hence, "'holding back one's tongue' created a fertile ground for corruption". But, the query is why the Naga leaders do not raise voice against such vice? Is it that they want to continue with it under the garb of 'honourable' culture that does not allow pointing out wrongs of others ?

(g) Another related exposition offered to the respondents was "People prefer such government jobs where there is opportunity to make extra illegal money". The table below explicits that nobody 'strongly disagreed' to this opinion, while 9% of the respondents 'disagreed'. Those opted 'Can't say' is 29%, those 'agreed' is 51%, and 11% 'strongly agreed'. As seen in the previous theme, majority (62%) are on the agreeing side. Here, a sizable number (29%) of respondents are wavering in their belief. However, the findings point out one more factor that causes corruption in public offices.

Table 2.18

Answers	*No. of respondents*	*Percentage*
Strongly Disagree	-	-
Disagree	13	9
Can't say	41	29
Agree	72	51
Strongly Agree	16	11

[48] Venüsa Tinyi and Chothazo Nienu, 2018 ; Making Sense of Corruption in Nagaland: A Culturalist Interpretation, *in* Jelle J P Wouters and Zhoto Tunyi (Ed.) Democracy in Nagaland: Tribes, Traditions, and Tensions, Highlander Books, (p. 171), http://www.highlanderbooks.org

Table 2.19

Variable 3	*1 SD*	*2 D*	*3 CS*	*4 A*	*5 SA*	$\bar{X}$ *mean*	*St. Dev*	*Skew*	*Kurt*	X^2 *Chi*	*P-value*
People prefer such government jobs where there is opportunity to make extra illegal money	-	13	41	72	16	3.640	.801	-.345	-.257	63.352	.000

The mean value of responses is 3.640 which is on the higher side of the standard average. The value of standard deviation is .801 (small variation), and skewness is -.345 which indicates that variation in the mean opinion is inclined towards higher side of mean. The value of Kurtosis is -.257 which is lower than zero and it illustrates that the distribution of opinion of respondents is platykurtic , i.e. scattered. The null hypothesis that people do not prefer such government jobs where there is opportunity to make extra illegal money is rejected as the P-value is .000, and instead, the hypothesis that people prefer such government jobs where there is opportunity to make extra illegal money is accepted. In Nagaland, as in other parts of the country, there is high competition for government jobs, and in this, as per the respondents' view, the job that enables to make extra illegal money is highly preferred.

At this point, it is very necessary to mention about the 'backdoor entry' system (which is illegal) existing in Nagaland. There had been complaints against the backdoor recruitment by the Police department, NPSC, etc. and those involved were from cities, towns and rural areas. When asked, a senior police officer said, "*Everybody knows about the corruption and the backdoor entry methods, irrespective they are from cities, towns or villages, and they have accepted corruption as a way of life. Further, the interaction of the villagers with the Block Development Offices has brought about massive changes in their approaches and value system. For them, corruption in its different forms has become a common phenomena, accepted it, and become an integral part of their culture.*" Here also, the small number of data shows that irrespective of urban or rural area, the link between culture and corruption, and culture of corruption in public offices are common facts.

(h) To another comment, "Vigilance & Anti Corruption agency in Nagaland is able to containing corruption", 8% 'Strongly disagreed', while 39% 'Disagreed' with the opinion. 35% of the respondents chose 'Can't say', 17% 'agreed', and 1% 'Strongly agreed' with the enunciation. Here, 18% approved the postulation, but 47% disapproved the explanation, i.e. the agency responsible for preventing corruption in government offices has not been fully successful in its mission. Why has it become ineffective? As the culture of corruption has plagued the government machinaries, has it impacted the Vigilance & Anti Corruption too?

Table 2.20

Answers	*No. of respondents*	*Percentage*
Strongly Disagree	11	8
Disagree	55	39
Can't say	50	35
Agree	24	17
Strongly Agree	2	1

Table 2.21

Variable 4	*1 SD*	*2 D*	*3 CS*	*4 A*	*5 SA*	*$\overline{X}$ mean*	*St. Dev*	*Skew*	*Kurt*	*X^2 Chi*	*P-value*
Vigilance & Anti Corruption agency in Nagaland is able to contain corruption	11	55	50	24	2	2.654	.899	.207	-.438	77.225	.000

It is observed that the mean value of responses is 2.654 which is less than the standard average, i.e. three at five point scale. The value of standard deviation is .899 i.e. variation is small, and skewness is .207 which indicates that variation in the mean opinion is on the lower side. The value of Kurtosis is -.438 which is less than zero and it illustrates that the distribution of opinion of respondents is platykurtic, i.e. scattered. The Chi square value as a goodness of fit indicates that majority of the respondents have preferred to disagree with the statement. Further, this is strengthened by the P-value of .000, which shows that the test is statistically significant. Hence, it can be concluded that the Vigilance & Anti Corruption agency in Nagaland has not been fully successful to contain corruption.

Analysis of the findings of above given postulations point out a possible relationship between culture and corruption and further substantiated the existence of 'culture of corruption' in government offices in the State. The Vigilance & Anti corruption agency, which is established to control corruption has found to be partially unsuccessful in its mission. However, acceptance of these findings is highly debatable as they are based only on a miniscule of sample literature and population. No doubt, this can be considered as a base for conducting a larger study that comprises more areas and populace.

(i) Another postulation given to the respondents was, "The Nagas carry in their minds the bitterness against the atrocities carried out on them by the Indian army in the beginning of insurgency". Three percent of the respondents 'strongly disagreed' and 22% 'agreed' with this comment, while a large number of respondents (36%) neither agreed nor disagreed. On the other hand, 29% 'agreed' and 10% 'strongly agreed' with this supposition. The percentage of respondents who strongly agreed/agreed (39%) is higher than those disagreed/strongly disagreed (25%) with this postulation. This shows that even after more than six decades they continue with the resentment against the Indian government. The reason could be principally due to the cruel atrocities unleashed on the common people by the Indian army. So, the respondents see that there is resentment among the people. It is very necessary for the governments to take appropriate measures to eradicate such resentments.

Table 2.22

Answers	*No. of respondents*	*Percentage*
Strongly Disagree	4	3
Disagree	32	22
Can't say	51	36
Agree	41	29
Strongly Agree	14	10

Table 2.23

Variable 16	*1 SD*	*2 D*	*3 CS*	*4 A*	*5 SA*	*$\bar{X}$ mean*	*St. Dev*	*Skew*	*Kurt*	*X^2 Chi*	*P-value*
The Nagas carry in their minds the bitterness against the atrocities carried out on them by the Indian army	4	32	51	41	14	3.204	.993	.019	-.602	52.296	.000

The mean value of responses is 3.204 which is on the higher side of standard average. The value of standard deviation is .993 (small variation), and skewness is .019 which indicates that variation in the mean opinion is inclined towards the lower side. The value of Kurtosis is -.602 which is lower than zero and it illustrates that the distribution of opinion of respondents is platykurtic , i.e. scattered. The null hypothesis that the Nagas do not carry in their minds the bitterness against the atrocities carried out on them by the Indian army is rejected as the P-value of chi square is .000, while the alternative hypothesis that the Nagas carry in their minds the bitterness against the atrocities carried out on them by the Indian army is accepted.

Similar opinion was pronounced by Jamir[49] (2016), "the Indian security forces began operations in a way that could very well be termed as a 'reign of terror'". This was futher defended by Wouters (2018)[50] when he said, "By the time Nagaland state was enacted, Nagas' experiences made them perceive of the postcolonial state as a repository of violence and despair, as an invading and ruthless force from which there was nothing truly to gain, only oppression and misery to reap" (p. 130). Regarding the funds being flowed in the state and looking at it as a compensation for the people's sufferings at the hands of the Indian army, Wouter quotes a villager, "In any case, it is high time for India to compensate us for making our life horrible for so long". All these echoe the voices of bitter experiences people had in the past and that they still carry in their minds.

(j) Another statement offered to the respondents was, "The Nagas are loyal to the Indian government", to which 1% respondents 'strongly disagreed', while 11% 'disagreed'. A good number of respondents (44%) 'agreed', 7% 'strongly agreed', while 37% were neutral. As a whole, it can be said that the Nagas are loyal to the Indian government. It needs to be remembered that the NSCN (IM) & (K) are still making demands to have separate flag and constitution for Nagaland, in spite of the fact that NSCN (IM) had signed a framework agreement with the Indian government in 2015 to work for bringing peaceful settlement to the issue. However, a fruitful result has not come yet.

[49] Jamir SC, 2016; A Naga's Quest for Fulfillment, Bhubaneswar, Apurba, p. 121-122

[50] Wouters, Jelle JP, 2018; In the Shadows of Naga Insurgency, Oxford University Press, New Delhi.

Table 2.24

Answers	*No. of respondents*	*Percentage*
Strongly Disagree	1	1
Disagree	15	11
Can't say	53	37
Agree	63	44
Strongly Agree	10	7

Table 2.25

Variable 20	*1 SD*	*2 D*	*3 CS*	*4 A*	*5 SA*	$\bar{X}$ *mean*	*St. Dev*	*Skew*	*Kurt*	X^2 *Chi*	*P-value*
Nagas are loyal to the Indian govern-ment	1	15	53	63	10	3.464	.804	-.298	-.081	108.141	.000

The mean value of responses is 3.464 which is higher than the standard average. The value of standard deviation is .804 (variation is small), and skewness is -.298 which indicates that variation in the mean opinion is inclined towards the higher side. The value of Kurtosis is -.081 which is lower than zero and it illustrates that the distribution of opinion of respondents is platykurtic , i.e. scattered. As the P-value of chi square is .000, the null hypothesis that the Nagas are not loyal to the Indian government is rejected, and the alternative hypothesis that the Nagas are loyal to the Indian government is accepted.

A look at both the above tables convinces that a good number of respondents have opted the neutral position (i.e. 36 & 37%), thereby making it very difficult to come to a clear conclusion. Other data give a loose impression that Nagas have bitter feelings against the Indian government. Nonetheless, they are loyal Indians.

So, what this small size of primary data show? Majority of the respondents feel that people have accepted corruption as a way of life, government officials/employees misused their power to illegally favour their family/clan members, and the government official not doing illegal favours to his family/clan would lose his prestige in his clan, and there is culture of corruption in government offices in Nagaland. A large number of the respondents have the impression that the Vigilance & Anti Corruption agency in Nagaland is partially incapable of containing corruption. Most of the respondents believe that those who accumulate wealth through any means are given high respect in the society, and people prefer such government jobs where there is opportunity to make extra illegal money. Some of the respondents consider that the Nagas carry in their minds the bitterness against the atrocities carried out on them by the Indian army, whereas a good number of respondents opine that the Nagas are loyal to the Indian government.

It needs to be emphasized here that though majority of the respondents are of the opinion that there exists a relationship between certain cultural elements and corruption, it is 'obscure' as the data is very small, and hence, could not be generalized.

Secondary data analysis

After the primary data analysis, the researcher wanted to examine the secondary data (qualitative) to verify whether it corroborates with the former or not. With this objective, a large number of literature were referred, and from these, 41 literature were identified using purposive sampling method, and these literature dealt with culture, corruption, and insurgency in Nagaland (thereby ensured that the relevant literature are selected). This part, being a qualitative one, the data were in the form of words, phrases, concepts, statements, opinions, themes, speeches, and so on that collected from books, journal articles, newspapers, websites and media. After collecting data, content analysis method was used, which helped to quantify and further analyse the presence, meanings and relationships of these words/concepts, etc. and its connection with culture, corruption and insurgency. After identifying these variables, its meanings were interpreted (Concept categorization), and frequency was found out. The Variables and its Interpretations are shown in table 2.26.

Table 2.26: Concept Categorization
(Variables and its Interpretations)

Code	*Variables*	*Interpretation*
1	Culture	What the people learnt, how they behave and live
2	Corrupt/ion	Corruption is prevalent in public offices
3	Practice	Public offices practice corruption
4	Accept	People accepted corruption as a part of life
5	Encourage/ favour	The culture is giving more emphasis to family/ community ties, but less to responsibilities in government offices. This leads to corruption getting embedded within local social bonds and kinship.
6	Attitude	Attitudinally people have accepted corruption in public offices
7	Values	Ethical values have gone down, people have become more materialistic
8	Norms	People have accepted the norm of bribing in public offices
9	Respect	Those who accumulate wealth through any means are given high respect in the society
10	Inequal	There is inequality in the society
11	Monster/ rampant	There is 'monster of corruption', or rampant corruption in public offices
12	Dishonest	Employees in government offices are dishonest in their work, misusing official power
13	Money/ wealth/ fund	Government officials are interested only in accumulating wealth by any means. Government funds are being misused, corruption made this easy
14	Tax/extort	Corruption has encouraged illegal 'tax'system and extortion in the name of insurgency
15	Internalize/ imbibe	Government officials have internalized corrupt practices from their office environment
16	Power/ful	People respect the powerful
17	Moral/ethical	Moral values have gone down in people's behaviour

18	Illegal/ illegitimate	People prefer such government jobs where there is opportunity to make extra illegal money
19	Feel	Indian government is pumping money in Nagaland to make the people feel Indian, but they do not have the sincere feeling of being Indian, they think that it is 'outside' money and (mis)use it as much as possible, they consider the money as 'compensation' for the sufferings they had with the hands of security forces in the past. "Deep down, we Nagas still want our independence" (Wouters, p. 169)
20	Belong	Nagas consider that they do not belong to India, but simply using the easy money, and corruption enables this.
21	Indian	Nagas have not forgotten the tyranny they suffered and do not want to be a part of India
22	Power distance	Power Distance exists in Nagaland, and corruption is one of the features of it
23	Insurgency / terror	There is insurgency in Nagaland, corruption is one of the factors that supported it
24	Influence	Insurgents influenced the government authorities so as to enable the former to accomplish their tasks easily, Corruption indirectly supported the insurgency

Variables and its Frequency are given in the table below:

Table 2.27: Variables and Frequency

Code	*Variables*	*Frequency*
1	Culture	1597
2	Corrupt/ion	1502
3	Practice	246
4	Accept	313
5	Encourage/ favour	86
6	Attitude	167
7	Values	485
8	Norms	280

9	Respect	203
10	Inequal	57
11	Monster/ rampant	23
12	Dishonest	13
13	Money/ wealth/fund	350
14	Tax/extort	121
15	Internalize/ imbibe	14
16	Power/ful	687
17	Moral/ethical	245
18	Illegal/ illegitimate	33
19	Feel	254
20	Belong	79
21	Indian	842
22	Power distance	378
23	Insurgency /terror	64
24	Influence	8

Table shows the frequency of the variables, highest being 'culture' and 'corruption', which are followed by 'Indian', 'Powerful', 'Values', 'Power distance', 'Money/wealth', 'Accept', 'Norms', 'Feel', 'Practice', 'Moral', 'Respect'', and so on.

On the basis of the aforesaid tables, correlation between different variables was established using Pearson Correlation tool, the result of which is shown in the below tables. Some researchers may argue that secondary data cannot be used for finding correlation between different variables. But, this researcher contends that what is wrong in making an attempt to find a distinct model. After all, data from the secondary sources are the result of efforts of various researchers.

Table 2.29 shows the correlation between different variables. It indicates that culture has significant correlation (p value <0.05) with Practice (0.786), Accept (0.429), Attitude (0.854), Value (0.726), Norm (0.722), Respect (0.567), Inequal (0.725), Monster/ rampant (0.540), Money/wealth (0.590), Tax/extort (0.669), Powerful (0.752), Moral/ethical (0.928), Feel (0.873), and Belong (0.567). (For the interpretations/meanings of the variables, refer Table- 2.26). On the other hand, the relationship between variables

Table 2.28: Descriptive Statistics

	Mean	*Std. Deviation*	*N*
Culture	38.95	101.568	41
Corrupt/ion	36.63	73.919	41
Practice	6.00	11.378	41
Accept	7.63	17.687	41
Encourage/favour	2.10	4.369	41
Attitude	4.07	9.740	41
Value	11.83	23.048	41
Norm	6.83	16.203	41
Respect	4.95	14.491	41
Inequal	1.39	3.137	41
Monster/rampant	.56	1.205	41
dishonest	.32	.879	41
Money/wealth/fund	8.54	9.737	41
Tax/extort	2.95	5.912	41
Internalize/imbibe	.34	1.175	41
Power/ful	16.76	44.156	41
Moral/ethical	5.98	22.732	41
Illegal/illegitimate	.80	1.806	41
Feel	6.20	18.813	41
Belong	1.93	4.251	41
Indian	20.54	82.661	41
Power distance	9.22	48.535	41
Insurgency/terror	1.56	5.762	41
influence	.20	.511	41

culture and corruption is insignificant (0.174, p value 0.05) which indicates that the relationship is very scant.

2. Variable Corruption does not have strong correlation with any of the other variables. It is very pertinent to note that the study is trying to find out the relationship between corruption in government offices and culture, which is, however, missing here,

Table 2.29

Correlation

Pearson Correlation	1	2	3	4	5	6	7	8	9	10	11	12	13	14	15	16	17	18	19	20	21	22	23	24
1.Culture	1	.174	.786**	.429**	.266	.854**	.726**	.722**	.567**	.725**	.540**	.258	.590**	.669**	.037	.752**	.928**	.216	.873**	.567**	.134	.177	-.103	-.145
2.Corrupt/ion	.174	1	.135	-.012	-.019	-.081	.272	.159	-.044	.095	-.021	.144	.056	-.023	.213	.044	.038	.189	-.091	-.134	-.088	-.003	-.067	-.064
3.Practice	.786**	.135	1	.707**	.692**	.907**	.758**	.625**	.780**	.700**	.640**	.098	.631**	.800**	.032	.882**	.762**	.336*	.791**	.692**	.490**	.464**	-.135	-.151
4.Accept	.429**	-.012	.707**	1	.866**	.693**	.445**	.637**	.939**	.334*	.684**	.046	.636**	.768**	.250	.852**	.554**	.488**	.661**	.737**	.865**	.133	-.094	-.116
5.Encourage/ favour	.266	-.019	.692**	.866**	1	.573**	.378*	.379*	.854**	.349*	.573**	.070	.582**	.726**	.027	.755**	.342*	.554**	.449**	.692**	.897**	.294	-.132	-.177
6.Attitude	.854**	-.081	.907**	.693**	.573**	1	.733**	.730**	.758**	.725**	.648**	.137	.655**	.859**	.105	.887**	.888**	.288	.913**	.684**	.413**	.373*	-.113	-.154
7.Value	.726**	.272	.758**	.445**	.378*	.733**	1	.639**	.438**	.893**	.293	.114	.354*	.518**	.295	.604**	.589**	.093	.547**	.295	.122	.660**	-.142	-.199
8.Norm	.722**	.159	.625**	.637**	.379*	.730**	.639**	1	.668**	.452**	.582**	.111	.541**	.626**	.305	.733**	.783**	.227	.764**	.557**	.363*	.041	-.116	-.156
9.Respect	.567**	-.044	.780**	.939**	.854**	.758**	.438**	.668**	1	.388*	.808**	.078	.770**	.852**	-.002	.942**	.695**	.537**	.774**	.847**	.870**	.065	-.095	-.134
10.Inequal	.725**	.095	.700**	.334*	.349*	.725**	.893**	.452**	.388*	1	.278	.253	.392*	.585**	.132	.569**	.572**	.234	.520**	.295	.074	.678**	-.123	-.173
11.Monster/ rampant	.540**	-.021	.640**	.684**	.573**	.648**	.293	.582**	.808**	.278	1	.111	.660**	.702**	-.068	.807**	.704**	.408**	.724**	.657**	.626**	-.088	-.129	-.182
12.Dishonest	.258	.144	.098	.046	.070	.137	.114	.111	.078	.253	.111	1	.094	.099	.159	.081	.173	.308	.132	.194	-.049	-.036	-.100	-.141
13.Money/ wealth/ fund	.590**	.056	.631**	.636**	.582**	.655**	.354*	.541**	.770**	.392*	.660**	.094	1	.807**	-.134	.772**	.665**	.575**	.689**	.719**	.605**	-.066	.079	-.001
14.Tax/extort	.669**	-.023	.800**	.768**	.726**	.859**	.518**	.626**	.852**	.585**	.702**	.099	.807**	1	-.008	.903**	.758**	.650**	.790**	.740**	.649**	.215	-.091	-.137
15.Internalize/ imbibe	.037	.213	.032	.250	.027	.105	.295	.305	-.002	.132	-.068	.159	-.134	-.008	1	-.020	-.030	-.003	-.055	-.090	-.069	.224	-.081	-.114

16.Power/ful	.752**	.044	.882**	.852**	.755**	.887**	.604**	.733**	.942**	.569**	.807**	.081	.772**	.903**	-.020	1	.851**	.468**	.872**	.777**	.707**	.206	-.062	-.104
17.Moral/ethical	.928**	.038	.762**	.554**	.342*	.888**	.589**	.783**	.695**	.572**	.704**	.173	.665**	.758**	-.030	.851**	1	.250	.959**	.622**	.299	.051	-.073	-.101
18.Illegal/ illegitimate	.216	.189	.336*	.488**	.554**	.288	.093	.227	.537**	.234	.408**	.308	.575**	.650**	-.003	.468**	.250	1	.265	.441**	.532**	-.053	-.095	-.174
19.Feel	.873**	-.091	.791**	.661**	.449**	.913**	.547**	.764**	.774**	.520**	.724**	.132	.689**	.790**	-.055	.872**	.959**	.265	1	.724**	.418**	.011	-.089	-.121
20.Belong	.567**	-.134	.692**	.737**	.692**	.684**	.295	.557**	.847**	.295	.657**	.194	.719**	.740**	-.090	.777**	.622**	.441**	.724**	1	.720**	-.073	-.084	-.120
21.Indian	.134	-.088	.490**	.865**	.897**	.413**	.122	.363*	.870**	.074	.626**	-.049	.605**	.649**	-.069	.707**	.299	.532**	.418**	.720**	1	-.038	-.050	-.064
22.Power distance	.177	-.003	.464**	.133	.294	.373*	.660**	.041	.065	.678**	-.088	-.036	-.066	.215	.224	.206	.051	-.053	.011	-.073	-.038	1	-.053	-.074
23.Insurgency/ terror	-.103	-.067	-.135	-.094	-.132	-.113	-.142	-.116	-.095	-.123	-.129	-.100	.079	-.091	-.081	-.062	-.073	-.095	-.089	-.084	-.050	-.053	1	.845**
24.Influence	-.145	-.064	-.151	-.116	-.177	-.154	-.199	-.156	-.134	-.173	-.182	-.141	-.001	-.137	-.114	-.104	-.101	-.174	-.121	-.120	-.064	-.074	.845**	1

**. Correlation is significant at the 0.01 level (2-tailed).

*. Correlation is significant at the 0.05 level (2-tailed).

i.e. such a direct relationship does not exist. At the same time, it has to be borne in mind that there are several other variables (e.g. Practice – meaning, public offices practice corruption; Accept – meaning, people accepted corruption as a part of life, etc.) that have got association with culture. This indicates that there is only a very thin relationship between culture and corruption, and that the corruption in public offices has major association with 'something else' than the culture.

3. Variable Practice has strong correlation with Culture, Accept, Encourage/favour, Attitude, Value, Norm, Respect, Inequal, Monster/rampant, Money/wealth/fund, Tax/extort, Powerful, Moral/ethical, Illegal, Feel, Belong, Indian, and Power distance.

4. Variable Accept has strong correlation with Culture, Practice, Encourage, Attitude, Value, Norm, Respect, Inequal, Monster/rampant, Money/wealth, Tax/extort, Powerful, Moral/ ethical, Illegal, Feel, Belong, and Indian.

5. Variable Encourage/favour has strong correlation with Practice, Accept, Attitude, Value, Norm, Powerful, Illegal, Feel, Belong, and Indian.

6. Variable Attitude has strong correlation with Culture, Practice, Accapt, Encourage, Value, Norm, Respect, Inequal, Monster/rampant, Money, Tax/extort, Powerful, Moral, Feel, Belong, and Indian.

7. Variable Value has strong correlation with Culture, Practice, Accept, Attitude, Norm, Respect, Inequal, Money, Tax, Powerful, Moral, Feel, and Power distance.

8. Variable Norm has strong correlation with Culture, Practice, Accept, Attutude, Value, Respect, Inequal, Monster, Money, Tax, Powerful, Moral, Feel, and Belong.

9. Variable Respect has strong correlation with Culture, Practice, Accept, Encourage, Attitude, Value, Norm, Inequal, Monster/rampant, Money, Tax/extort, Powerful, Moral, Illegal, Feel, Belong, and Indian.

10. Variable Inequal has strong correlation with Culture, Practice, Accept, Attitude, Value, Norm, Tax/extort, Powerful, Moral, Feel, and Power distance.

11. Variable Monster/rampant has strong correlation with Culture, Practice, Accept, Encourage, Attitude, Norm, Respect, Money, Tax, Powerful, Moral, Illegal, Feel, Belong, and Indian.

12. Variable Dishonest does not have strong correlation with any other variable.

13. Variable Money/wealth/fund has strong correlation with Culture, Practice, Accept, Encourage, Attitude, Norm, Respect, Monster/rampant, Tax, Powerful, Moral, Illegal, Feel, Belong, and Indian.

14. Variable Tax/extort has strong correlation with Culture, Practice, Accept, Encourage, Attitude, Value, Norm, Respect, Inequal, Monster/rampant, Money, Powerful, Moral, Illegal, Feel, Belong, and Indian.

15. Variable Internalize/imbibe has no strong correlation with any other variable.

16. Variable Powerful has strong correlation with Culture, Practice, Accept, Encourage, Attitude, Value, Norm, Respect, Inequal, Monster, Money, Tax, Moral, Illegal, Feel, Belong, and Indian.

17. Variable Moral/ethical has strong correlation with Culture, Practice, Accept, Attitude, Value, Norm, Respect, Inequal, Rampant, Money, Tax, Powerful, Feel, and Belong.

18. Variable Illegal/illegitimate has strong correlation with Practice, Accept, Encourage, Respect, Rampant, Money, Tax, Powerful, Belong, and Indian.

19. Variable Feel has strong correlation with Culture, Practice, Accept, Encourage, Attitude, Value, Norm, Respect, Inequal, Monster, Money, Tax, Powerful, Moral, Belong, and Indian.

20. Variable Belong has strong correlation with Culture, Practice, Accept, Encourage, Attitude, Norm, Respect, Rampant, Money, Tax, Powerful, Moral, Illegal, Feel, and Indian.

21.Variable Indian has strong correlation with Practice, Accept, Encourage, Attitude, Norm, Respect, Rampant, Money, Tax, Powerful, Illegal, Feel, and Belong.

22. Variable Power distance has strong correlation with Practice, Value, and Inequal.

23. Variable Insurgency/terror has strong correlation with variable Influence.

24. Variable Influence has strong correlation with Insurgency/terror.

As a whole, table 2.29 indicates the absence of correlation between culture and corrupt practices in public offices. Though the variable Corruption does not show any correlation with other variables, majority of other variables' meanings show an indirect relationship between cultural elements and corruption in public offices. Despite the fact that Indian government has been pouring huge funds in Nagaland, deep down they do not have the feeling of Indianness, but want independence. There is Power distance prevailing in the state. The table also prove that corruption in public offices is one of the factors that indirectly supported insurgency in Nagaland. After finding the correlation, Factor Analysis was also used to validate the findings.

Factor Analysis (Exploratory)

Factor analysis is a technique that is used to reduce a large number of variables into fewer numbers of factors. This technique extracts maximum common variance from all variables and puts them into a common score. As an index of all variables, we can use this score for further analysis (statisticssolutions)[51]. Hence, this method is used to shrink mass data into smaller data which becomes easy to manage and understand. The table thus prepared and its interpretations are as given below:

Communalities

In communalities we compute and analyse the extent to which a variable has been explained by the components. In the current communality analysis it can be noticed that the variable nos. 2 and 12 , i.e. corruption and dishonest have the lowest communality,

[51] https://www.statisticssolutions.com/factor-analysis-sem-factor-analysis/

Table 2.30: Communalities

	Initial	*Extraction*
Culture	1.000	.962
Corruption	1.000	.579
Practice	1.000	.899
Accept	1.000	.957
Encourage/favour	1.000	.948
Attitude	1.000	.955
Value	1.000	.934
Norm	1.000	.863
Respect	1.000	.980
Inequal	1.000	.927
Monster/rampant	1.000	.738
dishonest	1.000	.587
Money/wealth/fund	1.000	.780
Tax/extort	1.000	.889
Internalize/imbibe	1.000	.797
Power/ful	1.000	.970
Moral/ethical	1.000	.969
Illegal/illegitimate	1.000	.806
Feel	1.000	.967
Belong	1.000	.781
Indian	1.000	.957
Power distance	1.000	.956
Insurgency/terror	1.000	.917
Influence	1.000	.916

Extraction Method: Principal Component Analysis.

which indicates that the variables corruption and dishonest have been less explained by the analysis as compared to other variables. The variables respect (.980), power (.970), moral/ethical (.969), feel (.967), culture (.962), accept (.957) have registered greater communality meaning they are best explained.

Total Variance Explained

Table 2.31: Total Variance Explained

Component	*Initial Eigenvalues*			*Extraction Sums of Squared Loadings*		
	Total	*% of Variance*	*Cumulative %*	*Total*	*% of Variance*	*Cumulative %*
1	11.953	49.804	49.804	11.953	49.804	49.804
2	2.914	12.141	61.945	2.914	12.141	61.945
3	1.962	8.173	70.118	1.962	8.173	70.118
4	1.686	7.025	77.143	1.686	7.025	77.143
5	1.384	5.768	82.911	1.384	5.768	82.911
6	1.135	4.727	87.638	1.135	4.727	87.638
7	.914	3.808	91.447			
8	.545	2.271	93.717			
9	.359	1.497	95.214			
10	.262	1.091	96.305			
11	.239	.996	97.301			
12	.159	.661	97.962			
13	.139	.581	98.543			
14	.131	.547	99.090			
15	.074	.310	99.400			
16	.058	.240	99.641			
17	.040	.167	99.807			
18	.014	.060	99.868			
19	.011	.047	99.915			
20	.009	.038	99.952			
21	.005	.020	99.973			
22	.003	.014	99.986			
23	.002	.009	99.996			
24	.001	.004	100.000			

In this table there are six components which have been saved registering total variance upto about 87.4%. The six right-most columns of *Total Variance Explained* contain the most important information on this table and are interpreted as follows:

Six factors (i.e. components) have been saved. That is, the analysis assumes that 24 original variables can be reduced to 6 underlying factors (The number of components selected have been determined by the Kaiser rule). The six components explain 87.6% of the variance in the data. That is, when it is assumed that there are six components, we can predict 87.6% of the information in all the 24 variables. (By chance, we would expect to be able to predict 12.6%).

The first component explains more of the variance than the second component (49% versus 12%) followed by the third, fourth, fifth and sixth by contributing 8, 7, 5.7, and 4.7%.

Table 2.32: Total Variance Explained

Component	*Rotation Sums of Squared Loadings*		
	Total	*% of Variance*	*Cumulative %*
1	7.130	29.709	29.709
2	6.321	26.336	56.044
3	2.775	11.563	67.607
4	1.903	7.928	75.535
5	1.478	6.156	81.691
6	1.427	5.947	87.638
7			
8			
9			
10			
11			
12			
13			
14			
15			

16
17
18
19
20
21
22
23
24

Extraction Method: Principal Component Analysis.

Table 2.33: Component Matrix[a]

	Component					
	1	*2*	*3*	*4*	*5*	*6*
Power/ful	.978	-.072	.073	.043	-.027	-.023
Respect	.929	-.315	-.064	.077	-.018	-.083
Tax/extort	.924	-.099	-.001	.062	.004	.147
Attitude	.924	.248	.136	.001	-.149	-.009
Practice	.906	.215	.020	.144	-.078	.068
Feel	.887	.061	.263	-.287	-.138	-.073
Moral/ ethical	.853	.186	.302	-.334	-.043	-.046
Accept	.848	-.276	-.176	.234	.060	-.269
Belong	.812	-.331	.014	-.094	-.048	.034
Money/ wealth/fund	.794	-.265	.165	-.067	.147	.161
Culture	.794	.414	.252	-.305	.038	.059
Monster/ rampant	.785	-.266	.010	-.208	-.048	-.079
Norm	.767	.186	.083	-.205	.132	-.416
Encourage/ favour	.752	-.327	-.325	.406	-.020	.060

Indian	.666	-.620	-.219	.273	-.013	-.081
Inequal	.636	.629	.005	.191	-.021	.300
Illegal/ illegitimate	.506	-.341	-.319	.012	.422	.392
Value	.663	.668	-.028	.214	.025	-.043
influence	-.189	-.193	.778	.393	.287	-.017
Insurgency/ terror	-.138	-.185	.769	.399	.337	.019
Power distance	.224	.609	-.151	.663	-.196	.182
Corrupt/ion	.043	.274	-.191	-.082	.675	-.058
dishonest	.167	.162	-.184	-.311	.498	.394
Internalize/ imbibe	.058	.358	-.310	.190	.411	-.603

Extraction Method: Principal Component Analysis.a
a. 6 components extracted.

Rotated Component Matrix

Table 2.34: Rotated Component Matrix[a]

	Component					
	1	2	3	4	5	6
Moral/ethical	.952	.217	.086	-.016	.082	-.032
Feel	.917	.338	.053	-.046	-.020	-.077
Culture	.915	.069	.262	-.043	.221	.012
Attitude	.803	.386	.397	-.061	-.023	.001
Norm	.781	.283	.023	-.066	.005	.409
Power/ful	.701	.658	.212	.004	.030	.005
Practice	.651	.484	.484	-.055	.050	.019
Monster/rampant	.606	.582	-.125	-.116	.026	-.049
Indian	.108	.965	-.069	-.011	-.090	-.006
Encourage/favour	.126	.918	.282	-.093	.008	.019

Accept	.391	.847	.100	-.038	-.081	.262
Respect	.535	.829	.057	-.044	-.010	.022
Belong	.541	.680	-.054	-.054	.052	-.136
Tax/extort	.587	.671	.249	-.022	.149	-.097
Illegal/illegitimate	.038	.656	.002	-.056	.603	-.082
Money/wealth/fund	.561	.605	-.007	.147	.234	-.150
Power distance	-.045	.036	.965	-.026	-.111	.087
Inequal	.503	.082	.781	-.068	.229	-.005
Value	.556	.095	.715	-.081	.080	.302
Insurgency/terror	-.042	-.035	-.036	.954	-.036	-.037
influence	-.065	-.071	-.062	.944	-.100	-.042
dishonest	.128	-.019	.018	-.115	.746	.006
Corrupt/ion	.015	-.074	.032	.030	.565	.502
Internalize/imbibe	-.020	-.002	.142	-.076	.025	.877

Extraction Method: Principal Component Analysis.
Rotation Method: Varimax with Kaiser Normalization.a
a. Rotation converged in 6 iterations.

Rotated Component Matrix

The *Rotated Component Matrix,* sometimes referred to as the *loadings,* is the key output of principal components analysis. It contains estimates of the correlations between each of the variables and the estimated components. In the given table we find that:

1. The table envisages that there is strong correlation between the variables Moral/Ethical (.952), Feel (.917), Culture (.915), Attitude (.803), Norm (.781), Power/ful (.701), Practice (.651), and Monster/rampant (.606) and component one. Thus, it covers the issues of ethical, cultural, psychological and political. So what these show? Is it that the moral values have gone down in people's behaviour? Why it has gone down? People may be believing that the Indian government is pumping money in Nagaland to make them feel Indian, but they consider it as the 'outside money' and 'compensation' for

the sufferings they had at the hands of the security forces in the past. “Deep down, we Nagas still want our independence” (Wouters, 2018, p. 169). This is the idea evolved in the minds of the people. So, to get that easy money, they have to satisfy the officials of public offices. So, it is not that the entire Naga population is corrupt. It is the local elites who have ‘successful link’ with the state functionaries – these two entities are the epicentre of corruption in the public offices. Then how the common people are affected? Government offices are a place where citizens have to be in contact for different necessities of life. So, when the citizens are necessitated to approach these offices where corrupt culture is prevailing, they are forced by the circumstances to bribe. Here comes the other variable ‘attitude’ and ‘norm’. Because there is no other alternative, attitudinally people have accepted corruption as a norm in public offices, and it has become a part of their culture. The aforesaid ‘elites’ who have accumulated wealth through any means and have become powerful are accorded ‘high respect’ by the common people, and they simply agree with them (powerful). This is due to an ‘element of fear’ in the minds of common people towards the powerful, though it is not being expressed in their behaviour. So, the disagreement, if any in any context, is suppressed in their hearts. Thus, the component one validates the interlinkage between the corrupt practices in public offices, principally due to the huge funds allotted by the Centre, the practice of elites to have a share from it and become powerful, and the acceptance of all these as norms in such offices by the common people. Such belief system has become a part of their culture.

2. The correlation between other variables like insurgency/terror, influence, internalize/imbibe, etc. and the first component are very low. Normally, when interpreting a *component matrix*, correlations of less than 0.3 or 0.4 are regarded as being trivial (These correlations are commonly referred to as *loadings*; the correlations can also be negative and in such an instance correlations of between -0.4 or -0.3 and 0.0 are regarded as being trivially small). The variables like Indian (.965),

Encourage (.918), Accept (.847) Respect (.829), Belong (.680), Tax/Extort (.671), Illegal/illegitimate (.656), and Money/wealth/fund (.605) have close correlation with the second component. As seen in the first component, here it can be seen that the vindictiveness the Nagas had undergone at the hands of Indian security forces in those days has left serious injuries in their minds, and hence, they do not have the inclination to be with India. No doubt, the present government is making all possible efforts within the framework of Indian constitution. However, no fruitful results could be achieved so far. The latest dialogues and finally the demands of NSCN (IM) to have separate flag and constitution could be a sign of the intent at the bottom of their hearts.

The culture developed in the public offices has encouraged nonaccountability and corruption, people have accepted it, and this has got embedded within the local social bonds and kinship. This led to the extending of mutually beneficial support between the clan and their members in government offices, especially in the village context. The nature of support could be in the form of backing in case of failure in fulfilling the official responsibilities, or in any other way. As in component one, here also people gave high respect to those who accumulated wealth through any means. This further strengthens the corruption in public offices and the people who are 'respected' in the society. The development of corruption in public offices is already discussed. In spite of the fact that they accepted the 'easy money' they did not like to join in India. The reason of the sufferings they had in the past is already discussed. Could there be another reason – only the elites who have 'connection' with the state functionaries are financially benefitted. At the same time, the 'cut' goes to the local insurgent groups also. Nothwithstanding the several meetings happened, in the final stage the insurgent group takes a stand which India cannot agree. Does it mean that they do not want to settle the issue, but continue with the insurgency threat so that the Centre's funding will carry on and they will continue getting their share. At the same time, they could continue with the illegal 'tax' and 'extortion', which are also big sources of income.

3. Similarly component number three seems to have more correlation with the variables Power Distance (.965), Inequal (.781), and Value (.715). Power distance is the acceptance of inequality in the society by the people, and this is the cause of several societal problems. This shows that power distance exists in Nagaland and corruption in public offices is one of the results of it. This also indicates that there is inequality in the society and there is a group of rich and powerful who have a 'say' in the matters of public offices, especially in financial matters. Common people generally do not raise voice against the decisions of these powerful. Comparing to the earlier times, the ethical values have gone down among the rich and powerful and they have become more materialistic. People have accepted that the public offices practice corruption. So, it can be observed that though the term 'corruption' as such scored less points, certain elements of culture, e.g., attitude, belief system, etc. have relationship with corrupt practices in public offices.
4. The correlation between Insurgency (.954), Influence (.944) and component number four have close relationship. This shows that there is insurgency in Nagaland, and corruption is one of the factors that supported it. It further indicated that the insurgents influenced the government authorities so that the former could achieve their goals without much hindrance. As seen earlier, one of their important targets was to procure a share from the funds that were destined for the development purposes. They used their links with the government authorities in the hierarchical chain to get hold of the same, principally using coercive methods. Additionally, we have seen that illegal taxation, extortion and so on are also sources of income of insurgents. Common people were aware and accepted these, and hence, they did not go for complaining about the less utilization of funds for the development activities.
5. Component number five and variables Dishonest (.746), and Corruption (.565) have close relationship. This shows

that the element of dishonesty has become a part of the work culture in the public offices. As the people are fully aware about the atmosphere in government offices, they prefer such government jobs where there is opportunity to make extra illegal money. There are three reasons, (1) they want to become rich easily, (2) corruption is being seen as a norm in public offices, and (3) those who become rich by any means are getting high respect in the society. Thus, corruption is flourishing in public offices. In the words of Wouters (2018), in Nagaland corruption is not the exception, but the very norm of government and governance. It does not just exist, but thrives. Thus, dishonesty of public employees, preference for government jobs where illegal money can be collected, corruption and component number five have close interrelationship.

6. Component number six and variable Internalize/imbibe (.877) has close relationship. The variable that the government employees have internalized corrupt practices from their office environment and component number six has close interrelationship.

Overall, the table shows that there is strong correlation between the variables moral/ethical, feel, culture, attitude, norm, powerful, practice, monster/rampant and component one; component two and variables Indian, encourage, accept, respect, belong, tax/extort, illegal/illegitimate, money/wealth/fund; component three and the variables power distance, inequal, value; component four and variables insurgency/terror, influence; variables dishonest, corruption and component five; and component six and variable internalize/imbibe. All these corroborate the correlation between certain cultural elements (ethical, attitude, acceptance, norm, powerful, encourage, respect, value, inequal, practice, dishonest, illegal) and corruption in public offices, as per the sample literature. It may be recalled that there are literature, which show that due to the strong intra-family/clan bondage they support their clan men who are in government offices even if the latter are involved in malpractices, absenteeism, corruption, etc. Similarly, the officials too supported their clan men sometimes illegally in the official matters.

Similarly, this also validates the correlation between corruption (influence, belong) and insurgency (influence, Indian, tax/extort) in Nagaland.

Table 2.35: Component Transformation Matrix

Component	*1*	*2*	*3*	*4*	*5*	*6*
1	.720	.635	.248	-.075	.100	.034
2	.275	-.616	.649	-.165	.110	.291
3	.416	-.292	-.105	.792	-.198	-.253
4	-.452	.357	.619	.430	-.280	.152
5	-.085	.061	-.159	.394	.744	.505
6	-.149	.002	.314	.018	.554	-.756

Extraction Method: Principal Component Analysis.
Rotation Method: Varimax with Kaiser Normalization.

Geert Hofstede's Power Distance

In addition to finding the correlation, specific attempt was made to choose from the sample literature, the sentences/statements/opinions/phrases/discussions that have the ingrained relationship between culture and corruption. (The purpose of doing this exercise was to find out whether these sentences/statements' meanings have got any link with Hofstede's cultural dimension of Power Distance).

Hofstede's[52] Power Distance is defined as the extent to which the less powerful members of institutions and organisations within a country expect and accept that power is distributed unequally. Quoting Hofstede, Daniels and Greguras[53] (2014, 1203-04) state

[52] Hofstede-insights, https://www.hofstede-insights.com/country/india/

[53] Daniels, A Michael and Greguras, J Gart, 2014; Exploring the nature of Power Distance: Implications for Micro- and Macro-level

that power distance refers to the degree to which individuals, groups, or societies accept inequalities (e.g., inequalities in power, status, wealth) as unavoidable, legitimate, or functional. It is the perceived difference (inequality) in the amount of power (influence) that a supervisor has compared to that of a subordinate. Importantly, the magnitude of this inequality is accepted (valued) by both the supervisor and the subordinate and is reinforced by their social and national environments. Culture sets the level of power distance at which the tendency of the powerful to maintain or increase power distances and the tendency of the less powerful to reduce them will find their equilibrium. In high power distance cultures, individuals with power are seen as superior, inaccessible, and paternalistic and are expected to lead autocratically. Because individuals with power are perceived as superior and elite, those with less power accept their places in the hierarchy, trust their leaders, defer judgements to them and are generally submissive, loyal and agree with their leaders. Hofstede (2011, 9)[54] states that in a high power distance society, corruption is frequent, scandals are covered up, whereas in a low power distance society, corruption is rare and scandals end political careers.

Hofstede (p. 6) evolved the theory in 1980 after conducting a gigantic survey about values and related sentiments of people in over 50 countries around the world. These people worked in the local subsidiaries of one large multinational corporation-IBM. Most parts of the organization had been surveyed twice over a four-year interval, and the database contained more than 100,000 questionnaires. However, such a massive study based on primary data is not feasible in the present context, and hence, this report is based only on the literature review that shows the probability of high power distance, and as a consequence, corruption in Naga

---

Theories, Processes, and Outcomes, Journal of Management, Vol. 40, No. 5, July.

[54] Hofstede, Geert, 2011; Dimensionalizing Cultures: The Hofstede Model in Context, Online Readings in Psychology and Culture, 2(1), p. 9, https://doi.org/10.9707/2307-0919.1014; https://scholarworks.gvsu.edu/cgi/viewcontent.cgi?article=1014&context=orpc

public offices. The reason for identifying Hofstede's theory is that it is 'the most well-known, referenced, and adopted cultural value' (Daniels & Greguras) classification, and very much relevant to the present study as this tries to explore the relationship between culture and corruption. This researcher only want to mention that the findings of this study has similarity with the findings of Hofstede's research. In Nigeria, Babatunde Akanji (2017), drawing from Hofstede's culture theory, had carried out a qualitative study to explore the views of Nigerians on the extent to which cultural factors impacted corruption in that country, and the study had provided fruitful results.

India has Power Distance (PDI) as the highest Hofstede Dimension for the culture, with a ranking of 77 compared to a world average of 56.5. This Power Distance score for India indicates a high level of inequality of power and wealth within the society. This condition is not necessarily subverted upon the population, but rather accepted by the population as a cultural norm (India Business Etiquette & Culture)[55].

For the purpose of this study, as mentioned earlier, the statements/concepts/opinions etc. appeared in the literature in different forms of sentences and phrases and gave the similar meanings of linkage between culture and corruption were identified. Following the thematic approach, the sentences/statements/concepts, etc. that gave similar meanings (Table 2.11, Column A) enabled to formulate certain Themes (Column B). These themes not only showed the relationship between culture and corruption, but also indicated its relationship with the aforesaid Power Distance. The themes so formulated have been put into five categories, which are inter-linked. Thus, all these themes individually as well as jointly indicated that some of the cultural factors have encouraged corruption in Naga public life. A noteworthy factor is that the prevalence of all these themes supported Hofstede's (2011) cultural dimension of Power Distance.

[55] Stephen Taylor, India Business Etiquette & Culture; Geert Hofstede Analysis for India https://www.cyborlink.com/besite/india.htm

The statements/opinions/discussions/speeches and its related themes are shown in table 2.11below:

Table 2.36

Statements/Concepts/Sentences/Opinions/Phrases/ Discussions *A*	*Themes that link certain cultural factors with corruption in public offices* *B*
- Corruption has become day to day life style in Nagaland (Nagaland Post, 2018) - Crime and corruption have been sweeping Nagaland (ibid) - Everyone talks about corruption (ibid) - Corruption has become a topic of discussion in schools and colleges (ibid) - CAG reports have revealed the link between crime and corruption (ibid) - Government offices have become a bunch of robbers (ibid) - Central funds coming to Nagaland are deducted from top to bottom (ibid) - Corruption is 'skinning Nagas alive' without any prick of conscience – the worst social sin (ibid) - Need to promote and preserve the rich culture and traditions by living a cultured life (Nagaland Post, 2019) - Earlier, Nagas were sincere, hardworking and honest, but now has become a spoilt child (Tehelka, 2010) - Corruption has crept into the youths (ibid) - Corruption has become a culture (Wouters, 2018) - Corruption has created social and economic disparity (Eastern Mirror, 2019) - Scholars/commentators on Nagaland depict corruption as a 'way of life' (Northeast Window, 2018, Ezung, 2012, Wouters, 2018) - Corruption is caused due to "the attitude of the people" (Ezung, 2012) - Complacent attitude of the people, donation culture, expectation for jobs (ibid)	1. Prevalence of culture of corruption in government offices, permeated in the society, and has created social and economic disparity.

- Nagas have very strong family as well as intra clan ties (Horam, 1977)
- If my clan decided to clean its area, I would have to help (ibid)
- A family abstaining from repairing a footpath will have no right to use the path (ibid)
- Individuals are pushed towards corruption by the nature of their internalized values and by social pressures (Vannucci, 2015)
- The community people would support a government employee of the same community if he fails in his official duty (Wouters, 2018)
- Committee did not deduct the absent doctor/nurse' salary as they belonged to the same community of the chairman and members of the Health Committee (ibid)
- Justification-, the absentees have lots of household chores, have to take care of their children and aged (ibid)
- Did not punish absentee teachers- deduction of their salary would affect not only the teachers but their families too (ibid)
- It would be a shame on the part of the committee to take action against the absentee teacher who is from the same clan (ibid)
- The failure of village committees to stop absenteeism was the result of the thickly entangled social fabric of village life (ibid)
- The committees' motivation was nourishing of village social bonds and cohesion than enforcing good governance (ibid)
- Such loyalties of kinship and social bonds well exceeded the villagers' commitment to the state and its policies (ibid)
- Corruption has become a way of life for the Naga society (Ezung, 2012)
- Rational choice- when bribes are large, the chances of being caught small, and the penalties if caught meagre, many officials will succumb (Vennucci, 2015)

2. Internalization of values and social pressures encourage individuals towards corruption in public offices.

- "Within Naga culture, any talk that might embarrass or shame other persons was shunned or discouraged." Hence, "'holding back one's tongue' created a fertile ground for corruption" (Venüsa Tinyi and Chothazo Nienu, 2018, p. 171).
- Individuals who grow up in societies in which corruption is prevalent should be more likely to act corruptly than individuals who grow up in societies where corruption is rare (Barr & Serra, 2010)
- Not only do values and beliefs affect adherence to a social norm, but the proportion of people who adhere to the norm affects individuals' beliefs in the values underlying the norm (ibid)
- In some cultures, public servants experience a kinship-related obligation to favour family and friends, even when it entails corruption (Klitgaard, 2017)
- Person's decision to be corrupt is influenced by both cultural norms and a risk/reward evaluation (Juacaba, 2018)
- Corruption is not the exception but the very norm of government and governance, it does not just exist, but thrives (Wouters, 2018)
- Local politicians have developed a vested interest in the violence to continue (Purkayastha, 2007)
- Organized looting of public money by the ministers, MLAs and government servants (Morung Express, 2011)
- In other states people used to raise voice against rampant corruption (ibid)
- 80 % or more consider corruption as a normal system (PTI, 2018)
- Corruption had progressively increased and was now rampant in the society, besides becoming a way of life (Governor, 2018)
- No one questioned those who live beyond their means (ibid)
- Society itself had accepted and embraced corruption (ibid)
- 'Monster of corruption' had devoured the society (Governor, 2019)

- In Nagaland the corrupt have immense power, get 'high respect' (Morung Express, 2011`) - Those who have done 'well' out of their access to state and development monies were referred to as 'smart' and 'successful' (Wouters, 2018) - In Nagaland, exists a complex moral economy (ibid) - The pilfering of state is not condemned, but praised (ibid) - Corrupt are unlikely to be caught and punished (Northeast Window, 2018) - A government official who does not use his power to help his clan members are considered to be of 'no use' to their clan (Wouters, 2018)	3. Prevails the custom of giving high respect to people who accumulate wealth by any means
- The social status of those working in a department that earns extra cash is high and acknowledged (Ezung, 2012) - This attitude of people valuing those employees who earn extra money inspires people to be more corrupt (ibid) - 96% of the respondents preferred the department that provided an opportunity to earn side incomes (ibid)	4. Preference for jobs that enable to amass extra illegal money
- Indian security forces carried out operations that were 'reign of terror' (Jamir, 2016) - We Nagas are cunning in our own way, we simply take the money from them (Wouters, 2018) - We understand their strategies (ibid) - It is high time for India to compensate us for making our life horrible for so long (ibid) - Accepting this money does not make us feel Indian (ibid) - This made Nagaland the most corrupted state (ibid) - This is only Indian money (ibid) - Deep down, we Nagas still want our independence (ibid) - Lack of sense of belonging in the government by the people (ibid) - India made every effort to reach out to the lowest levels, but loyalty to the Indian state proves tenuous and fragile (ibid)	5. The Moral Economy of Resentment exists, and uses corruption to get its 'compensation'

Above table has cited the sentences/statements/opinions, etc. briefly that were made by several authors/authorities at different places. These have been quoted from books, articles, media and websites that denote the relationship between certain cultural elements and corruption in Naga public life. After sorting the statements that gave similar meanings they were put together that helped formulating certain Themes that have relationship with Hofstede's cultural dimension of power distance. Elaborate discussion on each Theme is given below:

1. Prevalence of culture of corruption in government offices, permeated in the society, and has created social and economic disparity.

Nagas, in olden days, gave much importance to sincerity, loyalty, honesty and simplicity in all their dealings. But, as the time changed and they came in contact with outer world, its impact started to manifest in the lives of some Nagas. It needs to be emphasized here that all the Nagas are not corrupt, but a few who have connections with politicians, and authorities in government offices. They left aside their simplicity and honesty of good old days and they started to look for ways to make 'better life' through short cuts. Leaving aside the merits, innocence and admired life of their ancestors, they got attracted towards the materialistic life, thereby eager to acquiring more and more wealth. Needless to say, this is made possible through a variety of corrupt means. When a few corrupt individuals start walking on this path and accumulating wealth easily, there are possibilities that others also get attracted and tempted towards this idea. Gradually, the number of people getting attracted towards corruption could go up and its strength swells. Progressively, it becomes an integral part of their culture, which gives rise to a society of inequals. No doubt, politics, maladministration, red-tapism and many more have their roles in shaping the society in this way.

"The hot waves of crime and corruption have been sweeping Nagaland for so long. Everyone talks about corruption. It has become a topic of discussion in schools and colleges. Everyone blame everyone without much doing. This has become day to day life style in a small State, Nagaland. The report of the Comptroller of Auditor General has revealed the very system of crime and corruption in Nagaland. Few Naga officials who hold respectable position in the Government offices have become a bunch of robbers, and they efficiently dry up all the funds and schemes without any guilt and shame. A sincere servant is put to shame by the dishonest officers. They pretend to work for the welfare of the Nagas but inside them are full of selfishness and greed. Central funds and schemes that come to Nagaland are deducted from top to bottom. It exists from Pension to Scholarship, mid-day meal to Village Development Board (VDB) funds, Mahatma Gandhi National Rural Employment Guarantee Act (MGNREGA) to the Funds meant for Differently Abled Persons. This is how we skin others alive inside our esteemed offices. This is called 'skinning Nagas alive.' Even the funds meant for Differently Abled Persons were eaten by some officers without any prick of conscience – the worst social sin" (Nagaland Post, 2018)[56].

On one hand, this is the situation in Nagaland, whereas on the other, the Minister of Higher & Technical Education and Tribal Affairs, Temjen Imna Along stressed on the need "to promote and preserve the rich culture and traditions by living a cultured life, as who loses one's culture and traditions, will lose everything" (Nagaland Post, 2019)[57]. What this shows? By exhorting students to live a valued and cultured life, does the minister advertently admit that these have already lost in Nagaland? Is it that the politicians and government authorities are absolved from preserving the rich culture and traditions? Or, is it that the minister realises the harm that could bring in due to corruption, and sincerely wanted to go to the past rich cultured life?

In an interview, Naga National Council veteran Thinoselie

[56] Nagaland Post, 2018; Holy Crime and Saintly Corruption in Nagaland!, 25th September. http://www.nagalandpost.com/holy-crime-and-saintly-corruption-in-nagaland/182190.html

[57] Nagaland Post, 2019; Promote and preserve rich culture: Temjen Imna, 15th August). http://www.nagalandpost.com/promote-and-preserve-rich-culture-temjen-imna/201849.html

Keyho[58] said that earlier, the Nagas were described as sincere, hardworking and honest people. These qualities have disappeared today. Nagaland has become a spoilt child; corruption and laziness are rampant and the Indian government supports this. When officials come from India, they are bluffed by the local officials. Even if 50 percent of what the Indian government gives to Nagaland is utilised effectively, this would be one of the most developed states in the country. Instead, the state has 300-400 crorepatis awash in corrupt money. Corruption is not restricted to government officials and politicians, but it has crept into the youths as well (Nagalimvoice, Tehelka Magazine, 2010).

For sure, Nagaland has earned reputation for governmental disarray, failing development, and vast networks of corruption. Based on the dialogue he had with prominent personalities, Wouters (2018, p. 170) mentions, "corruption has become a culture, one that pervades at all levels, nooks, and niches of the state machinery. Scholars and commentators on Nagaland similarly depict corruption as a 'way of life'"[59].

In his study on Nagas, Wouters (p.183) explicitly shows the material benefit of development. At the same time he mentions about several incidents that show how the people have become immoral and selfish and how it has created social harms to the society. The inflow of huge monies in the name of development has resulted in to 'falling apart of the village community and the rise of immoralities. The materialities of development and morality carried an inverse relation'.

No doubt, corruption has engulfed several spheres of life in Nagaland. As of late, the Convenor of Public Action Committee (PAC) of Naga Council requested the Governor of Nagaland to intervene and prevent the illegal tax collection by various Naga

[58] Quoting Thinoselie Keyho, Nagalim voice, Tehelka Magazine, 2010; Gandhi supported the Naga desire for independence, Vol 7, Issue 43, 30th October http://www.nagalimvoice.com/interviews/%E2%80%98gandhi-supported-the-naga-desire-for-independence%E2%80%99/

[59] Wouters, Jelle JP, 2018; In the Shadows of Naga Insurgency, Oxford University Press, New Delhi.

Political Groups (NPGs) and different agencies. The Convenor said that the state of corruption has reached extreme indescribable heights, which has affected genuine development of all and created social and economic disparity in Nagaland (Eastern Mirror)[60].

As seen from the preceeding discussions, the secondary data collected from different sources and its analysis have proved that there was 'culture of corruption' in government offices in Nagaland. Further, to validate this finding, primary data was collected by interviewing respondents from Kohima and Shillong during the field work.

2. Internalization of values and social pressures encourage individuals towards corruption in public offices

Nagas have very strong intra family as well as clan ties. As the family was a closely knit unit, it was insufficient to meet any serious problem or threat like fight, raids, head-hunting and so on. With an aim to counter any external threat, several families have joined together that formed the clan, which has strong bonds. Nagas have internalized such values that give high significance to the family and clan ties. This strong bond and cooperation can be observed in all spheres of life like, agricultural work, festivities, village work, ceremonies such as marriage, death and so on. Everybody took part in the work that was belonging to their clan. Absence of anybody in the work was noted seriously. To quote Horam (1977)[61], "If my clan decided to clean its area, I would have to help; if they were repairing the road approaching the clan area, I must take part in it. I remember how members of a certain family failed to join the rest of the clan in clearing the well on which the entire clan was dependent for water. Whether their absence was deliberate or due to carelessness nobody knew for sure; their behaviour, however,

[60] Eastern Mirror, 2019; Nagaland: PAC takes 'illegal collection' issue to governor's doorstep, 9th September. https://www.easternmirrornagaland.com/nagaland-pac-takes-illegal-collection-issue-to-governors-doorstep/

[61] Horam M, 1977; Social and Cultural Life of Nagas, BR Publishing Corporation, Delhi.

was viewed as 'indiscipline' by the clan elders. They forbade the members of that family from drawing water from that for one whole year as a punishment. Similarly, a family abstaining from repairing a footpath will have no right to use the path and will have to use a different track of their own". This shows the strength of mutual aid and responsibilities among the members of a clan. It is also worth mentioning that internalization of such values is certainly good for boosting mutual trust, help and support for a better society.

While the attachment with members in a family, clan or community is strong, there is possibility that such a situation may encourage the government officials of that family or clan to misuse his official power for the benefit of his family/clan members. In this context, there may be two important elements, (1) the internalization of societal norms and values towards family/clan ties, and (2) the way in which these ties impact the internalization of norms and values of official procedures and regulations. It further depends on the intensity of internalization, i.e. how strongly an individual is motivated due to the internalization. So, in situations where there is quandary in mind what has to be given more importance, the level of intensity in which the norms have been internalized would take preference, and this depends on the prevailing circumstances. Internalization is the process of recognition and acceptance of a set of norms and values that are established through socialization. This gradually becomes the traits of personality of the individual. Quoting Ostrom, Chabova[62] says that norms are defined as shared understanding about actions that are obligatory, permitted, or forbidden within society. Naga culture shows that the bondage towards the family is much stronger while the internalization of norms about the office rules and procedures may be weak. Additionally, a government employee working in a feeble ethical environment will internalize such

[62] Chabova, Kristyna; Norms and values connected to corruption: Is there difference between post-communist countries and the rest of Europe? https://www.europeansocialsurvey.org/docs/about/conference/CHABOVA_Norms-and-Values-corruption.pdf

values. Otherwise, how corruption at a massive scale is observed in government institutions? As Vannucci[63] says, "individuals belonging to different societies and organizations can be pushed towards corruption by the nature of their internalized values and by social pressures" (p. 11). This may lead some government officials to misuse their position for their own and family/clan interests, even at the cost of engaging in corruption, favouring a person belonging to the official's family/clan to get a job in the office or for some other purpose. This is due to the internalized values towards the family/clan, and social pressures. At the same time, the public office environment is such that the phenomenon of 'favouritism' is flourishing. Similarly, imitation of others may also lead to a 'push' factor from the family/clan and 'pull' factor from the office environment towards corruption. Resultantly, the kinship and social bonds get embedded with corruption. And this acts as a vicious cycle both strengthening each other. So, in brief, it is attitude of the individual towards corruption that matters, and the attitude comes from the culture. To quote a study conducted by Cameron, et al (2005)[64] in Australia, India, Indonesia and Singapore, it was found that 'attitudes towards corruption play a critical role in the persistence of corruption'. It further establishes that the 'subjects in India exhibit a higher tolerance towards corruption than the subjects in Australia'. Further, the family/clan members ensure that they support and justify their clan men who work in government offices, even if the latter has committed any wrong or there is failure in fulfilling his/her responsibilities. In Naga society, this bonding was very strong, and was given more importance by everybody. Wouter mentions that the Communitization of Public Institutions Act 2002 was passed by the Nagaland Assembly to counter the widespread absenteeism in government offices. To implement this

[63] Vannucci, Alberto, 2015; Three paradigms for the analysis of corruption, Labour and Law Issues, vol.1, no.2, ISSN: 2421-2695.

[64] Cameron Lisa, Chaudhuri Ananish, Erkal Nisvan, Gangadharan Lata, 2005; Do Attitudes Towards Corruption Differ Across Cultures? Experimental Evidence from Australia, India, Indonesia and Singapore https://papers.ssrn.com/sol3/papers.cfm?abstract_id=778464

Act, different village committees were constituted under different departments such as Health Committee, Education Committee, Water Committee, Electricity Committee, and so on. These committees were empowered to deduct salary of employees who were found to be absent in their duties. However, when the Health Committee found that the doctor or nurse was absent from village dispensary, the committee members were not ready to deduct the absentees' salary. Their argument was that the doctor/nurse were belonging to the same community of the chairman and members of the Health Committee, the absentees have lots of household chores, have to take care of their children and aged. Similar was the stand of the Education Committee in punishing absentee teachers, arguing that the deduction of salary would affect not only the teachers but their families too, and it would be a shame on the part of the committee that due to its action the person's (whose salary is deducted) relatives and clan members would feel bad. "Here the failure of village committees to stop absenteeism was the result of the thickly entangled social fabric of village life. The committeees' motivation was nourishing of village social bonds and cohesion than enforcing good governance. Such loyalties of kinship and social bonds well exceeded the villagers' commitment to the state and its policies." (Wouters, p.195). So, in the process of preserving social bonds, the corrupt practice of absenteeism is permitted to an extent by not implementing the rules strictly. As the family/clan related bonds and obligations amongst the Nagas are strong, there emerged a temptation amongst their government servants to misuse their official power for the former's gain, and this might have transformed into their cultural mandate. This can be termed as a 'spin-off effect' of the strong social bonds of those involved in corrupt practices. Thus developed a strong relationship between both these entities in legal as well as illegal matters that are mutually beneficial. This could be one way how the the social bonds encouraged corruption in public offices.

These are just a couple of examples about absenteeism from duties. Similar is the case with other modes of corruption, bribery, illegal action, manipulation, fraud with government funds, etc. and inaction against the same. It is observed that there is a consensus approach among the rich and powerful towards such (mis)behaviour, and gradually it has ingrained into their culture. Secondly, the benefitted stakeholders, be it the contractor, ministers, bureaucrats, officials or anybody in the hierarchical unholy chain do not feel that there is a need to implement any program as per the laid down policies of the government. As the huge money is coming from 'outside' Nagaland, the stakeholders are keen to have their 'share' from it. The misuse of funds and its sharing with the underground groups may be with the oblique consent of the government for 'buying' peace, which turns out to be an indirect support to the insurgent groups. Why is this being allowed? Is it due to the incapability of the government or because they do not want to stop it? In both the situations, the aforesaid stakeholders are economically benefitted and it is the common people who are suffering. For example, the development of infrastructures in villages and urban areas did not take place the extent to which it should have due to which life of the people suffer. The 'taxation' enterprise by the insurgent groups has made the commodities transported from neighbouring states so costly that the ordinary citizens bear its brunt. Even if the common men do not want to be a part of the corrupt system, they are forced to accept it, as there is no alternative. Gradually a situation emerges wherein corruption in the society is not being looked upon as a 'sickness' that corrodes the core strength of the society. To quote Ezung(2012), "corruption, which is defined as the abuse of public power for personal ends, has become a way of life for the Naga society".[65] The gradual process of weak internalization of anti corruption values strengthens the corrupt practices. No doubt, imbibing values prevailing in the society is a part of societal culture, and this encourages corruption in public offices. Additionally, the huge funding in government offices further leads to a 'culture of corruption', which permeats in the society and acts a vicious cycle.

While this is the cultural paradigm, another reason for

[65] Ezung, . Zarenthung T, 2012; Corruption and its Impact on Development: A Case study of Nagaland, International Journal of Rural Studies (IJRS), vol. 19, no. 1, April.

corruption is the rational individual choice. Rational choice theory states that an individual's beliefs and preferences lead to certain behaviours and actions, which can have positive or negative impact on the society. These beliefs and preferences can be due to 'culturally transmitted tastes for personal habits and commitments'[66]. This prompts a person whether to involve in corrupt practices or not. Quoting Klitgaard, Vannucci (p. 6) postulates, "True, there are both saints who resist all temptations and honest officials who resist most. But when bribes are large, the chances of being caught small, and the penalties if caught meagre, many officials will succumb". So, when the government officials found from their experiences that the chances of being caught were less, they also developed the practice of earning 'easy money'.

According to Barr and Serra (2010)[67], 'culture of corruption' appears to exist and persist in some countries and not in others, because in the former, individuals have not internalized the anti-corruption norm and so the impact of intrinsic motivations on their decision to abstain from corruption is weak, whereas in the latter, the opposite applies. If this is the case, all other things being equal, individuals who grow up in societies in which corruption is prevalent should be more likely to act corruptly than individuals who grow up in societies where corruption is rare. They further opine that not only do values and beliefs affect adherence to a social norm, but the proportion of people who adhere to the norm affects individuals' beliefs in the values underlying the norm, and, as a consequence, the likelihood that the norm will be internalized by others including future generations. And these strategic complementarities may lead to multiple equilibria characterized by varying levels of adherence to the norm and belief in the underlying values... Their study of 2007 found that social norms, values and beliefs internalized during childhood may play

[66] Wittek, Rafael, 2013; Rational Choice Theory, *in* Theory in Social and Cultural Anthropology : An Encyclopedia Account: Sage Publications, Inc., January, p.688.

[67] Barr, Abigail & Serra, Danila, 2010; Corruption and Culture: An Experimental Analysis, Journal of Public Economics 94, 2010, p.862-863.

a determining role in individuals' decisions about bribery later in life and that corruption is, in part, a cultural phenomenon.

Klitgaard (2017)[68] says, "In certain cultures it's okay to put yourself and your family above your obligations to serve in the public interest. Public servants have a role-related obligation to be impartial and not corrupt. And more strongly in some cultures, they may also experience a kinship-related obligation to favour family and friends, even when it entails corruption".

According to Juacaba (2018)[69], "national culture is expected to influence corruption. For instance, cultural dimensions may affect the subjective perception of ethical situations by an individual". Quoting Klitgaard, Juacaba further mentions that person's decision to be corrupt is influenced by both cultural norms and a risk/reward evaluation. In this sense, in a 'corrupt culture', a kind of prisoner dilemma might occur, in which a corrupt equilibrium may arise even if all the officials wished they were honest and efficient and all the people paying bribes wished they did not. This implies that, sometimes, not being corrupt may be a costly choice, resulting in a loop of corrupt practices (p.31). Quoting a study on family ties conducted by Alesina & Giuliano (2010), Juacaba further states that countries with stronger family ties tend to be more corrupt (p.33). Thus, it can be safely said that the internalization of cultural norms supporting corruption and its benefit highly influences an individual to become corrupt.

Another factor that causes corruption is the belief that helping the near and dear ones, irrespective of misusing official power, would enable to enhance their status in their community. This way of thinking exists in closely knit societies because they give more importance to their near and dears' wellbeing and happiness, and their own status amongst their community. Needless to mention,

[68] Klitgaard, Robert, 2017; On Culture and Corruption; BSG Working Paper, BSG-WP-2017/020 July https://www.bsg.ox.ac.uk/sites/default/files/2018-05/BSG-WP-2017-020.pdf

[69] Juacaba, S Rodrigo, 2018; The contingency effect of national culture on corruption, Masters dissertation, p.31, 33, https://pdfs.semanticscholar.org/702d/773ac43f5380f34df237a9608cf1c8e190cc.pdf

this system also amounts to corruption, which leads to inefficient people in government offices while competent candidates are rendered unemployed. This sends out a message in the society that it is the influence that matters than competence. Such an environment, gradually allows strengthening corrupt culture in the society.

3. Custom of giving high respect to people who accumulate wealth by any means

Cooperation, help, responsibility, and reciprocity are considered to be mandatory in Naga culture. Anybody who does not agree with or violates this norm has to bear the brunt. One of the facets of the Naga culture is that anybody in a better position by wealth or power has to use it for the benefit of his family/clan, even if the means adopted to acquire it is illegal. A person in high position in a job is obliged to help his family/clan member to get a job in that organization. If he is not doing this, he would not be getting good respect from other members of the clan, because he is considered to be of 'no use' to their clan. Several times the person in high position is forced to give job to a job-seeker who is from the same clan, despite the fact that there are better competent other candidates. It may also happen that a person upholding high ethics and moral values may not succumb to such practices. On the other hand, there are also officials who bend the law to suit his desires and do 'undue' favour to his clan-men, though it is illegal.

The people who have accumulated wealth through corruption are accorded high respect in the Naga society. According to Wouters (p. 171), "those who have done 'well' out of their access to state and development monies were referred to as 'smart' and 'successful'". "What must be explained in Nagaland is the existence of a complex moral economy and reasoning that does not condemn all pilfering of state as corrupt and immoral, but regularly praises those able to secure private gains out of their dealings with the state" (p. 172).

In a survey conducted by The Morung Express (2011)[70] on

[70] The Morung Express, 2011; Do you believe that Nagaland is the

the level of corruption in Nagaland, one of the answers echoed by a large number of interviewees was, "In other states people used to raise voice against rampant corruption, whereas in Nagaland the corrupt have immense power, get high 'respect' wherever they go, people simply could not dare them, and the corrupt just get away with it". This shows that the people just agree with these rich and powerful and they are not questioned (due to fear?). Hofstede shows that in societies with high power distance, people do not disagree with the powerful, but show loyalty to them.

Many times, officials in public institutions engage in corrupt practices to maintain 'high esteem' in their clan. So, in a way, the practice of corruption is approved by their culture, though indirectly. In the initial stage, when an employee involves in such practices, he will be facing a peculiar kind of hesitation because his inner conscious is not allowing him to do this. At the same time, the environment where he works 'pushes' him to engage in such wrong practices, as he observes other other employees also practicing the same thing, and thus he too succumbs to it. Over a period of time, the corrupt practices become a part of his habit and accepts it as an easy way to make money, the strength of such people swells, and gradually this practice becomes a part of their culture. Thus, the corruption prevailing in government institutions results into evolving a society where culture of corruption exists. And when such a situation becomes widespread, people will not hesitate to engage in any kind of illegal activities, even if it is harmful to the society. They will only be interested in making their pockets hot, and they will look the other way when the underworld, organized crime syndicates, smugglers, criminals and so on carry on with their illicit activities. These illegal actors are also very much keen to keep the corrupt practices alive so that their activities can be carried out with less hindrance. For this, they always found various methods to grease palm of authorities from top to bottom in government offices, thereby corruption begot corruption, and

---

'corruption capital' of India?, 7th November http://morungexpress.com/do-you-believe-nagaland-corruption-capital-india

in certain cases, it had a link with the insurgency too. Nagaland has been witnessing this during the last few decades.

4. Preference for jobs that enable to amass extra illegal money

The preference of people towards certain jobs also encourages corruption. Those who have extra income in their job command high respect in their community. "The social status of those working in a department that earns extra cash is high and acknowledged. This attitude of people valuing those employees who earn extra money inspires people to be more corrupt" (Ezung, 2012)[71]. This kind of beliefs also facilitate creeping in and expanding corruption in the society in multiple ways. In his study, Ezung found that 94% of the Naga respondents viewed a government job as the most preferred job in the state and 96% of the respondents preferred the department that provided an opportunity to earn side incomes(through cuts, commissions, and other corrupt practices).

5. The Moral Economy of Resentment:

Didier Fassin[72] (2017) uses the term 'moral economy of resentment' to explain 'the affect corresponding to a condition related to a past of oppression and domination'. In Nagaland, the people suffered unimaginable atrocities at the hands of Indian security forces when the insurgency was at its peak. According to Jamir[73] (2016), 'the Indian security forces began operations in a way that could very well be termed as a 'reign of terror'. 'By the time Nagaland state was enacted, Nagas' experiences made them perceive of the postcolonial state as a repository of violence and despair, as an invading and ruthless force from which there was nothing truly to gain, only oppression and misery to reap' (Wouters, 2018, p.

[71] Ezung, T Zarenthung, 2012; Corruption and its Impact on Development: A Case Study of Nagaland; International Journal of Rural Studies, vol. 10, no. 1, April.

[72] Didier Fassin, 2017; The Moral Economy of Resentment, https://piirs.princeton.edu/event/moral-economy-resentment

[73] Jamir SC, 2016; A Naga's Quest for Fulfillment, Bhubaneswar, Apurba, p. 121-122

130). However, later on the Indian government started to pour in huge funds for the development of the state. How certain people look at such money? Wouters (p. 169) quotes what one of the village Naga contractors said, "Delhi no longer sends bullets but monies. In Delhi they think the more money they give us the more we will start feeling India. They think we do not understand their strategies. But we Nagas are cunning in our own way. We simply take the money from them. In any case, it is high time for India to compensate us for making our life horrible for so long. But accepting this money does not make us feel any more Indian. The only thing it has done is to make Nagaland the most corrupted state of India. Everyone is corrupt; politicians, bureaucrats, police, and even our villagers... But who cares? This is only Indian money. Deep down, we Nagas still want our independence".

This conversation depicts the minds of people. They consider the money as a compensation for the tyranny the Indian security forces carried out on them and the sufferings they had. This way of thinking and accepting easy money has gradually became a part of their life and they do not regret for it. Thus, there is a belief of 'compensation for resentment', and 'we have suffered, so we are getting' attitude amongst them. To get this 'easy' money, they have to 'grease palm' of concerned government functionaries. This attitude may have got ingrained in their way of thinking, which has a relationship with the corruption in public offices.

"Diagnosing the corruption and mis-governance all across, Nagaland's Development Commissioner ascribed this to a 'lack of sense of belonging in the government by the people' and lamented the 'very debilitating' effect this had on the state's development" (Wouters, p. 173). According to Manchanda and Bose[74], "most Nagas accept the scaling down of the sovereignty position as inevitable. According to the CSDS 2008 election survey in Nagaland, 41% of the respondents were for independence, 35% for greater autonomy and 15% for the status quo. In the last five

[74] Manchanda, Rita & Bose, Tapan, 2011; Expanding the Middle Space in the Naga Peace Process, Economic and Political Weekly, December 31, Vol xlvi No 53, p. 58.

decades, especially after the creation of the Nagaland state, the government has made every effort to reach out and penetrate to the lowest levels possible, but loyalty to the Indian state proves tenuous and fragile".

After Indian independence and statehood, the situation was made worse because most Nagas adopted an attitude that funds coming from Delhi was 'Indian Money', and did not feel a sense of ownership. The legacy of war economy, and induced inflation, continues to wreak havoc on Naga society today through widespread corruption and inability to manage resources (Chasie, 2005, p. 256)[75].

This shows the ill-feeling many of the Nagas been carrying in their minds for more than half a century. Perhaps, this could be the reason why several agreements signed between the Indian government and sections of Naga insurgent groups were violated after certain period of its signing. Further, after the signing of the framework agreement in 2015, there were several meetings between Indian government and the insurgent groups, especially NSCN (IM), and accordingly, a final settlement was to happen on 18th October 2019. However, NSCN (IM) came up with the demand for a separate flag and constitution for Nagaland, which marred the hope for a solution to the decades long Naga issue. As of late, there are inputs indicating that the NSCN (IM) is considering to setting up camps in the border areas of Myanmar. Thus, to a certain extent, the presence of resentment against India can be observed amongst the Nagas opposing the framework agreement. Could it be that they had put this resentment under wrap for decades for gaining easy money, and who are interested in it?

The five themes formulated on the basis of the secondary data indicate that there is a linkage between culture and corruption in Naga public life. Analysis of the primary data collected during the field work show an indirect relationship between culture and corruption in Nagaland. It is important to mention here that there

[75] Chasie, Charles, 2005; Nagaland in Transition; Indian International Centre, Quarterly journal, Vol. 32, No. 2/3, https://www.jstor.org/stable/23006032?seq=1#metadata_info_tab_contents

are numerous causational factors of corruption in public offices. But, this study has focussed only on the cultural elements, and it was found that these (cultural elements) had its role in facilitating the growth of corruption in government offices. This further shows the justification of facilitation theory in the context of Nagaland. Additionally, it is noteworthy that the aforesaid five themes as well as the analysis of the secondary data have shown its relationship with Hofstede's (2011) cultural dimension of Power Distance. Further, as mentioned previously, before taking these findings at its face value, it needs to be remembered that this is the result of studying a very small number of sample respondents and literature.

Justification of the Primary and Secondary data link with the Power Distance

In the context of Nagaland, all the five themes and the findings of the primary data mentioned above indicate the existence of high power distance, which is a part of the culture.

The first theme and related primary data show that there is culture of corruption in public offices and this proves the existence of high power distance in the society. As Hofstede opined, there is corruption, vast inequality in the the social order, and people approved and accepted it in such societies. Being aware of such a situation, for getting any work done, people preferred the dishonest method, i.e. giving and accepting bribe, be it in the form of money or material. This has become a part of their culture and a way of life.

As seen earlier, an important factor that supported the culture of corruption is the culture of silence, wherein people do not raise voice against the wrongs, due to fear of the powerful. Moreover, the dictum of clans to support their own people even if the later are wrong, may also strengthen the culture of corruption, as echoed by a senior professor.

The second theme - internalization of values and social pressures encourage individuals towards corruption in public offices – can have a close relationship with the mutual bond and support among members of the same clan and its link with corruption in public offices. This is because they give more importance to the clan ties than the official's responsibilities towards the organization's mission. This is supported by the findings of the primary data too. Because of the internalization of such norms and values from the surroundings and customs of the workplace, they are less concerned about fulfilling the official obligations than gratifying the clan/family wishes. At the same time, such employees get support from their clan when the former fails to accomplish their duties honestly. So, there can be mutual understanding and help from both sides that aided thriving of corruption. Thus, the norms that are internalized may have become a part of the culture and people do not feel 'bad' or 'wrong' for behaving the way they behave. Thus, the internalization of such values enabled to have a system wherein there is high power distance, and thereby inequality and corruption at public offices.

Further, in high power distance societies, the officials at the higher positions misuse their power as they wish, and being so, it is followed by those in lower positions too, thereby facilitate the growth of corruption. Quoting Getz and Volkema, Seleim and Bontis (2009)[76] state that in high power distance cultures, high-level public officials may believe that it is a privilege of their class to obtain personal benefits from their official positions. On the other hand, members of the underclass who are part of the bureaucracy may try to improve their own positions through extortion. Similarly, those who are not public officials may try to find creative ways, outside of the law, for raising their living standard. Thus, they may be inclined to offer or pay a bribe to low-level officials.

Thirdly, giving high respect to people who have accumulated wealth by any means show two facets, inequality prevails in

[76] Ahmed Seleim, Nick Bontis, 2009; The relationship between culture and corruption: A cross-national study, Journal of Intellectual Capital, Vol. 10 No. 1, pp. 165-184, Emerald Group Publishing Limited, https://www.emerald.com/insight/content/doi/10.1108/14691930910922978/full/html

the society, and there is no matter of shy in getting involved in corrupt practices as they see it in their surroundings. Moreover, the wealthy cannot be challenged by anybody as they are very powerful. People, being aware of this, agree with whatever way the rich and powerful act, even if it is unethical or wrong. This also shows that the culture accepts inequality and respects powerful people, be it in any way they have become rich and influential. Individuals want to be at the higher level in the prevailing unequal system, accumulating wealth is considered as 'success' in life, and for this they do not hesitate to assume corrupt methods, and thereby command 'high' respect in the society, and resultantly, the prevalence of high power distance.

Fourthly, some people preferred such government jobs wherein they could earn extra illegal money, so as to be rich and powerful in the society, as this was what they have seen and believed. Primary data also supported this finding. Since the goal is to become rich by any means corruption in public offices make the task easy. Otherwise also, as corruption in public offices is considered to be regular, why should the officials be devoid of it when it is not being reflected as something wrong? This may be what they experienced in the government institutions and being aware of such prevailing culture, they did not want to challenge it but preferred to swim with the current. This situation resulted into a system of high power distance in which such employees were accorded high respect. Hence, there is a preference for jobs in such public institutions where they could earn 'easy money'. So, they may have the attitude that the more an employee is rich, higher the respect he commands amongst their clan.

The fifth theme shows that there was a time when the people were suppressed, subjugated and tyrannized by the Indian security forces because the former were weak. There is possibility that the people had been carrying the resentment in their heart all through the decades. So, when the Centre started to pour in huge funds, those who had influence and connections believed that it was the time to get 'compensation' for their sufferings, and they saw the money as so. To get a portion of this 'easy' money they embraced different unfair methods, because they were cognizant about the prevailing system and how to get the work done without much hindrance from public institutions. Challenging the authority would spoil their wishes. Therefore, a covert link can be seen between the moral economy of resentment and corruption in public offices, whose operationalization is simplified with the already existing high power distance.

Thus, a link between these themes, primary and secondary data, and the power distance can be observed, which they imbibed in and that fostered corruption in public offices.

Here it is worth mentioning that this kind of study requires extensive field work and data collection, which is not possible in the present context. So, this finding is based on the small sample that was selected during the short duration of the field work and some secondary data. Though the results show that there is link between culture and corruption in public offices and there exists power distance in the state of Nagaland, it is highly recommended to have a wide-ranging study to make generalizations.

Mechanism to investigate Corruption - SVC[77]

As this section is dealing with corruption in Nagaland, it is necessary to give a brief about the mechanism prevailing in the state to counter the menace of corruption. In the Department of Personal and Administrative Reforms (DPAR), there is Nagaland State Vigilance Commission (SVC) that was established in 1976. The Director of Vigilance & Anti-Corruption, under the State Vigilance Commission, as the Officer-in-Charge of the Vigilance Police Station for the whole State of Nagaland and the Officers of the Directorate having been declared to be Police Officers are empowered to investigate or cause to investigate the following offences committed by a public servant:

1. All offences under the Prevention of Corruption Act, 1988.
2. Section 406 to 409 IPC and 417 to 420 IPC.
3. Section 471 to 477 A IPC.

[77] State Vigilance Commission, Government of Nagaland, 2016 https://dpar.nagaland.gov.in/state-vigilance-commission/

4. All offences under the Official Secrets Act, 1923.
5. All offences under the Assam maintenance of Public Order Act, 1947.
6. Attempts, abetments and conspiracies of offences in item 1 to 5 above, by whosoever committed.
7. Any other particular offence or offences that may be specified by the State Government.

The State Vigilance Commission is headed by a Vigilance Commissioner with the following wings under him:

- *Administrative Wing*: Headed by a Secretary.
- *Tribunal Court*: Headed by Tribunal for Disciplinary Proceedings & Special Judge.
- *Directorate of Vigilance & Anti-Corruption Police*: Headed by the Director & DIGP.
- *Technical Wing:* E.E (Technical) to assist the I.Os on technical matters.

The State Government has also appointed the Secretaries of the departments and the Deputy Commissioners of the districts as Vigilance Officers in their respective Departments and Districts. The Vigilance Officers are to coordinate with the Vigilance Commission, in cases involving allegations of bribery, corruption, forgery, cheating, criminal breach of trust, falsification of records, etc. and also cases where it is alleged that the officer has acquired assets disproportionate to their known sources of income (SVC, Nagaland).

The Organizational set up of the State Vigilance Commission[78]

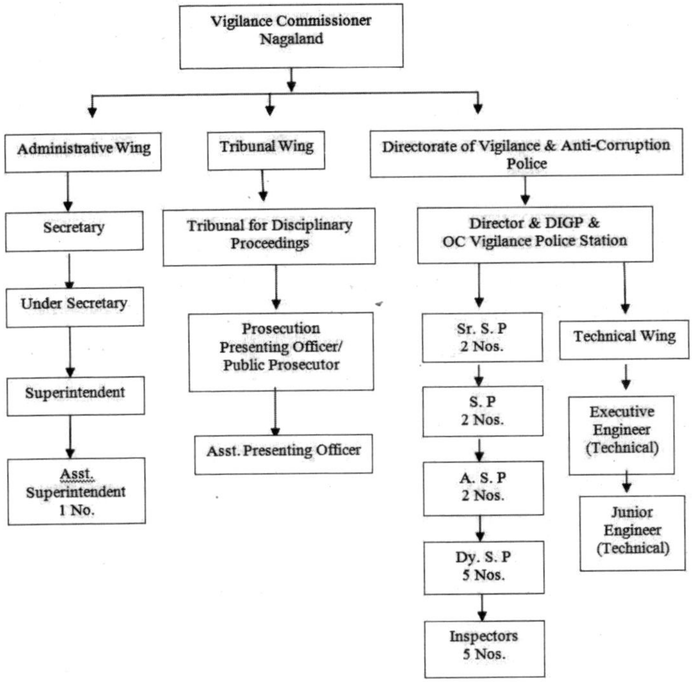

As per the latest information available, 105 cases were registered and investigated with various Government Departments in Nagaland during March 2015 to February 2016, including the cases brought forward from the previous year. Of these, maximum number of cases was from the Department of School Education (20), Health and Family Welfare (17), PWD (13), and Rural Development (8) (SVC, 2016).

The government is fighting against the insurgency while the insurgents are working against the government. So, both

[78] State Vigilance Commission, Government of Nagaland https://dpar.nagaland.gov.in/state-vigilance-commission/

are fighting against each other and do not meet eye to eye. But in reality, there could be doubts about the possible covert or unintentional meeting points wherein the actions of one support the other. On one side the state wants to contain insurgency, and to have development. For this lots of money is poured in by the Centre, and a portion is being parted to the insurgents so that they do not harm the government and people. As other stakeholders are also monetarily benefitted, they do not want to forego such benefit, and this is enabled under the disguise of 'threat' from the insurgents. And for this, the survival of the insurgency is necessary.

When the development work is happening, the contractors have to give money to the insurgents to ensure their security, as the state is either incapable of providing security or they do not want to provide security. In both these situations, the insurgents are benefitted because either they are getting money, or else they would be carrying out attacks, which propagate their organization's actions and name. Through this, the insurgents are conveying their message to the people and the government that they do not want the present regime to continue, would dislodge it, and seek to establish their own administration in their own way and thus, eager to be in power. Through their destructive actions and persuasions they force the people to support them.

The government should be for the welfare of its people, and act according to the laid down rules and guidelines. The Centre is providing huge funds to Nagaland for its development for which the State is accountable. But in lot many cases the so called developmental works are only on paper. The CAG's reports provide ample proofs for this (Chapter III). In large number of cases, a small portion of the big money is spent to show that the work is done and excessively billed. Thus, there is a double standard operational system adopted in showing the expenditure. The ordinary citizens do not have any means to counter the government. So with such quandary, the machineries and agencies entrusted the responsibility of national security could not accomplish their responsibilities in an impartial way, and gradually they become dissatisfied and lethargic, which adversely affect their efficiency and thereby public opinion about them. This certainly affects the national security.

Findings

The objective of this chapter is to explore the relationship between Naga culture and corruption in public offices in the state of Nagaland. As no study to find such relationship was carried out in India, it was decided to collect and analyse primary data as well as secondary data so that the findings of the study can be authenticated. With this aim, primary data was collected during the fieldwork using questionnaire schedule prepared with 5-point Likert scale answers. The data thus collected was used to find out the Mean, Standard Deviation, Skewness, Kurtosis, Chi square, and P value. Thereafter, for collecting secondary data, certain variables were identified from the sample literature, its interpretation was done using content analysis, and frequency made out. Thereafter, with the help of Pearson's correlation, the relationship between different variables was searched. Factor analysis was done to further validate the study. Using thematic approach, statements/ opinions/ discussions/speeches from different literature were cited, which helped to formulate certain themes that could show the links between culture and corruption. These themes have been put into five categories that are inter-linked, and they are: (1) Prevalence of culture of corruption in government offices, (2) Internalization of values and social pressures encourage individuals towards corruption in public offices, (3) Prevails the custom of giving high respect to people who accumulate wealth by any means, (4) Preference for jobs that enable to amass extra illegal money, and (5) The Moral Economy of Resentment exists, and uses corruption to get its 'compensation'. After formulating these themes, it was found that these have relationship with Hofstede's cultural dimension of Power Distance.

The findings of both the data show that there is an 'obscure relationship' between certain cultural factors and corruption in government offices in Nagaland. The study further shows that the Naga society gives more importance to family and clan ties, but less to anti-corruption principles (this needs much more indepth study to justify). Internalization of such norms and values and the prevailing corrupt environment in the public offices prompt several government employees to behave and adopt such practices that boost corruption. There had been cases in which government employees botched to fulfil their official duties honestly, but their clan members defended their failure suggesting that they had several family obligations. This is the misuse of public office for personal interests, which got indirect support from the clan members due to the strong intra-clan relationship. At the same time, the family/clan expect that their own men in public offices help the former even by misusing official power. This is further strengthened with the belief that extending such help to the near and dear ones, irrespective of misusing official power, would enable enhancing their status in their clan. Moreover, the belief that officials who do not (mis)use his power for the benefit of his clan members is of no use and does not deserve any respect, also encourages corruption. However, the data being very small and the respondents are from only one field, at this point it can only be said that there is an 'obscure relationship' between Naga culture and corruption in public offices.

Here, a big question – Do Nagas consider the mutual help between family/clan and their men in public offices as an offence? Nagas identified themselves from their clan and then the village they belong to, and these are integral part of their culture. Even after the statehood, the importance of these affinities is valued high as it is their traditional custom. In such a situation, the aforesaid mutual help is to remain because of the strong bond. Further, to maintain such strong ties, the mutual help is essential even if it goes against the modern law. The laws may be turning such 'mutual help' as corruption, but they (Nagas) do not discern it as an offence as (1) they are more concerned to maintain intra family/clan relationship, and (2) it is the 'laws of outsider'. The context in which it is being termed as 'corruption' is the secondary effect of the strong clan ties. Here it needs to be added that there are a large number of Nagas who look at the laws as 'laws of outsider', because they believe that the statehood was forcefully imposed on them. Hence, for them, ties to clan and village are of paramount importance than the laws.

It is worth mentioning that the respect given to those who have become rich through dishonest means may be only hype for gaining material benefits, due to the fear factor that they (riches) may harm them, and internalizing the belief that the 'end justifies the means'. And these changes happened in the mindset of lot many Nagas in the recent past - running behind wealth and power.

Another cause of corruption is found to be the rational individual choice, wherein the individual engaged in corruption after weighing the cost-benefit aspect, found that the chance of being caught was remote. He got this opinion from the experience he had from his office surroundings. But, the dimensions of internalization of norms and the rational choice facet need in-depth empirical study with the help of enormous primary data.

Preference for government jobs that enable to amass extra illegal money encourages corruption. The social status of those working in departments that earn extra cash is high and acknowledged. This attitude of people valuing those employees who earn extra money inspires people to be more corrupt.

The moral economy of resentment that prevailing amongst the Nagas has been another cultural factor that encouraged corruption. Nagas had suffered a lot from the hands of Indian security forces. Now, that the Indian government has been pouring huge monies in Nagaland in the name of development has been accepted and misused in different ways. Literature shows that they consider the money as compensation to their sufferings they had in the past. At the bottom of their heart, still they want to be a sovereign state. The peace accords between the Indian government and sections of Naga insurgents and its violation during the last several decades could be an indication of this. May be, they want to continue the fear phobia of insurgency for their personal interests.

Corruption in the government offices needs further emphasis in the light of the reports of the Comptroller and Auditor General (CAG), which is really worrisome due to its adverse impact on the development of the State. Central funds and schemes that come to Nagaland are deducted from top to bottom. It exists from

Pension to Scholarship, mid-day meal to Village Development Board (VDB) funds, Mahatma Gandhi National Rural Employment Guarantee Act (MGNREGA) to the Funds meant for Differently Abled Persons. Earlier, Nagas were described as sincere, hardworking and honest. But today, these qualities have disappeared, and Nagaland has become a spoilt child; corruption and laziness are rampant. People talk a lot about corruption and find out new ways to accumulate easy money. Awareness of the corrupt practices existing in government offices have forced the people to adopt dishonest methods to get any work done. Massive corruption and 'cuts' in sharing the government funds have made several developmental programmes showing simply on paper. It is also found that the insurgent groups have some claim on the funds that are allotted to the state for developmental works. The illegal taxation as well as extortion have encouraged corruption in many ways. Today, corruption has become a way of life that led to the 'culture of corruption' in the public offices, and this menace has adversely affected the progress of the state. It needs to mention here that these findings are based only on the small sample population of a particular place and less number of literature, and hence, could not be generalized on the Naga society, but can be taken as a lead for a larger study.

CHAPTER III

Corruption and Insurgency in Nagaland

Corruption is the misuse of official power for vested interests. Corruption can be in the form of bribery, embezzlement, graft, extortion, cronyism, nepotism, parochialism, patronage, influence peddling, and so on. Discussion on corruption has already been made in the previous chapter. However, a brief on the misappropriation of funds in Nagaland as brought out in the reports of the Comptroller and Auditor General (CAG), the apex body that does the financial assessment of government offices in India, has been included in this section. This chapter will be exploring the relationship between corruption and insurgency, in Nagaland.

Corruption is one of the factors that hinders good governance and gives birth to several problems. The term 'corruption' has been defined by Ackerman (1978)[1] as 'using public goods or capacity for private benefits.' Insurgency is a rebellion or movement with mass support to overthrow the legitimately established government. It is a 'struggle between a nonruling group and the ruling authorities, in which the nonruling group uses political resources and violence' and is a 'protracted political-military activity' that uses irregular military forces (World Report News)[2]. Wherever there is insurgency, corruption is a precursor. But it does not mean that wherever there is corruption there has to be insurgency. Teets

[1] Ackerman, Rose, Susan; 1978; Corruption: A Study in Political Economy, Academic Press Inc. Sandiego.

[2] World Report News; http://www.worldreportnews.com/us-foreign-policy-archived/the-difference-between-terrorists-and-insurgents

and Chenoweth (2009)[3] opine that corruption and terrorism (insurgency) coexist in a mutually reinforcing relationship.

Corrupt officials look the other way when illegal activities are happening due to the personal gains they will be having. Corruption enables the entry of inefficient people in jobs that further greater corruption and corrupt systems. In an insurgency-infested area, the insurgents influence authorities in power so that the former can easily carry out their activities such as recruitment, imparting training, transportation of weapons, as well as collecting information from within the department on the strength and movement of government forces. In corrupt societies, the government may be unwilling to strictly implement the laws. In another context, many times the government agencies are incapable of executing the laws stringently due to their inability to fight against the insurgents, who have grown in their strength and capability with the help of corruption. So, corruption begets more corruption and makes the government machineries too weak to fight insurgency. Thus, corruption results in unwillingness and/or incapability of the government to strictly implement the laws. Similar link can be seen between corruption and border security. National borders play an important role in the growth of insurgency, as cross border smuggling of weapons, drugs, money, and humans happens due to weakened security resulting from rampant corruption. Borders are more vulnerable to corruption due to various reasons, like the influence of organized crime syndicate, lack of external oversight, size and type of borders, benefit of discretionary powers empowered to the border authorities, high tariffs on goods that are lawfully transported, ban on transportation of drugs and weapons, and so on. To overcome these issues, the stakeholders many times prefer corruption. In case of the Nagaland insurgency, the insurgents sneaked to the neighbouring countries like Myanmar, Bangladesh, China, Pakistan and so on for insurgency training.

[3] Teets, Jessica & Chenoweth, Erica; 2009; To Bribe or to Bomb: Do Corruption and Terrorism Go Together?; *in* Corruption, Global Security, and World Order, Ed. Robert I Rotberg, Brookings Institution Press, Washington DC.

Similarly, smuggling of weapons was done in a massive way. In all these activities, corruption at the border played a significant role in accomplishing their tasks. Thus, an 'invisible' link between corruption and insurgency can be observed.

How Insurgents influenced the Naga mindset towards Insurgency?

Insurgency is often described as a state of mind, and the support of the common people is imperative for its success. Utmost love for their family, clan and land is the characteristic of Naga life. Their existence revolve around these foundations and do not like anybody's interference in it, a feature imbibed and inherited from their forefathers and it is in their genes. But, the annexation of Naga Hills by the British was a blow to their self-esteem that they could not ingest, and a kind of vengeance engendered in their minds. This mind-set was further strengthened with the actions of Naga Club and NNC. It was this conviction that got them the wholehearted support of the people in the beginning of insurgency.

There is a need to understand how the insurgent groups in Nagaland bent, interpreted and demonstrated the prevailing belief system to suit and fulfil their purposes. As it was the British who annexed Naga Hills with Assam, Nagas asserted that when the former left, the Naga hills had to be free and independent as earlier. They better preferred death than losing their freedom. These attitudes and related ideas prevailing among the Nagas were exploited and used as propaganda by the insurgent groups to draw the people towards them and support insurgency. According to Verrier[4] (1961), the deep-rooted belief system of free and uninterfered life were revived and given much publicity by the insurgent groups, so as to rouse the people. The propaganda systematically explained how they will be suppressed and lose their freedom if they joined India and how their communal harmony will be disturbed. The usage of the land, forests and natural resources

[4] Verrier Elwin, 1961; Nagaland, Research Department, Adviser's Secretariat, Shillong.

that they had been enjoying freely since time immemorial will be taxed. The significance of family, land, cultivation, food pattern and so on will be disturbed. They will have to pay taxes for the fishing that they had been doing over the 400 miles of river. By depicting that the Hindu government would bring an end to Christianity, the insurgents were able to create panic among the Christians and to bring them to their fold. Further, they raised the issues like cow protection movement and prohibition policy to warn the common people that their custom of beef eating and consuming rice-beer will be prohibited by the Indian government. Thus, the issues of everyday life were taken up and projected as being endagered under the Indian rule. The powerful chiefs were warned that they will be losing their power under the Indian government. To make the situation worse, the insurgents created the propaganda that the Indian armed forces had been given a free hand to rape Naga women, steal food, drinks, grains, fruits and vegetables, and to torture and harass the local people as much as they can. Ultimately there will be a situation wherein the Nagas will lose their prestige as warriors. It is a fact that Nagas are intensely attached with their land, village and mountain, as also to the freedom to lead life the way they want, their traditions, and everything that they have been enjoying since centuries. The insurgents raised all these issues, and propagated that allowing Indian rule would destroy everything that belonged to them and their social and cultural practices would be in danger. To prevent such destruction, everybody was to support the insurgents and contribute physically, mentally as well as monetarily. Here we can observe how meticulously the insurgent groups have identified the features of their culture, linked it with the sentiments of the people and used to provoke them. Once they succeeded with this tactics, youths came forward in a massive way and took up arms. After portraying themselves as the saviour of people, they urged each household to send at least one youth to join insurgency. This not only enhanced the strength of the insurgent group but also created a sympathy wave amongst the people, towards the insurgent groups. This empathy and strong fellow feeling enabled the insurgent groups to continue with their fight even when there were 'reports of wanton killings, unprecedented levels of violence, torture, abductions, village regrouping, ambushes and burning villages and granaries of what seemed to be a murky geography of misery.' In spite of such tyrannies, the NNC and its military could carry on its battle because "for every Naga life that was taken, ten others joined the Naga Army" (Wouters)[5]. At the same time, the people had highest regards and faith in the strong leadership of A Z Phizo, which too played a positive role in attracting people towards the movement.

No doubt, the later periods of Naga movement witnessed lots of intra-organizational politics and factional conflicts that resulted in the stealthy inclusion of vested interests of insurgents and their leaders. Thus, the individual interests overpowered the organizational interests and a situation emerged, wherein the criminals sneaked into the 'insurgency umbrella' and started to play their roles under the pretext of insurgency. Gradually a variety of malices too found their way into the functioning of the insurgent groups. With the pouring in of unaccountable money in the state, in the name of controlling insurgency, there were a large number of people who wanted to keep the insurgency alive. For them, insurgency had become a money-minting mechanism. This was followed by massive corruption and bribery in the government functioning that indirectly supported the insurgents to spread their wings further. Corruption weakens the government machineries, and this weakness is exploited by the insurgent groups for strengthening their infrastructure. The literature review shows that the government funds that poured into the state for developmental works were, in several instances, diverted to the insurgents. This can be an indication of the relationship between corruption and insurgency in the state.

Teets and Chenoweth (2009)[6] opine that the existence of

[5] Wouters Jelle JP, 2018; In the Shadows of Naga Insurgency, Oxford University Press, New Delhi, p. xii.

[6] Teets Jessica & Chenoweth Erica; 2009; To Bribe or to Bomb: Do Corruption and Terrorism Go Together?; *in* Corruption, Global Security, and World Order, Ed. Robert I Rotberg, Brookings Institution Press, Washington DC.

corruption "indirectly increases the ability of insurgent groups to carry out attacks. Corrupt states create opportunities for terrorist organizations because of an inability or unwillingness to enforce the rule of law, which reduces the costs of operating within such territories. In addition, the presence of corruption allows for the creation of a criminal infrastructure that groups use for funding, weapons, transport, and forged documents, thereby strengthening terrorist organizations. This criminal infrastructure supports illicit trade in arms, people, and drugs, and creates three conditions of which terrorist groups take advantage: (1) a signal to potential terrorists that the state does not have the capacity to enforce the rule of law, (2)an infrastructure in money laundering, secretive transportation, and forged documents, and (3) a flow of materials and independent funding by which terrorists can conduct their activities, thereby lowering the costs to terrorists of operating from within these countries. The *facilitation* explanation argues that corruption and terrorism coexist, but that the relationship between the two is indirect.'

Coming to the study context, it is the Directorate of Nagaland Lokayukta Police (Vigilance Commission) that conducts investigation of the corruption cases in the state. This was established in 1975. Between 1975 and 1999, several preliminary enquiries and a few regular cases were registered, the data of which is given in the below table:

Table 3.1: Corruption Cases in the State

Sr No.	*Period*	*Preliminary Enquiry*	*Regular Case*	*Total no. of cases*
1	1975 - 1979	7	-	7
2	1980 – 1984	7	-	7
3	1985 – 1989	138	-	138
4	1990 – 1994	160	3	163
5	1995 – 1999	59	-	59
	Total	371	3	374

Source : Nagaland Lokayukta, Directorate of Investigation

The data shows that though the number of preliminary enquiries are large, the regular cases registered are very meagre. A regular case is registered when the preliminary enquiry shows that a crime has been committed.

In the present context, let us examine whether there is any link between corruption in public offices and insurgency in Nagaland. Hence, the **Hypothesis** of this chapter is:

Null Hypothesis: *Corruption in public offices has no relationship with the domestic insurgency in Nagaland.*

Alternative Hypothesis: *Corruption in public offices has relationship with the domestic insurgency in Nagaland.*

Primary Data Analysis

The method adopted for collecting primary and secondary data was the same as mentioned in chapter II. To find out the relationship between corruption and insurgency, the respondents were given a statement, "Corruption has got link with insurgency in the state". As shown in the below table, 1 per cent of the respondents 'strongly disagreed', and 7 per cent 'disagreed' with this statement. A good number of respondents (29 per cent) were neutral, whereas 57 per cent 'agreed' and 6 per cent 'strongly agreed' with this supposition. This shows that a major part of the respondents (63 per cent) were on the agreeing side, while only 8 per cent respondents disagreed with the statement. Thus, according to them there is a linkage between corruption and insurgency in the state.

Table 3.2

Answers	*No. of respondents*	*Percentage*
Strongly Disagree	2	1
Disagree	10	7
Can't say	41	29
Agree	81	57
Strongly Agree	8	6

Table 3.3

Variable 12	*1 SD*	*2 D*	*3 CS*	*4 A*	*5 SA*	$\bar{X}$ *mean*	*St. Dev*	*Skew*	*Kurt*	X^2 *Chi*	*P-value*
Corruption has got link with insurgency in the state	2	10	41	81	8	3.584	.764	-.868	1.078	154.127	.000

It is observed that the mean value of the responses is 3.584 which is higher than the standard average, i.e. three at five point scale. The value of standard deviation is .764 (variation is small), and skewness is -.868 which indicates that variation in the mean opinion is inclined towards the higher side of the mean. The value of Kurtosis is 1.078 which is higher than zero and it illustrates that the distribution of opinion of respondents is laptykurtic or concentrated. As the P-value (Asymp. Sig. - full form asymptotic significance) is .000, the hypothesis that corruption has no link with insurgency in the state is rejected, and the alternative hypothesis that corruption has got link with insurgency in the state is accepted.

A study conducted by Usman[7] (2017) on the Boko Haram insurgency in the Northeast Nigeria between 2009 and 2015 found that corruption perpetuated by the office of the former National Security Adviser was one of the most important reasons for the growth of insurgency.The study adopted content and observational analysis. Documentary ideas, as expressed in text books, journal articles, magazines, internet and newspapers were analyzed. The study very clearly established that corruption had negatively impacted the war against insurgency in the region, and this was due to the sharing of the 2.1 billion dollars and the questionable contracts awarded, which were not executed by some companies and persons.

[7] Usman Umaru, 2017; Impact of Corruption on Insurgency in the North-Eastern Region of Nigeria, IOSR Journal of Business Management, Vol. 19, Issue 1, Ver. I, January, p. 19-25.

This finding is further strengthened by another study by Victoria[8] (2018), wherein it was found that corrupt military officials had taken advantage of the situation to create and award non-existent and fraudulent contracts to themselves and their cronies. The proceeds of these unlawful gains are laundered in the UK, USA and elsewhere around the world. There have been insinuations from different quarters that Nigeria may never witness the end to Boko Haram insurgency since some elites have designated the fight against 'insurgency' as one of the ways of making quick and cool money. They are sure that once the insurgency is stopped, their guaranteed source of income would automatically cut off. Quoting different sources, Victoria maintains that the Nigerian police officers on the joint task force mission had to confront insurgent group with over 1000 bullets on a daily basis with just 30 bullets. Any officer that required more of the bullets had to bribe to get it.

Events across the globe show that prevalence of corruption is one of the preconditions for the growth of insurgency. The Iraqi forces had to face defeat in the first battle of Mosul, principally, due to the prevalence of corruption in their army in many ways, like recruitment, promotion, ghost soldiers, theft of weapons and supplies, which further caused the rise of ISIS. Thus, corruption brought down the regime as well as stimulated the growth of insurgency. This was revealed in an investigation by the Iraqi Parliamentary Committee for Security and Defense that financial and administrative corruption fed the rise of ISIS (MacLachlan, 2018)[9].

Quoting another example, MacLachlan mentions that in South Sudan, in the early years after independence, the ruling elite

[8] Victoria Nkemdilim Ogbuehl, 2018; Corruption and Escalating Boko Haram Insurgency in Nigeria, Research & Reviews: Journal of Social Sciences, Vol. 4, Issue 3, October.

[9] MacLachlan, Karolina, 2018; Corruption and Conflict: Hand in Glove, NATO Review, 6th December https://www.nato.int/docu/review/2018/Also-in-2018/corruption-and-conflict-hand-in-glove-nato-defense-security/EN/index.htm

diverted oil revenues to fund patronage networks through defence sector expenditures. A bloated military budget was used to pay the salaries of 230,000 soldiers and militia members belonging to various patronage networks. Loyalty was bought and violence kept in check. But in 2012, increasing prices of loyalty, a spat with the Sudanese government over the use of oil infrastructure, and a global decline in oil prices led to decreasing production and lower revenues. This diminished the ability of President Salva Kiir's government to buy the loyalty of its opponents, so Kiir resorted to dismissing his opponents. Within a year, civil war and a humanitarian crisis engulfed the country, and today it is a failed state.

Afghanistan is another example, where corruption undermined the US mission by fuelling grievances and channelling support to the insurgency. The US experience in Afghanistan shows that the systematic corruption was a strategic threat to their mission. In 2016 former US ambassador to Afghanistan Ryan Crocker said, "The ultimate point of failure for our efforts wasn't an insurgency. It was the weight of endemic corruption" (SIGAR, 2018)[10].

Coming back to India, the Governor of Nagaland BK Nehru, in the midst of ongoing tension following the non-acceptance of Indian government's offer by the 'underground' Nagas, in August 1972 cautioned 'the overground supporters of the underground,' particularly 'certain members' of the Nagaland Legislative Assembly. He warned that if any members through their action showed that an oath sworn to the constitution of India and its integrity was false, the question arose whether such members 'can continue to be members of the Indian Legislature'. No Governor 'can ever entrust such a person with the responsibilities of holding charge of any office in the State'"[11]. This warning implied that there were certain MLAs who were alleged to have supported the

[10] Special Inspector General for Afghanistan Reconstruction-SIGAR, 2018; Corruption in Conflict, September. https://www.sigar.mil/interactive-reports/corruption-in-conflict/index.html

[11] Aram, M, 1974; Peace in Nagaland, Arnold-Heinemann Publishers (India) Pvt. Ltd., New Delhi, p. 303.

underground insurgents, and such patronage inferred a linkage between corruption and insurgency.

Another postulation made in this connection was, 'The insurgents got their 'cut' from the funds given to the government offices' to which it is seen that nobody 'strongly disagreed', while 2 per cent of the respondents 'disagreed', whereas 25 per cent neither agreed nor disagreed. On the other hand, 64 per cent of the respondents 'agreed' and 9 per cent 'strongly agreed'. To the previous assertion it is seen that 63 per cent were on the agreeing side, while 73 per cent agreed to this statement, which signifies that the insurgents got their 'cut' from the funds given to the government offices.

Table 3.4

Answers	*No. of respondents*	*Percentage*
Strongly Disagree	-	-
Disagree	3	2
Can't say	36	25
Agree	90	64
Strongly Agree	13	9

Table 3.5

Variable 18	*1 SD*	*2 D*	*3 CS*	*4 A*	*5 SA*	$\overline{X}$ *mean*	*St. Dev*	*Skew*	*Kurt*	X^2 *Chi*	*P-value*
Insurgents got their 'cut' from the funds given to the government offices	-	3	36	90	13	3.795	.625	-.355	.482	127.690	.000

It is observed that the mean value of the responses is 3.795 which is higher than the standard average. The value of standard deviation is .625 (variation is small), and skewness is -.355 which indicates that variation in the mean opinion is inclined towars the higher side. The value of Kurtosis is .482 which is higher than zero and it illustrates that the distribution of opinion of respondents is laptykurtic or concentrated. As the P-value of chi square is .000, the hypothesis that the insurgents did not get their 'cut' from the funds given to the government offices is rejected, and the alternative hypothesis that the insurgents got their 'cut' from the funds given to the government offices has been accepted.

The huge amount of money poured in the state by the Centre has given opportunity to politicians, bureaucrats, contractors, agents, and so on to accumulate wealth according to their vested interests. According to Rammohan (2003)[12], 'the policy of the Central Government, or rather the political party who ruled from Delhi then, thoroughly corrupted the local politicians and bureaucrats. After splitting the NNC and the Underground Naga leadership, and granting statehood, development money was poured into the state, without any accountability. A notorious gang of contractors sprang up, all based in Delhi, all followers of the party in power. It soon attained the dubious distinction of being called the 'Delhi Durbar.' All the major contracts of the state and contracts for supply of stores went to this unholy gang, who brought 95 per cent of all development money sanctioned to the state back to Delhi, by simply carrying out projects and supplying stores on paper, and the money was used for their personal benefits. The effect on the state was devastating, and the insurgency, which began without any grounds of discrimination or poor governance, got all the reasons for an insurgency because of this single facet.' A portion of the funds, 'rebel cuts,' had to be spared for the insurgent groups. This shows how the flourishing of corruption in the name of development has strengthened insurgency in the state.

Further, certain cases have come out in Nagaland that show evidence of link between corruption and insurgency. The NIA investigation has found documentary evidence indicating former chief minister and Naga People's Front (NPF) leader T.R. Zeliang's

[12] Rammohan EN, 2003; The Naga Insurgency – Part I, USI Journal, July – September https://usiofindia.org/publication/usi-journal/the-naga-insurgency-part-i/

involvement in a terror funding case in which he siphoned government funds to NSCN (K) (Manoj Anand, 2018)[13]. But, the other side of this and similar other incidents was that the money was paid to the insurgent groups due to fear for life, i.e. the government failed to prevent insurgents from making threatening demands to pay money. Here, it is the Chief minister himself, and this shows his helplessness. Or is it that the state administration had also been 'benefitted' from the funds and to continue with this benefit, consented to share a portion of the fund to the insurgents?

In 2018, the NIA arrested three senior Nagaland government officials in connection with its probe into alleged funding of terror groups such as the NSCN-K by defrauding the state exchequer. The Director of the Directorate of Agriculture G Ikuto Zhimomi, Executive Engineer in the Directorate of Rural Development Ketouzo Peseyie and Divisional Accounts Officer of the Directorate of Urban Development Sangtemchuba were arrested from Dimapur. The officials were arrested for paying huge amount of money to various underground factions such as NSCN-K, NSCN-R, Federal Government of Nagaland (FGN), Naga National Council (NNC) and others between 2012 and 2016. The facts regarding the payment were revealed during the scrutiny of the official documents including demand letters and payment receipts which were seized during the search operation carried out at 13 government offices in January 2017. Earlier, the agency had arrested two NSCN-K cadres from whom several incriminating documents were seized. Their interrogation revealed the involvement of above government officials in paying large sums of money to the tune of crores, to the various terrorist factions and led to their arrests (Firstpost, 2018)[14].

[13] Manoj Anand, 2018; NIA Claims Former Nagaland CM Zeliang help in funding terror, Deccan Chronicle, 19th March https://www.deccanchronicle.com/nation/current-affairs/190318/nia-claims-former-nagaland-cm-zeliang-help-in-funding-terror.html

[14] Firstpost, 2018; NIA probes large-scale extortion, illegal tax collection by NSCN-K, arrests 3 senior Nagaland govt officials, 26th March. https://www.firstpost.com/india/nia-probes-large-scale-

According to Purkayastha (2007)[15], 'there has been constant accusation of the politicians sponsoring, supporting and receiving kickback from certain insurgent groups' (p. 52). This explains how politicians are involved in corruption and how it is linked with insurgency.

The emergence of a middle class and a nexus between politicians, drug dealers, contractors and the insurgent groups has vitiated the body politic and Naga civic life. Some members of the State Administration are nothing more than middlemen in the flow of funds to insurgent groups. This has been made possible by ensuring that no system of accountability exists (Pillai, 2001)[16].

It is being alleged that the leaders who wanted Nagaland to be a separate nation, started to use the central government funds for violent purposes. The flow of money without any oversight enabled them to divert it as they wished. The central government did not seek accountability of the state for these funds. It can be assumed that such flow of funds contributed in some way in boosting insurgency in the state.

The insurgent groups are involved in forcefully collecting 'taxes' from different sources in Nagaland. One of the sources is the developmental works. Insurgent groups have a direct say in the distribution of funds for development works. Hence, budgets for the development works did not wholly reach the ground destination, because 'taxes' for the Naga underground groups were deducted from the original amount by the government officials e.g. Block Development Officer (BDO) and only the remaining money was utilized for the developmental work. As there is no account for the deducted money, it is obvious that the 'cut' includes the money meant for the authority himself too. So, the action of the

---

extortion-illegal-tax-collection-by-nscn-k-arrests-3-senior-nagaland-govt-officials-4405343.html

[15] Purkayastha, Rakhal, 2007; 3rd Presentation, *in* Roots of Insurgency in Northeast India, Ed. Bhattacharjee JB, Akansha Publishing House, New Delhi.

[16] Pillai S K; 2001; Anatomy of an Insurgency Ethnicity & Identity in Nagaland; SATP http://www.satp.org/satporgtp/publication/faultlines/volume3/fault3-enpillaif.htm#33

government official itself supports insurgency. Thus, on record the fund is spent for development work, whereas in reality no such work has taken place or has happened partially. In this way he uses the underground taxes as a cover for his own corrupt practices.

Construction contract is the most lucrative job for the contratror to make easy money to the contractor, as well as for all the authorities in the hierarchical chain. In addition to the contractor, the minister holding the department, bureaucrats, section heads, clerks, engineers, Sub Divisional Officer, insurgent groups in the area and so on have their own 'cuts', and it is a matter of conjecture, what is left out for the real work. Then certainly the quality and quantity of the work suffer and in many cases the work is shown only on the paper.

According to Wouters (2018)[17] 'the Naga underground groups put pressures on development funds, which led to lowered (development) budgets. The Development Office itself was locally known as a breeding ground of corruption, where the cuts and commissions taken by its officers and engineers…The Block Development Officer himself was appropriating large sums. The position of BDO is of modest rank, yet perhaps no other post offers such lucrative possibilities for (illegal) side incomes.' This is one of the ways in which corruption fostered insurgency in the state. It is noteworthy that this system has been existing since long back. Quoting Charles Pawsey (1960), the last serving British District Commissioner of the Naga Hills district, Wouters added, 'the underground really are supported by the Government of India. The enormous sums spent on the civil administration meant a surplus of cash in the villages. No rich contractor is going to refuse a request for help if an underground leader is backed by an escort of armed guerrillas. There nevertheless exists a clear perception that such 'rebel cuts' were systematized and increased, and steeply at that, after the 1997 ceasefire.' (p.112-3) Quoting sources, Wouters further mentions that Delhi has been pumping in huge funds in Nagaland thinking that it would help the Nagas

[17] Wouters Jelle JP, 2018; In the Shadows of Naga Insurgency, Oxford University Press, New Delhi, p.111.

feel Indian. But this has made Nagaland the most corrupted state of India. Everyone is corrupt; politicians, bureaucrats, police, and even the villagers. However, Nagas still want their independence (p.169).

In a public rally, the Action Committee Against Unabated Taxation (ACAUT) contended that the Naga underground (UG) has left aside the Naga nationalism and were interested in 'private material gains and to fight over interpersonal and intertribal differences' (Wouters, p.4). Development offices have become a prime source of 'rebel revenue', especially after ceasefire (p. 82). The present day insecure, chaotic politics of insurgency in the everyday Naga life, are the result of the keen vested interests of the authorities in different walks of life. The competing discourses, political rhetoric and standpoints that emerge from the Indo-Naga conflict belong to, and are manipulated by Naga militant leaders and Indian politicians, army officers, and negotiators (p. 86).

Moving further, another assertion was presented to the respondents to express their views, i.e. 'Corruption in government offices has encouraged insurgency in the state.' This assertion was 'strongly disagreed' by 1 per cent, and 'disagreed' by 8 per cent of the respondents. 21 percent of the respondents opted 'Can't say', while 61 per cent 'agreed' and 9 per cent 'strongly agreed.' Here also, a major part of the respondents (70 per cent) were on the agreeing side, and only 9 per cent on the disagreeing side.

Table 3.6

Answers	*No. of respondents*	*Percentage*
Strongly Disagree	1	1
Disagree	12	8
Can't say	30	21
Agree	86	61
Strongly Agree	13	9

Table 3.7

Variable 19	*1 SD*	*2 D*	*3 CS*	*4 A*	*5 SA*	*$\bar{X}$ mean*	*St. Dev*	*Skew*	*Kurt*	*X^2 Chi*	*P-value*
Corruption in government offices has encouraged insurgency in the state	1	12	30	86	13	3.690	.782	-.833	.804	161.169	.000

The mean value of the responses is 3.690 which is higher than the standard average. The value of standard deviation is .742 (variation is small), and skewness is -.833 which indicates that variation in the mean opinion is inclined towards the higher side of mean. The value of Kurtosis is .804 which is higher than zero and it illustrates that the distribution of opinion of respondents is laptykurtic or concentrated. As the P-value is .000, the null hypothesis, that corruption in government offices has not encouraged insurgency in the state, is rejected, and the alternative hypothesis, that corruption in government offices has encouraged insurgency in the state, has been accepted.

While discussing the relationship between corruption and insurgency in the state, one of the senior police officers said, '*No government can be in power without the sympathy of the insurgent groups, and this (sympathy) is purchased with money. When funds are given to the State and its allocation to different departments is done, it is known to th insurgent groups. In fact, the insurgent groups are capable of procuring copy of the fund allocation letter. Armed with this information, they contact the authorities of the concerned offices and ask to make contribution of particular amount to them. Due to fear of life, the authorities are forced to share a 'cut' of the fund with the insurgents, and accordingly manipulate the figures on paper. This way the receipt of the funds and its expenditure are made clear in the documents. The sufferer is the project/programme for which the fund was actually meant, and hence, the underdevelopment of the state.*"

Explaining another angle of corruption and insurgency, the police officer added, '*the person who is dealing with the funds and siphoning a part of it to the insurgent group,s diverts precise amount into his own pocket. This is the 'extra' amount he is getting, in addition to his 'entitled cut'. In this situation, all those benefitted would secretly prefer to continue with the 'hype of insurgency' under the garb of 'peace' agreements.*"

To quote another police officer, "*Peace agreement says that the cadres have to be in their camps. But in reality, some cadres are in their camps, their leaders have become overground (OG), and enjoy luxury life. They get huge money through illegal tax collection, cuts from the government funds, extortion, and several other means. The insurgents hold their budget session, wherein they decide the entity and the amount that have to be collected.*'

Elucidating the link between corruption and insurgency, the police officer related, '*Insurgency survives because of the financial support they get. People contribute because of fear for life. Politicians, government officials, contractors, and everybody give money to insurgents due to fear for life. The insurgents have link with every office and they get useful information from the officials. Officials take away some amount in the name of 'cuts to the insurgents.' Illegal taxation/extortion flourish due to the failure of the government to take any stern action. As everybody in the hierarchical chain is benefitted, there is no political will to control insurgency.*'

In the initial days of their struggle for sovereignty, the Nagas were very honest. However, over a period of time due to various reasons, they deviated from the path of nationalism, and today they are involved in certain criminal activities, which are enabled due to the prevalence of corruption in government offices.

While studying the relationship between income inequality and domestic terrorism, Krieger and Meierrieks (2019)[18] found that this connection 'is in parts due to the ill effects of income inequality on institutional outcomes (e.g., corruption) which in

[18] Krieger, Tim and Meierrieks, Daniel, 2019; Income inequality, redistribution and domestic terrorism, Elsevier, World Development, Volume 116, April 2019, Pages 125-136.

turn motivate domestic terrorism.' This explicits that corruption in institutions causes inequality in people's income and that becomes one of the factors that encourages insurgency/terrorism, which we observe in Nagaland. Here, the insurgents encouraged corruption in government offices using coercive methods that benefitted them, politicians, contractors, bureaucrats, government officials, and all those coming in the network, which ultimately resulted in income inequality in the society, which in turn played a significant role in encouraging people to support or join insurgency. This is a vicious cycle wherein corruption encouraged insurgency which further fostered corruption.

'The Naga HoHo, the apex body of the Naga tribal organisations, upbraided the 'national workers' (the UGs) for rampant extortion and imposing unbearable taxes on old and emerging Naga entrepreneurs... what was striking was the frankness with which disappointment and disillusionment with the "national workers" of all the militant groups was voiced by the people. Some people also accused the "national workers" of corruption and extortion.'[19]

According to Nuh (2016)[20], in a joint meeting held under the auspices of the Nagaland Peace Council and Peace Commission on 7th August 1993 in Kohima, a resolution was passed to stop the extortion of money from public, government servants, businessmen, etc. causing insecurity and tensions (p. 536)

The post 1997 ceasefire period witnessed continued fights amongst different Naga rebel groups, systematic violation of ceasefire conditions and severe damage to the economic and social fabric of Naga society. The division and factional feuds among the Naga cadres help the authorities at different levels to encash the situation to their favour. The parallel government, hand in glove with the authorities of different departments in the state, have created a conducive atmosphere for the rapid spread of corruption.

[19] Manchanda, Rita & Bose, Tapan, 2011; Expanding the Middle Space in the Naga Peace Process, Economic and Political Weekly, December 31, Vol xlvi No 53, p. 52.

[20] Nuh VK, 2016; The Naga Chronicle, 2nd revised edition, Regency Publications, New Delhi.

How is it possible that the state and central governments are unaware of this? Is it that they wanted to continue with the situation so that their inflated personal ambitions could be flourished unhindered? If the fence starts eating crops, how will the crops be protected? This fence-eating-crops phenomena started mainly in the post-statehood period, which gradually corrupted all wings of the government and thus led to a culture of corruption. In fact, this was and still is an appeasing method to make the people happy by fulfilling their certain demands, so that in the long run they can be forced to forego their principal demand, which is the bone of contention in amalgamating the state with Indian Union.

This was made possible by creating a group of moderate people who were ready to concede lesser than sovereignty and independence by fulfilling all their peripheral demands. So, in the initial stage, security forces were used to suppress insurgency, Naga Hills-Tuensang Area was established, the demand for statehood was agreed to, still insurgency and counter insurgency continued, then ceasefire, pouring in of colossal funds for 'development', siphoning of part of it to the undergrounds, emerging of factional feuds in the name of group, community, and tactics to gain maximum funds, and making their presence felt in the society. Wouters cites several instances to prove that corruption has become a culture in all government offices to get any work done, which made Nagaland to earn the dubious distinction of 'the symbol of corruption', 'paradise of corruption', 'whirlpool of rampant corruption', and corruption is the 'very norm of government and governance'(p. 170).

All these show that corruption in government offices is one element that fosters insurgency in the State. There are vested interests as well as the element of fear that force people/authorities to contribute to the insurgents. It also shows that the failure of the government to take action against insurgency is an indirect support to this menace.

Though there are several factors that fostered insurgency, this study has focussed on corruption in public offices, which has been found to be a crucial element in encouraging insurgency, in addition to illegal tax collection and extortion in Nagaland.

Secondary Data Analysis

As mentioned in Chapter II, the same methodology was used here to find out the relationship between corruption and insurgency in the State. The prevalence of corruption in public offices has been established in the previous chapter. Table 2.29 explicts that variable no. 23 'insurgency/ terror' (0.845) (i.e. 'there is insurgency in Nagaland, and corruption is one of the factors that supported it') has a close relationship with variable no. 24 'influence'. The interpretation of 'influence' is that the 'insurgents influenced the government authorities so as to enable the former to accomplish their tasks easily, corruption indirectly supported the insurgency'. Further, it is seen in table 2.34 that component no. 4 has a close relationship with variable 'insurgency/terror' (0.954) and variable 'influence' (0.944). As the study does not show any direct correlation between the variable 'corruption' and variable 'insurgency', but since correlation is shown between variable 'insurgency/terror' and 'influence', it can be safely said that there is indirect relationship between corruption in public offices and insurgency in the State of Nagaland. So, inference can be drawn that corruption is one of the factors that supported insurgency indirectly.

Factor Analysis

In the Factor Analysis of Chapter 2 (Table 2.30) it has been shown that the variables 'insurgency/terror' (.917) and 'influence' (.916) have close relationship. This indicates that there is insurgency in Nagaland, and corruption is one of the factors that supported it. It further indicated that the insurgents influenced the government officials so that the former could achieve their goals without much hindrance. As seen earlier, one of their important targets was to procure a share from the funds that were destined for development purposes. They used their links with the government authorities in the hierarchical chain to get hold of the same, principally using coercive methods. Additionally, we have seen that illegal taxation, extortion and so on were also sources of income of insurgents. So, the Factor Analysis also shows the relationship between corruption in public offices and insurgency in Nagaland. Further, as seen earlier, primary data also indicated that corruption in government offices has been one of the factors that encouraged insurgency in the state.

Statements and Themes

As done in Chapter II, using thematic approach, here also specific statements/phrases were selected, that show the relationship between corruption and insurgency, which helped to formulate the relevant Theme. This is expressed in the below table:

Table 3.8: Statements and Themes

Statements/Opinions/Phrases *A*	*Theme that link corruption in public offices and insurgency* *B*
- The existence of corruption 'indirectly increases the ability of insurgent groups to carry out attacks' (Teets and Chenoweth, 2009) - Corrupt states create opportunities for terrorist organizations because of an inability or unwillingness to enforce the rule of law (ibid) - The presence of corruption allows for the creation of a criminal infrastructure that groups use for funding, weapons, transport, and forged documents, thereby strengthening terrorist organizations (ibid) - This criminal infrastructure supports illicit trade in arms, people, and drugs, and creates conditions, which terrorist groups take advantage (ibid) - In the Northeast Nigeria, corruption was one of the important reasons for the growth of Boko Haram insurgency (Usman, 2017) - The policy of the Central Government, or rather the political party who ruled from Delhi then thoroughly corrupted the local politicians and bureaucrats in Nagaland (Rammohan, 2003)	Corruption in government offices is one of the factors that strengthened insurgency in the state.

- Development money was poured into the state, without any accountability (ibid)
- The effect on the state was devastating, and the insurgency which began without any grounds of discrimination or poor governance, got all the reasons for an insurgency because of this single facet (ibid)
- The NIA investigation has found documentary evidence indicating former chief minister and Naga People's Front (NPF) leader T.R. Zeliang's involvement in a terror funding case in which he siphoned government funds to NSCN-K (Anand, 2018)
- In 2018, the NIA arrested three senior Nagaland government officials in connection with its probe into alleged funding of terror groups such as the NSCN-K by defrauding the state exchequer (Firstpost, 2018)
- There has been constant accusation of the politicians sponsoring, supporting and receiving kickback from certain insurgent groups (Purkayastha, 2007)
- Some members of the State Administration are nothing more than middlemen in the flow of funds to insurgent groups (Pillai, 2001)
- The Naga underground groups put pressures on development funds, which led to lowered (development) budgets. ¯The Development Office itself was locally known as a breeding ground of corruption, where the cuts and commissions taken by its officers and engineers (Wouters, 2018)
- 'The underground really are supported by the Government of India,' quoting Charles Pawsey (1960), the last serving British District Commissioner of the Naga Hills district, Wouters, 2018, p.112)
- Corruption has become a culture in all government offices to get any work done, which made Nagaland to earn the dubious distinction of 'the symbol of corruption', 'paradise of corruption', 'whirlpool of rampant corruption', and corruption is the 'very norm of government and governance' (ibid)

- Governor of Nagaland BK Nehru, in the midst of ongoing tension following the non-acceptance of Indian government's offer by the 'underground' Nagas, in August 1972 cautioned 'the overground supporters of the underground,' particularly 'certain members' of the Nagaland Legislative Assembly. He warned that if any members, through their action, showed that an oath sworn to the constitution of India and its integrity was false, the question arose whether such members 'can continue to be members of the Indian Legislature.' No Governor 'can ever entrust such a person with the responsibilities of holding charge of any office in the State' (Aram, 1974)
- The Naga HoHo, the apex body of the Naga tribal organisations, upbraided the 'national workers' (the UGs) for rampant extortion and imposing unbearable taxes on old and emerging Naga entrepreneurs. Some people also accused the 'national workers' of corruption and extortion (Manchanda & Bose, 2011).

Above Statements/Themes/Opinions/Phrases quoted from different literature enabled to formulate the Theme. These statements individually as well as jointly indicate the relationship between corruption in government offices and insurgency in Nagaland.

CAG's Report about Corruption - A Brief

It is not that the evil of corruption has emerged in Naga society in the recent times or that it is confined to a few departments only. It had been prevailing since decades across all the departments. The best evidence are the reports of the Comptroller and Auditor General (CAG) of India, in successive years, which have authenticity. It is found that embezzlement of huge funds has happened every year. The researcher made all out efforts to collect maximum reports of the CAG belonging to Nagaland. The websites of CAG and the Accountant General Nagaland provide audit reports from the year 1998-99 onwards. However, the website does not provide reports of prior to this year. So, manual search at certain libraries facilitated the collection of the copy of the audit reports from the year 1978-79. These reports have brought out anomalies and misappropriation of huge funds that happened in Nagaland. Further, this is not the case of any particular span of time, but year after year, the same situation has continued till today. All these prove beyond doubt the prevalence of extensive corruption in the Nagaland administration. In spite of the fact that the CAG had, in numerous cases, written reminders to provide justification for the (mis)steps taken by the state government, the latter did not find it necessary to answer.

Nagaland state was formed in 1963, and the briefs of the CAG's report from the year 1978-79 till 1998-99 are given in the **Appendix**.

Findings

Ours is a democratic country and it has deep connection with corruption. Corruption chips away at democracy to produce a vicious cycle, where it undermines democratic institutions and, in turn, weak institutions are less able to control corruption (Patricia Moreira, Managing Director, Transparency International). Corruption and democracy are inversely proportional. When the democracy score is going down the corruption level goes up and vice versa. The prime indicators of democracy are Free and fair elections, Strong and independent institutions, and Political rights – like right to protest, Civil rights – like access to a fair trial (Freedom House, 2019)[21]. So, when democracy weakens, several players get in to that space which gives birth to a situation wherein wrong and illegal things happen.

One of the reasons for the success of insurgency in Nagaland in the initial stage was that Phizo was able to build proper structure of a fighting force and attract youths into it. His propaganda office

[21] Freedom House, 2019. https://www.transparency.org/news/feature/cpi_2018_global_analysis

meticulously used Naga life and their cultural aspects to attract the attention of people. They were made to feel that the freedom they enjoyed will be taken away, Indian rule would destroy everything that belonged to them, their social fabric and cultural practices will be in danger, and that they will be suppressed by the Indian government. The NNC and its armed wing portrayed themselves as the saviour of the people and exhorted to spare one male youth from each house for protecting their life, land and dignity. Thus, various precisely planned programmes succeeded in gaining sympathy of the people and attracting youths towards insurgency.

The pumping in of massive funds by the Central government, specifically after the formation of the State, encouraged corruption in public offices, and both these aspects continued supporting each other and acted as a vicious cycle. Corruption enabled the insurgent groups to have a big stake in the incoming funds, through coercion, and the government office authorities in the hierarchical chain with their claims, evolved an environment of culture of corruption in public offices. As mentioned earlier, the study shows the relationship between the practicing of corruption in public offices and the insurgency in the state. It needs to be emphatically mentioned here that corruption is only one of the factors that encouraged insurgency in Nagaland.

As far as corruption is concerned, the CAG reports have continuously showed the existence of massive corruption in government institutions. There have been cases in which politicians and government officials were involved in channelizing funds to insurgent organizations (media reports). At the same time, illegal tax collection and extortions by the insurgents also contributed significantly in the expansion of corruption and strengthening insurgency.

The methodology adopted in Chapter II with regard to primary and secondary data has been used here also. Analysis of the primary data collected during the field work found that majority (63 per cent) of the respondents agreed with the statement that corruption has got link with insurgency in the state. While 73 per cent of the respondents consented that insurgents got their 'cut' from the funds given to the government offices, 70 per cent accepted that corruption in government offices has encouraged insurgency in the state. It has to be noted that only a meagre percentage of respondents disagreed with all these statements, whereas some of the respondents were neutral. Thus, the finding shows that out of several reasons, corruption in government offices is one of the factors that supported insurgency in Nagaland.

Analysis of secondary data also shows that there is a relationship between corruption in public offices and insurgency in the state.

In brief:

1. Corruption in public offices has been one of the factors that helped strengthen insurgency in Nagaland.
2. Pouring in of huge funds into the State by the Centre corrupted the politicians, bureaucrats, officials and so forth.
3. Sparing of 'rebel cuts' for the insurgents from the funds allocated to the state was one of the factors that strengthened insurgency in Nagaland.
4. The prevalence of corruption enabled illegal 'tax' collection and extortion in different forms, and all these further helped to reinforce insurgency.

CHAPTER IV

Nagaland

Connectedness Between the Government and People

A government is said to be successful if it is capable of delivering good governance and ensuring welfare of its citizens. Getting feedback from the citizens would enable the government to modify its decisions and actions. Engagement and participation of citizens in the government's decision making process and its acceptance, make good governance easier. In short, the mutual confidence, communication and support between a government and its people are essential for the welfare of a state. Where these are lacking, there will be mistrust and breakdown of relationship leading to illegality, manipulation, corruption, crime and other terrible incidents. And hence, a healthy relationship between the government and its citizens assumes high significance.

The impacts of insurgency in Nagaland are disastrous. Innumerable people have lost their lives, value of properties has been destroyed, and it has seriously affected all facets of Naga life; be it cultural, economic, social, or political. And this has influenced the governance of the state, adversely affecting common people's welfare. Good connectedness between government and its people enhances mutual confidence, respect, sense of belonging, and overall wellbeing of the people, thereby facilitating good governance. In this background it is necessary to study the relationship between the Nagaland government and its people.

It is the prime responsibility of the government to ensure welfare of its people. Welfare is the holistic well-being of individuals, concering security, health, food, economy, education, housing, and so on. When the government fails to fulfil any of these needs, the trust of the people in their government diminishes and in the long run leads to a gulf between these two entities. Chapter-2 has discussed the relationship between culture and corruption in public offices in Nagaland (It needs to be reiterated that there are several factors that encourage corruption, but this study has focussed only on the role of culture). How did the practice of corruption become so rampant in the government offices? The government as a whole has to be blamed for it, because all its stakeholders gradually allowed this evil to creep into their daily practice and then get strengthened over a period of time. This resulted in a full blown 'culture of corruption' causing impediments in the developmental programs and directly affecting the lives of common people. This could cause a dwindling in the trust of the people in their government.

Government is the political body or institution of the state that has the legal authority to implement programs for the welfare of its people and security of the nation. On the other hand, governance is the execution or application of the responsibilities of the government by exercising its political power, regulating the actions of the people/organizations, and thereby achieving their (government and society's) shared goals. Governance has a pivotal role in the implementation of developmental programs. When the government does not or is incapable of executing such programs, it directly affects the welfare of the people. This, in the long run, also leads to plummeting of the trust of the people in their government and its machinaries. It is 'bad governance', whatever be the reasons, that causes a variety of tribulations in society, and hence, every nation needs to put in tremendous efforts to achieve 'good governance'. The (UNESCAP) has identified 8 major characteristics[1] of Good Governance. They are:

Participation: Participation by both men and women, freedom of association and expression, etc. are the cornerstones of good governance.

[1] Yap Kioe Sheng, The United Nations Economic and Social Commission for Asia and the Pacific; What is Good Governance?, https://www.unescap.org/sites/default/files/good-governance.pdf

Rule of law: Impartial judiciary and police force, protection of everybody's human rights need to be maintained.

Transparency: Decisions are taken and implemented within the framework of rules and regulations, and factual information is made available to everybody.

Responsiveness: It is required that the institutions and processes try to serve all stakeholders within a reasonable timeframe.

Consensus oriented: Interests of different sections of the society need to be mediated to reach a broad consensus for achieving sustainable development of all humans.

Equity and inclusiveness: Ensure the well being of all members and nobody should feel excluded from the mainstream.

Effectiveness and efficiency: Make the best use of available resources to produce necessary results and protect the environment.

Accountability: Government and private institutions, NGOs, etc. should be accountable to all their stakeholders.

Governance refers to the political field and political activity as the vital task of every national government.

The earlier chapters show that many of the indicators of good governance identified by the UNESCAP, are missing in Nagaland. To elaborate further, it is necessary to mention certain cases of corruption; how they weakened the government machineries, strengthened insurgent groups and criminal gangs, and how they engaged in extortions in different forms.

Corruption

There have been several cases of corruption and misappropriation of funds in Nagaland. From 1998 to 2010, Rs. 442.56 crores was withdrawn from various government offices using fake documents. The greatest fraud took place in the Border Affairs department, involving Rs. 164.74 crores during 2005-10 followed by the same in the rural development department, involving Rs. 141.91 crores from 2008 to 2010. Education, Horticulture, Police,

Commerce and Industries, PWD and PHED followed up with Rs. 46.599 crores during 2003-10, Rs. 23.04 crores during 2006-08, Rs.18.17 crores during 2006-09, Rs. 14.005 crores during 2004-07, Rs. 12.98 crores during 1998-09 and Rs. 11.56 crores during 2004-09 respectively (Ezung, 2012)[2]. All these show that there exists pervasive corruption with high intensity in almost all departments in Nagaland.

According to Ezung (2012), there have been cases of pervasive corruption in Nagaland. Investigations by the NIA have found that politicians were involved in many corruption cases (The Northeast Today, 2018)[3]. Corruption strengthens the insurgent activities, and criminal gangs and their networks flourish. Parallel governments are run by insurgent groups and they collect taxes from individuals, businessmen, and government employees (Dey, 2018)[4]. In the state, corruption has become a part of life, be it education, health, police, etc. (Eastern Mirror News, 2015)[5]. Extortion in the form of taxes, collecting money at various police check gates are very common (Ezung, 2012).

In Chapter 3, we found that the former Chief minister was involved in paying State money to the insurgent group. Further, the NIA had arrested several government officials for giving

[2] Ezung, Zarenthung T, 2012; Corruption and its impact on development: A case study of Nagaland, International Journal of Rural Studies (IJRS) vol. 19 no. 1, April.

[3] The Northeast Today; 2018; NIA stumbles upon evidence of Zeliang's involvement in terror funding case; 19th March https://thenortheasttoday.com/nagaland-nia-stumbles-upon-evidence-of-zeliangs-involvement-in-terror-funding-case/

[4] Dey Kallol; 2018; Illegal taxation continues to haunt Nagaland, government employees deride NIA; 7th January http://indianexpress.com/article/north-east-india/nagaland/illegal-taxation-continues-to-haunt-nagaland-government-employees-deride-national-investigation-agency-4951172/

[5] Eastern Mirror News, 2015; Police Corruption: Kyong students want action against Home ministers , November 17 http://www.easternmirrornagaland.com/police-corruption-kyong-students-want-action-against-home-ministers/

government money to the insurgent groups. However, actions of the NIA were opposed by the Nagaland government employees on the ground that payments of money to the insurgent groups were made, not willingly, but under duress and fear of life and limb. It is a well-known fact that all the separatist groups run their own parallel governments from designated camps and collect taxes from individuals, small to big businesses, as well as state government departments and their employees. It seems that the state government has 'conveniently forgotten' the fact that it is their first and foremost responsibility to ensure security of the people of the state. But, when this did not happen, to safeguard their lives, the citizens, including politicians, found an alternative by satisfying the insurgents with money.

According to Ezung (2012)[6], there is nepotism, manipulation and bribery in the Nagaland Public Service Commission (NPSC) examination system which is the highest recruiting body in the state. Incidents like typing question papers of NPSC by a clerk at Alder College, Kohima without sanction from the Commission in 2004, making bribery attempt on the Controller of Examinations (CoE) NPSC by a candidate in February 2005, denying seat to a candidate who was declared passed as extra assistant commissioner in 2005, allowing over aged candidate to appear for viva-voce, adjusting a DSP candidate to UDA in 2006 NPSC examination, selection and keeping in abeyance of 24 candidates for the posts of lecturers in 2004 and clearing only in 2006, appointing and regularizing 263 employees against the total vacancy of 63 in 2006, making 1181 illegal appointments from the State Health and Family Welfare department without any advertisement in 2007, illegally appointing 2140 employees in the education department in 2004 against the actual vacancies of 719, giving fake teacher appointments to 2125 persons, giving out of turn promotion to police personnel and so on have been reported from the state.

[6] Ezung, Zarenthung; 2012; Corruption and Its Impact on Development: A Case Study of Nagaland, International Journal of Rural Studies (IJRS) vol. 19 no. 1, April. http://www.vri-online.org.uk/ijrs/April2012/Corruption%20and%20its%20impact%20on%20development%20in%20Nagaland%20India.pdf

To protest against the prevalence of corruption in public offices, in March 2016, the Eastern Nagaland College Students' Union (ENCSU) lashed out at the Nagaland government, alleging that the State administration was protecting the guilty officials responsible for corruption. Up till November 2015, 20 PILs were filed by Human Rights Law Network (HRLN) alleging utter neglect and rampant corruption in the Nagaland Government health sector (Morung Express News, 2015)[7].Many exposures were made by ACAUT (Against Corruption and Unabated Taxation,) a mass based movement in Nagaland, regarding corruption in Food and Civil supplies, fuel adulteration, and illegal appointments at various departments. Same is the case with policing. Nagaland police department is mired in allegations of illegal appointments or 'backdoor' appointments. There had been many corrupt appointments in the police department (Eastern Mirror News, 2015)[8].

Extortion at the check gates

Extortion in the form of collecting taxes, collecting money at various police check gates are very common. Incidents involving non-payment of bills, cheating, fake currency business, fake certificate business and other illegal businesses have become widespread in Naga society. Abuse of power in different forms, non movement of files without bribing, etc. are examples of rife corruption in government offices, from top to bottom. The consequences are worse. Higher the corruption rate, lower will be the development. It breeds monopoly and concentration of wealth in the hands of a few people, causes inequality in the distribution

[7] *Morung Express News, 2015;* Nagaland Health Sector in Shambles?, 30th November http://morungexpress.com/nagaland-health-sector-in-shambles/

8 Eastern Mirror News, 2015; Police Corruption: Kyong students want action against Home ministers, November 17 http://www.easternmirrornagaland.com/police-corruption-kyong-students-want-action-against-home-ministers/

of wealth, inefficient manpower, corruption abets corruption, higher inflation due to illegal taxation, and common people suffer a lot (Ezung, 2012).

Politicians try to hoard public development funds as much as possible. This encourages bureaucrats to conduct red-tapism, and the practice of 'share of cuts' becomes an accepted norm, that results in poorer quality developmental works. Contractors/ suppliers look for profit after paying all the 'cuts', and hence the work and goods supplied are of low quality. Government employees also look for 'cuts' and bribes, without which no file moves. Works of the common people do not get done without bribing, so they are forced to be part of the incorrect system. During elections, votes are purchased and after winning, the candidates make all efforts to grab money from all quarters to fill their pockets and the very people who have elected them to serve, are neglected. The 2015 Report of the Comptroller and Auditor General of India (CAG) safely asserts that Nagaland is the most fertile ground for corruption to thrive unabated.

Nagaland's politicised ethnicity has created new 'tribes' of corrupt officials, drug runners and a stratification of the early egalitarian Naga society. The emergence of a middle class and a nexus between politicians, drug dealers, contractors and the insurgent groups has vitiated the body politic and Naga civic life. Some members of the State Administration are nothing more than middlemen in the flow of funds to insurgent groups. This has been made possible by ensuring that no system of accountability exists (Pillai, 2001)[9].

The extent to which the eight characteristics of good governance prescribed by the UNESCAP are prevalent in Nagaland, can be logically deduced from the aforesaid corruption and extortion cases. It further substantiates the level of sufferings the common people have to bear due to the lacklusture attitude

[9] Pillai S K; 2001; Anatomy of an Insurgency Ethnicity & Identity in Nagaland; SATP http://www.satp.org/satporgtp/publication/faultlines/volume3/fault3-enpillaif.htm#33

of the government toward these threats. In such a pathetic environment, the kind of faith and relationship existing between the government and the common public would be fragile.

Due to inflow of huge funds in the name of security and development, the stakeholders got lots of money; especially politicians, bureaucrats, contractors, agents and many other backers, and they used all methods possible to pocket maximum money for their personal purpose. Ihe Indian government has been of the belief that by pumping in huge money leading to implementation of several developmental programs, it would be able to capture the heart of people of Nagaland. But people do not have sympathy for or loyalty towards India, and are very critical, and have, intead, developed an approach to take advantage of the money that is being poured in. From the bottom of their heart, they did not like India because they believed that India cheated them on two counts – after British left India, the latter forcefully exerted their control on Nagaland. Secondly, they believed that according to point no. 9 of Hydari agreeement, after ten years, the Nagas had the right to choose their future, but India did not allow the same by (mis)interpreting the condition in its favour. So, even if Nagas have been utilizing India's money for such a long time, some of them still prefers to be independent (refer chapter 2).

The relationship between the people and their government principally depends on how and what efforts the government makes for the welfare of its people and how the latter responds to it. If the government succeeds in this mission, common people will be satisfied and would support different programmes of the government. This in turn depends on the extent to which the government is transparent and accountable in its functioning. Both these elements enable the common people to understand the mission of the government and whether it sincerely functions for their welfare. As Vijayalakshmi[10] puts it, 'Transparency and

[10] Vijayalakshmi V, 2013; Transparency, Accountability, and Governance: Local Government in Kerala and Karnataka, *in* Local Governance in India, *Ed. by* Niraja Gopal Jayal, Amit Prakash, Pradeep K Sharma, Oxford University Press, New Delhi, p. 385.

accountability are vital factors in the effective performance of the local government including both political representatives and the bureaucracy.' Dearth or absence of these factors in governance leads to inefficiency and failure in fulfilling the expectations of the common people. This gradually results into dissatisfaction and they lose confidence in their government, which is an unhealthy situation that creates conducive atmosphere for the growth of illegal activities. Thus, analysis of the secondary data shows that the government has been unsuccessful in fulfilling its genuine responsibilities towards the people, which led to dissatisfaction amongst them, which caused the lack of confidence between the people and their government.

Primary Data Analysis

During the course of field work, with the purpose of knowing the opinion of the people, a few statements were offered to the respondents. One of the statements was, 'The State government has taken steps to minimize corruption in government offices,' to which 6 per cent 'strongly disagreed', while 24 percent respondents 'disagreed'. A large number of the respondents (40 per cent) replied 'Can't say', while 29 per cent 'agreed', and 1 per cent 'strongly agreed' with the postulation. Here, one factor that has to be pointed out is that those in the agreeing as well as disagreeing side is 30 per cent each, equal, whereby a clear result has not emerged.

Table 4.1

Answers	*No. of respondents*	*Percentage*
Strongly Disagree	8	6
Disagree	34	24
Can't say	57	40
Agree	41	29
Strongly Agree	2	1

Table 4.2

Variable 9	*1 SD*	*2 D*	*3 CS*	*4 A*	*5 SA*	$\overline{X}$ *mean*	*St. Dev*	*Skew*	*Kurt*	X^2 *Chi*	*P-value*
State government has taken steps to minimize corruption in government offices	8	34	57	41	2	2.964	.902	-.283	-.497	74.690	.000

During further analysis it is found that the mean value of the responses is 2.964 which is less than the standard average, i.e. three at five point scale. The value of standard deviation is .902 (variation is small), and skewness is -.283 which indicates that variation in the mean opinion is inclined towards the higher side of mean. The value of Kurtosis is -.497 which is lesser than zero and it illustrates that the distribution of opinion of respondents is platykurtic i.e. scattered. As the P-value of chi square (Asymp. Sig. – full form asymptotic significance) is .000, the null hypothesis that the State government has not taken steps to minimize corruption in government offices is rejected, whereby it maintains that the government has taken steps to minimize corruption in its offices.

After enquiring about the action on the part of the government, another related statement on the impact of the steps taken was made, i.e. 'The State government succeeded in controlling corruption in government offices.' 16 per cent of the respondents 'Strongly disagreed' to this statement, and 60 per cent 'agreed'. 20 per cent of the respondents replied 'Can't say', while 3 per cent 'agreed', and 1 per cent 'strongly agreed' with the postulation. Only 4 per cent of the respondents agreed with varying intensity to this assertion, whereas 76 per cent of the respondents disagreed with fluctuating intensity, which shows its unacceptability to them.

Table 4.3

Answers	*No. of respondents*	*Percentage*
Strongly Disagree	22	16
Disagree	85	60
Can't say	29	20
Agree	5	3
Strongly Agree	1	1

Table 4.4

Variable 10	*1 SD*	*2 D*	*3 CS*	*4 A*	*5 SA*	$\bar{X}$ *mean*	*St. Dev*	*Skew*	*Kurt*	X^2 *Chi*	*P-value*
State government succeeded in controlling corruption in government offices	22	85	29	5	1	2.140	.739	.728	1.372	159.972	.000

In detailed analysis it is found that the mean value of the responses is 2.140 which is less than the standard average, i.e. three at five point scale. The value of standard deviation is .739 (small variation), and skewness is .728 which indicates that variation in the mean opinion is inclined towards the lower side of mean. The value of Kurtosis is 1.372 which is more than zero and it illustrates that the distribution of opinion of respondents is laptykurtic i.e. concentrated. On applying Chi square test as a goodness of fit, its value clearly indicates that more inclination of responses is towards disagreeing with the statement. This disagreement is further strengthened by the P-value of .000. Here it needs to be mentioned that the level of statistical significance is expressed as a P-value between 0 and 1. A P-value less than 0.05 is statistically significant and it indicates strong evidence against the null hypothesis. Here the P-value .000 shows that the test is statistically significant. It also indicates that, according to the respondents, the State government has partially failed in controlling corruption in its offices. When we read this version with the preceding finding, it becomes clear that though the government had taken some steps, those failed to bring down the level of corruption in its offices. This may be due to the absence of any concerted efforts by the successive governments to stop corruption, because they might have more interest in their personal gains.

Another statement made was, 'Civic organizations like Public Action Committee/Nagaland Public Rights Awareness & Action Forum/ACAUT have succeeded in containing corruption.' To this 3 per cent 'Strongly disagreed', 36 per cent 'disagreed', and a large segment (44 per cent) responded 'Neutral'. 16 per cent of the respondents 'agreed' and 1 per cent 'Strongly agreed'. Overall, only 17 per cent were on the agreeing line, while 39% were on the disagreeing line.

Table 4.5

Answers	*No. of respondents*	*Percentage*
Strongly Disagree	4	3
Disagree	52	36
Can't say	62	44
Agree	23	16
Strongly Agree	1	1

Table 4.6

Variable 11	*1 SD*	*2 D*	*3 CS*	*4 A*	*5 SA*	$\overline{X}$ *mean*	*St. Dev*	*Skew*	*Kurt*	X^2 *Chi*	*P-value*
Civic organizations like Public Action Committee/ Nagaland Public Rights Awareness & Action Forum/ ACAUT have succeeded in containing corruption	4	52	62	23	1	2.753	.782	.195	-.387	107.789	.000

In detailed analysis it is found that the mean value of the responses is 2.753 which is less than the standard average. The value of standard deviation is .782 (small variation), and skewness is .195 which indicates that variation in the mean opinion is inclined towards the lower side of mean. The value of Kurtosis is -.387 which is less than zero and it illustrates that the distribution of opinion of respondents is platykurtic i.e. scattered. The Chi square value shows that majority of the respondents disagree with the statement. Further, .000 P-value justifies the finding about the disagreement of the respondents. Hence, it can be concluded that the activities of these civic organizations have failed to control corruption in public offices.

To a statement, 'The present Central government's policies are helping in confidence building between people and the Central government,' 42 per cent disagreed in wavering degree, and 191 per cent agreed in varying proportion, while a large section (39 per cent) remained undecided.

Table 4.7

Answers	*No. of respondents*	*Percentage*
Strongly Disagree	7	5
Disagree	53	37
Can't say	55	39
Agree	26	18
Strongly Agree	1	1

Table 4.8

Variable 13	*1 SD*	*2 D*	*3 CS*	*4 A*	*5 SA*	*$\overline{X}$ mean*	*St. Dev*	*Skew*	*Kurt*	*X^2 Chi*	*P-value*
Central government's policies are helping in confidence building between people and the Central government	7	53	55	26	1	2.725	.843	.127	-.543	88.986	.000

Here it is found that the mean value of the responses is 2.725 which is less than the standard average. The value of standard deviation is .843 (small variation), and skewness is .127 which indicates that variation in the mean opinion is inclined towards the lower side. The value of Kurtosis is -.543 which is less than zero and it illustrates that the distribution of opinion of respondents is platykurtic i.e. scattered. The Chi square value shows that majority of the respondents disagree with the statement. This is strengthened by the P-value of .000 which shows that the test is statistically significant. Hence, it can be concluded that the Central government's policies have failed to a certain extent in enhancing confidence building between them and the people.

To a statement, 'The present State government's policies are helping in confidence building between people and the State government,' 5 per cent 'strongly disagreed', and 43 per cent 'disagreed' to this opinion, whereas response of 40 per cent was neutral. At the same time 12 per cent 'agreed' but nobody 'strongly agreed.' This shows that 12 per cent were on the agreeing line, while 48 per cent were on the disagreeing line.

Table 4.9

Answers	*No. of respondents*	*Percentage*
Strongly Disagree	7	5
Disagree	61	43
Can't say	57	40
Agree	17	12
Strongly Agree	-	-

Table 4.10

Variable 14	*1 SD*	*2 D*	*3 CS*	*4 A*	*5 SA*	*$\bar{X}$ mean*	*St. Dev*	*Skew*	*Kurt*	*X^2 Chi*	*P-value*
Present State government's policies are helping in confidence building between people and the State government	7	61	57	17	-	2.591	.764	.170	-.440	63.859	.000

Here it is found that the mean value of the responses is 2.591 which is less than the standard average. The value of standard deviation is .764 (small variation), and skewness is .170 which indicates that variation in the mean opinion is inclined towards the lower side. The value of Kurtosis is -.440 which is less than zero and it illustrates that the distribution of opinion of respondents is platykurtic i.e. scattered. The Chi square value as a goodness of fit indicates that majority of the respondents have preferred to disagree with the statement. Further, this is strengthened by the P-value of .000, which shows that the test is statistically significant. Hence, the study shows that the State government's policies have failed up to a level in enhancing confidence building between them and the people.

While discussing on the interplay between people and the government, a senior police officer explained, *'people have little faith in their MLAs and the government because they (people) do not get real benefit of any developmental programmes. During election, politicians go to the people, and people take advantage of the opportunity by putting forward their demands for money and material. So, there is only purpose-specific timebound relationship. People have seen particular individuals who were poor, but after joining politics they amassed wealth and became influential. Thus, people have the tendency to utilize opportunity and accumulate wealth through any means. They have less faith in the government that it would take any step for the improvement of people's life.'*

To a related yet another assertion, 'The State bureaucracy is taking steps to contain corruption in public offices,' 7 per cent 'strongly disagreed', while 40 per cent 'disagreed' to this opinion, and response of 42 per cent was neutral. At the same time 11 per cent 'agreed' to this statement, i.e. 11 per cent were on the agreeding line, while 48 per cent were on the disagreeing line, which indicated that a good number of respondents did not agree with this opinion.

Table 4.11

Answers	*No. of respondents*	*Percentage*
Strongly Disagree	10	7
Disagree	57	40
Can't say	59	42
Agree	16	11
Strongly Agree	-	-

Table 4.12

Variable 15	*1 SD*	*2 D*	*3 CS*	*4 A*	*5 SA*	*$\overline{X}$ mean*	*St. Dev*	*Skew*	*Kurt*	*X^2 Chi*	*P-value*
The State bureaucracy is taking steps to contain corruption in public offices	10	57	59	16	-	2.570	.784	.031	-.415	57.606	.000

Here it is found that the mean value of the responses is 2.570 which is lower than the standard average. The value of standard deviation is .784 (small variation), and skewness is .031 which indicates that variation in the mean opinion is on the lower side. The value of Kurtosis is -.415 which is less than zero and it illustrates that the distribution of opinion of respondents is platykurtic i.e. scattered. On applying Chi square test as a goodness of fit, its value indicates that more inclination of responses is towards disagreeing with the statement. The P-value of .000 justifies this inclination towards disagreement, and it is statistically significant too. As 11 per cent respondents agreed with the statement, it can be established that though the State bureaucracy has been taking steps to contain corruption in public offices, it has not yielded the required positive results.

To a related comment, 'The Nagaland government is taking steps to prevent 'illegal tax' collection,' 7%per cent 'Strongly disagreed', and 38 per cent 'disagreed' with this opinion, whereas a good number (33 per cent) responded 'Can't say'. On the other hand, 22 per cent 'agreed' but nobody 'strongly agreed'. This shows that 22 per cent are on the agreeing line, while 45% are on the disagreeing line. Here also it shows that a good number of respondents did not agree with this opinion.

Table 4.13

Answers	*No. of respondents*	*Percentage*
Strongly Disagree	10	7
Disagree	54	38
Can't say	47	33
Agree	31	22
Strongly Agree	-	-

Table 4.14

Variable 17	*1 SD*	*2 D*	*3 CS*	*4 A*	*5 SA*	$\overline{X}$ *mean*	*St. Dev*	*Skew*	*Kurt*	X^2 *Chi*	*P-value*
The Nagaland government is taking steps to prevent 'illegal tax' collection	10	54	47	31	-	2.697	.891	.027	-.889	32.254	.000

Here it is found that the mean value of the responses is 2.697 which is less than the standard average. The value of standard deviation is .891 (small variation), and skewness is .027 which indicates that variation in the mean opinion is inclined towards the lower side. The value of Kurtosis is -.889 which is less than zero and it illustrates that the distribution of opinion of respondents is platykurtic i.e. scattered. As seen in the previous cases, here also the Chi square value as a goodness of fit indicates that more respondents have disagreed with the statement. The P-value being .000 has also justified this. However, as 23 per cent of the respondents have supported the comment, it can be said that though the Nagaland government is taking steps to prevent illegal tax collection, it has not shown any required positive result, as we see today on the ground that this illicit action is continued unabated.

In this context, in a latest development, a Public Interest Litigation (PIL)[11] was filed in the Gauhati High Court, Kohima bench in December 2020 by three organizations – Against Corruption and Unabated Taxation (ACAUT) Nagaland, Public Action Committee (PAC) and Business Association of Nagaland (BAN) over rampant collection of taxes in Nagaland. The petition pointed out that the menace of illegal taxation prevailing in the State has been creating fear and resentment amongst businessmen and the public, paying the cost for the unlawful taxation imposed on the entrepreneurs and businessmen. It further pointed out that Manipur trucks carrying goods and essential items pay money to the organizations, associations, police, undergrounds and others starting from entering Nagaland gate-Dimapur- Kohima-Khuzama Police check gate. The petitioners said that the prices of essential items in Manipur were cheaper than Nagaland. This was because in Nagaland, taxation does not end after collection from the wholesale dealers/truck drivers at various check gates, but the chain goes down to collection of money illegally from retailer shops, markets, wholesale dealer shops, street vendors and all other commercial outlets. Filing of the petition shows that the limit of collecting forceful illegal taxation has already gone beyond acceptable limits, and people are the sufferers as they have to shell out extra for their daily necessary commodities.

The above mentioned series of questions were asked to know the respondents' opinion and thereby understand the way in which people look at their government. As the saying goes, 'Action

[11] Nagaland Post, 2020; HC serves notice on state govt: ACAUT, PAC, BAN File PIL with HC against rampant illegal taxations, 11th December, 2020 http://www.nagalandpost.com/hc-serves-notice-on-state-govt/225942.html

speaks louder than words,' it is the real work on the ground and development, not big promises, that create faith amongst the people about their government. A senior government official rightly puts, '*There is a need for 'Internalized Reforms',instead what is happening in Nagaland is 'forced development'. In the former, the government/authorities genuinely realize that particular programs are needed for the welfare of the society and initiate actions. The benefit of internalized reforms is that the steps taken for it are with full commitment and satisfaction, and hence, the result of such initiatives will be truly beneficial to the people. Visualizing the problems that could crop up, proper security arrangements are made well in advance, the work will be carried out prudently, no effort to delay, will not budge to any interruption, nor will be abandoned on the midway. But what is happening in the state is the forced development, and so, there is no sincere commitment, projects are taken up due to compulsion, no interest in quality work, delaying tactics are used, blame the situation for any wrongs, interested in show offs and the common people are devoid of the benefits of the governmental programmes. In this scenario good rapport between people and the government is unimaginable.*'

Findings of the primary data show that the relationship between the government and people is not up to a satisfactory level.

A few more questions were asked, viz., Is corruption a virtue or vice? To this, nobody replied that it was a 'Virtue'. 79 per cent of the respondents answered that it was a 'Vice', while 21 per cent opted for 'Can't say'. The neutral way in which 21 per cent answered may be due to the reason that they have been observing the practicing of corruption as a routine affair in every aspect of functioning of public offices, and thereby have vacillating mindedness.

Table 4.15: Is corruption a virtue or vice?

Answers	*No. of respondents*	*Percentage*
Virtue	0	0
Vice	112	79
Can't say	30	21

Another question asked was, 'What do you see the causes of corruption?', to which 7 respondents said that it was the 'cultural issues' that caused corruption, whereas 47 respondents believed that it was the 'political issues', 27 respondents believed it was 'social issues', and 33 assumed 'moral issues' that caused corruption.

Table 4.16

Sr. No.	*Issues*	*Number of respondents*
1	Cultural issue	7
2	Political issue	47
3	Social issue	27
4	Moral issue	33

Several respondents have chosen multiple reasons for corruption, like 10 respondents have given all the four issues as causes for corruption, one respondent has specified 1,3, & 4 as the causes of corruption, 9 respondents identified 2 & 3, four respondents stated 2, 3, & 4, and three respondents have given 2 & 4 as causes of corruption.

Table 4.17

Sr. No.	*Number of respondents*
1,2,3,4	10
1,3,4	1
2,3	9
2,3,4	4
2,4	3

With an aim to gather more information, a few open-ended questions were asked, wherein the respondents were free to give any of their answers. The first question asked was, 'What are the important causes for corruption in government offices?' to which the respondents opined several reasons. The similar answers were clubbed together, and some of them are: Greed for power and money, earning money and respect in the society, family ties, favouritism to family and clan, backdoor appointments, nepotism, tribalism, absence of moral values, lack of accountability and punitive measures, and inefficient bureaucracy. In brief, weak (low level) democracy, little civil participation, and low political transparency leads to corruption. Frédéric Boehm[12] pronounces that corruption in government adversely affects development, and if the government officials entrusted the responsibility to work for public interest are abusing their power for their personal gains, the citizens will lose trust in their government.

Similar situation is observed in Nagaland. There is democracy and for its sake, elections are also being held, but votes are bought; funds are pumped in to the state for developmental purposes; but nobody knows where it is spent; there is culture of corruption in government offices due to which common citizens are forced to grease the palm of officials for getting any work done. A parallel government is being run by the insurgents and criminal gangs who are involved in extortion, illegal tax collection, and forcefully collecting money from government offices that meant for development works. All these, in addition to the findings of earlier queries on the steps taken by the governments in confidence building between them and the people, show vividly the gap in relationship between people and the government.

Another open-ended question asked was, 'Since 1963, why did the successive governments not succeed in preventing insurgency?' The answers given by the respondents are: government of India could not agree with Naga's demand; lack of strong willpower; struggle for political power and money; non-implementation of govt policies properly; weak leaders and government; it is a political movement for self determination but not insurgency for Nagas; political leaders used insurgents during elections to come to power to which they reciprocated later; insurgents were not willing to unite within themselves and hence several factions; corrupt governments and their lack of attention towards

[12] Boehm, F., 2015; Democracy and Corruption, Dimensión Empresarial, 13(2), p. 75-85, JEL: K42, P16, P17, DOI: http://dx.doi.org/10.15665/rde.v13i2.558

insurgency; government played safe and not ready to risk for a change; through the insurgents the government in a way has control over the people under the shadow of fear, by preventing insurgency they will loose that control, government wants to rule, not serve; and lack of educated and visionary leaders. When there are weak and corrupt leaders, they will be interested in fulfilling their own personal gains, for which they seek anybody's help, including insurgents/criminals. Once they come to power they have to reciprocate the help taken and thereby are not able to take any strong action against them.

Another open ended question asked was, 'What are the steps to minimise corruption in public offices?' Some of the replies are: transparency in governance, access to information and empower citizens; stop backdoor appointments and remove those who got employment using this path; free and fair election; transparency in decision making process and seek feedback of people; disposal of corruption cases at the earliest, take immediate action on those found guilty and thereby set examples; setting up of accountable staff selection board, their strict verification and bringing out names of corrupt officials; eliminate power of appointment by ministers; reformation in finance management; encourage private industries in Nagaland so as to reduce unemployment; strictly check absenteeism of employees; use of technology like biometric and computerized system; support honest and upright officials/political leaders; strict vigilance on the financial matters of all officials; stern implementation of anticorruption policies and punish the corrupt; and make Lokayukta more accountable.

While having discussion with a police officer on the means to minimize corruption in public offices, he said, '*there is a need for the people to come out and break their silence. Social media is playing some role, but this needs to be used in a massive way to educate people and to encourage them to fight against corruption. Encourage people not to vote for corrupt candidates, even if they offer money. Churches can play a crucial role in bringing the attention of the people towards ethics and morality. There should be a mechanism to verify the property return statements filed by the candidates during election, and keep watch on the election spendings. Most important is the political will, for which honest candidates have to contest and win elections. Similarly, the Vigilance & Anti Corruption Bureau (ACB) has to be given a free hand, along with necessary infrastructures.'*

To an additional open-ended question on the steps to be taken, to contain insurgency, the respondents suggested several measures, like strong political determination and counterinsurgency steps; accountable governance; genuinely implement developmental projects; stop illegal tax collection and extortion; facilitate platform for people to speak out with safety; meet demands of insurgents in a proportionate way; educate children not to take up arms; create job opportunities as most join insurgency due to unemployment; determined mobilization of people against insurgency seeking popular support; government, bureaucrats, intellectuals, students, civilians should come together and stand up against insurgency; stop politicians using insurgents during elections and check their movements; respect Naga aspirations; create feeling of belonging amongst Nagas towards India, mutual respect, and willingness to work together for the betterment of the society and nation.

Before ending, there is a need to look at another angle of the government and people relationship. In the 1950s, when the situation became uncontrollable and highly dangerous in Nagaland, the central government enacted the controversial Armed Forces Special Powers Act (AFSPA), 1958. Having been invested with vast powers, the security forces carried out unimaginable tyrannies on the people of Nagaland. In chapter two, we have seen how the people have been carrying bitterness against the Indian army, and this was caused due to the AFSPA.

AFSPA, the draconian law gives impunity to the security forces in whatever act they commit. Under section 4 of the Act, the authorised officer of the armed forces is empowered to (a) open fire at any individual even if it results in death if the individual violates the law which prohibit the assembly of five or more persons or the carrying of the weapons, (b) destroy arms dump, training camp, etc., (c) arrest, without warrant, any person who has committed a cognizable offence, and (d) enter and search without warrant any suspicious premises.

Sec. 5. The person taken in to custody has to be handed over to the nearest police station.

Sec. 6. Prosecution of the authority can be conducted only with the prior permission of the Central government.

The security forces misused this Act, and it did not serve its genuine purpose. This was revealed by various Committees:[13]

(i) **Justice Jeevan Reddy Committee (2005)**: An alarming statement was made by this committee, with regard to the arbitrary and unfettered powers vested in the Act. The statement in exact words was 'the law had become 'a symbol' of oppression, an object of hate and an instrument of discrimination and highhandedness,' and recommended the repeal of this Act.

(ii) **Justice J S Verma Committee (2012)** in its 657 pages report had made the reference of sexual violence in the conflict zones, and said that AFSPA legitimized sexual violence in such zones. According to the recommendation, amendment was made in the Code of Criminal Procedure, which removed the need for prior sanction for the prosecution of government officials for committing crimes involving violence against women i.e. rape, sexual assault, sexual harassment, stalking.

(iii) **Justice Santosh Hegde Commission (2013):** The Commission report said that the AFSPA was widely abused by security forces and had made a mockery of the law. It also pointed out the failure of the Act in providing protection to citizens against possible misuse of these arbitrary powers.

(iv) **International Opposition Against AFSPA**: AFSPA violates various International laws, like Universal Declaration of Human Rights (UDHR), The Convention Against Torture, The UN Code of Conduct for Law

[13] Rao Abhimanyu & Charles Mwirigi K, 2019; Critical evaluation of armed forces (special powers) act, 1958: Sovereignty first, Research Review Journals, vol. 4, issue 2, February, https://rrjournals.com/wp-content/uploads/2019/02/125-129_RRIJM190402029.pdf

Enforcement Officials, The International Covenant on Civil and Political Rights (ICCPR), UN Principles on Effective Prevention and Investigation of Extra-legal and summary executions, and Principles for Protection of All Persons Under any form of Detention. The law has been subjected to a lot of criticism by many UN experts, which includes Special Rapporteurs on violence against women, extra-judicial executions, etc.

So, the common people already have a prejudiced attitude towards the government. Thereafter, however, the different governments came to power, not only failed to pacify the people, but also were unsuccessful in providing good governance, due to which the people have to live under threat and bear the brunt of exorbitant prices of essential commodities. In a letter addressed to the Chief Minister, the Nagaland Governor[14] says, 'there is over 200 per cent cost escalation in transportation the moment a goods laden truck enters Nagaland due to gun point extortions by the armed miscreants,' and certainly this burden will be put on the common people, leading to the suffering of the people, owing to the failure of the government. Thus, it can be seen that the earlier disconnect, prevalent between the people and the government in the later 1950s, continued in a different form after the statehood and even till today.

Findings

All the variables discussed in this chapter have dealt with the opinion of the respondents on the policies/steps taken by the Nagaland government to prevent corruption in its offices. How the respondents see it is very important as it interprets their confidence in their government and the relationship between both of them. However, in all the instances – be it the steps taken by

[14] Singh Vijaita, 2020; Armed Gangs Rule Nagaland: Governor, The Hindu, New Delhi, 25th June, https://www.thehindu.com/news/national/other-states/nagaland-governor-slams-collapse-of-law-and-order-in-state/article31915402.ece?utm_source=taboola

the State government and bureaucracy to minimize corruption in government offices, and whether it achieved success; the role of civic organizations in containing corruption; the initiatives of the Central and State governments in confidence building between them and the common people; or be it the steps taken by the State government to prevent 'illegal tax' collection – the respondents see everything with utmost despair. Further, as seen in Chapter 3, the way in which a portion of the funds meant for development is being forcefully given to the insurgent groups and the helplessness of the government therein; collection of illegal tax, extortion happening under the nose of the government – all have had negative impact on the image of the government. Due to these illegal and threatening activities, people are living in fear, and have to pay a high price for every commodity needed for daily life. In such a situation, it can be presumed that the people are dissatisfied with the functioning of the government, and this underlines the disconnect between the people and the government, evident from their responses. But, because they are left with no alternative they succumb to the situation.

Here it is worth mentioning that a good number of Nagas still consider the statehood as 'forcefully imposed' on them, and hence, less importance to it from the very beginning. Those in power, then and now, were keen to fulfil their personal interests, and this further worsened the already existing 'delicate' state of affairs. Thus, what is observed is that the gulf, existent in the past, continued to the present due to several reasons, like suppression of the common people, forceful carving of the state, pocketing of state funds, sparing 'cuts' to the insurgents, incapability to eliminate fear from the people's mind, nepotism, and lack of development.

Findings of the close–and open–ended questions show that there is less ray of hope of reducing corruption in government offices, people want to stop insurgency and extortion, are not happy with the mode of governance, and all these indicate the prevalence of a gulf between the government and people.

CHAPTER V

Counterinsurgency

Theoretical Perspectives

For countering insurgency, it is very necessary that the counterinsurgency (COIN) forces and agencies are aware of the people, geography, insurgent groups, their capability, local support, and various other factors related to the insurgency. One of the methods the government has to adopt is to establish a force comprising of local people, because they know the actual ground situation. They need to be trained and provided necessary infrastructure to capacitate them to fight the insurgency. This is possible only if the government has a will to eliminate insurgency. This has specific significance as the study is focused on Nagaland, where certain activities of the government indirectly support insurgency in the state.

If we look at the counterinsurgency operations in India and the US, there is a vast contextual difference. India has carried out counterinsurgency operations inside the country, barring Sri Lanka, whereas the US has the experience of conducting COIN operations in foreign countries, like Vietnam, Iraq, Afghanistan and so on. According to Ray (2016)[1], counterinsurgency is 'primarily a strategy to defeat guerrilla fighters who hide among civilian populations over an extended period of time.' This has been possible as the insurgents are able to win over the local people, who in turn give them shelter and other necessary facilities. This is one of the biggest challenges the security forces face to distinguish

[1] Ray, Ayesha, 2016; Culture, Context and Capability: American and Indian Counterinsurgency Approaches, ISDA Monograph Series, No. 57, December.

between the insurgents and common people. And knowingly or unknowingly, if actions of the security forces result in harm to the common people, this creates hurdles on the former's strategies.

A modest attempt is made here to briefly discuss the counterinsurgency strategies of the US and India.

American military doctrine during the 1950s had relied heavily on the doctrine of 'massive retaliation' which was directed primarily against the Soviet Union and was essentially a war-deterring rather than a war fighting doctrine (231)[2]. In 1961, Kennedy ordered a fivefold increase in Army Special Forces strength which was designed primarily for a counterinsurgency role, and the U.S. Air Force and Navy created parallel COIN groups. To increase the U.S. intervention capability – the so-called Rapid Deployment category – the Pentagon pushed through crash programmes designed to speed the deployment of men and material to obscure trouble spots in the Third World, as well as providing a rapid reinforcement capability for the NATO front (p.232).

In the initial stages, the US army focussed on improving social and economic factors that caused insurgency. Certainly, this is a long-term process. A serious problem observed by the thinkers of counterinsurgency was the alienation of insurgents from the people. If this is done, the insurgents could be dried of food, hideouts, weaponry, information about security forces, training, and so on.

Insurgency emerges as they (insurgents) create a situation in which they justify their actions and prove that the government has failed to satisfy the demands of the people, and hence, compelling them to take up this responsibility. Quoting Charles Wolf Jr., Mack (1975) has said that the main concern of counterinsurgency efforts should be to influence the behaviour and action of the populace rather than their loyalty and attitudes (p. 234). Here the focus would

[2] Mack, Andrew, 1975; Counterinsurgency in the Third World: Theory and Practice, British Journal of International Studies , Cambridge University Press, Vol. 1, No. 3, Oct., pp. 226-253, https://www.jstor.org/stable/20096746

be to identify ways in which common people can be influenced so that they do not extend any support to the insurgents.

In the 1960s and 70s, the US Army experimented with different counterinsurgency approaches in Vietnam – from 'pacification' to 'search and destroy'[3]. But the failure of each plan forced them to focus on advanced technologies, which would detect anything that 'perspires, moves, carries metal, makes a noise, or is hotter or colder than surroundings'.[4] Such technologies helped to create such battlefields where the actions were conducted by the technologies, not man, and this reduced casualties of their army personnel.

Despite having well trained army personnel and advanced technologies, the US had to retreat from Vietnam. Why so? To quote Mack, "Almost without exception COIN theorists concentrate on the insurgency itself, on its causes and a variety of means to defeat it. What these theorists do *not* examine is the impact the war has on the metropolis involved" (p.239). Needless to mention, there are serious effects of COIN operations on the people of the area, and this develops opinions among people against the COIN operators, domestically as well as internationally. It further enlarges the sympathy and support of the people for the insurgents, thereby strengthening their actions. Hence, the COIN agencies have to ensure that their actions are not counterproductive, which may go in favour of the insurgents.

The Vietnam war convinced the US to bring changes in its counterinsurgency policy due to the high cost it had to bear at the domestic front. It had to suffer loss of large number of military personnel; national economy was impacted very badly; social security was disturbed; and there was political instability. All these forced the nation to adopt a 'low profile' approach towards counterinsurgency, thereafter. This made the then president Richard Nixon realize – to help another nation fight the war but not to fight the war for them – and he laid down three principles as guidelines for future American policy toward Asia[5]:

[3] Ibid.

[4] Ibid, p. 237.

[5] Nixon Doctrine, President Richard Nixon, November 3,

- First, the United States will keep all of its treaty commitments.
- Second, the US shall provide a shield if a nuclear power threatens the freedom of a nation allied with it or of a nation whose survival the US consider vital to their security.
- Third, in cases involving other types of aggression, the US shall furnish military and economic assistance when requested in accordance with the treaty commitments. But the US shall look to the nation directly threatened to assume the primary responsibility of providing the manpower for its defence.

This way the US decided to abstain from direct military intervention in other countries, yet support the threatened nation in building its capacity to defend its freedom by providing advice, technology, and training to its people.

What is the right time to begin an insurgency? The 'foco' theory of insurrection was used successfully by Castro to defeat the Batista regime in Cuba. The 'foco' theory, developed by the French writer Regis Debray, maintains that instead of waiting until conditions become right to launch an insurrection, a dedicated group of revolutionaries can launch very small scale, roving semi-guerrilla warfare at any time, which will supposedly serve as a *focus* and inspiration for the rapid growth of more general guerrilla warfare and at some relatively early time a general uprising capable of seizing political power[6].

In prolongation with the US Army's Field Manual (FM) 3-24, FM 3-24.2[7] describes *insurgency* as an organized movement aimed at the overthrow of a constituted government through use of subversion and armed conflict (p. 1-1). It defines *counterinsurgency* as military, paramilitary, economic, psychological and civil actions taken by a government to defeat an insurgency. COIN includes tactical planning; intelligence development and analysis;

1969, http://cf.linnbenton.edu/artcom/social_science/clarkd/upload/Nixon%20Doctrine.pdf

[6] Foco Theory, Dictionary of Revolutionary Marxism, http://www.massline.org/Dictionary/FO.htm

[7] Department of the Army, 2009; Tactics in Counterinsurgency, Field Manual Interim, No. 3-24.2, Headquarters, Washington DC, March.

training; material, technical, organizational assistance; advice; infrastructure development; tactical-level operations; and information engagement (p. 3-1). Counterinsurgency operations are a combination of offensive, defensive, and stability operations. Counterinsurgent offensive operations focus on eliminating the insurgents. Counterinsurgent defensive operations focus on protecting the populace and infrastructure from insurgent attacks. Stability operations focus on addressing the root causes that allowed to insurgency to come into existence (p. 3-6). Coordination between military forces and a wide range of non-military agencies is essential for the success of any COIN operations.

The Manual discusses three theories that would help illuminate the challenges inherent in defeating an insurgency (p. 3-9 & 10).

1. Robert Thompson's Five Principles for Successful Counter-insurgency based on his experience in the Malayan emergency follow:
   - The need for government to have a clear political aim.
   - To function within the law.
   - To establish an overall plan, whereby all political, socio-economic and military responses were coordinated.
   - To give priority to the elimination of political subversion.
   - To secure the government's base area before conducting a military campaign.
2. David Galula's *Four Laws for Successful Counterinsurgency* based on his experience in Indochina and Algeria follow:
   - The support of the population is as necessary for the counterinsurgent as it is for the insurgent.
   - Support is gained through the active minority.
   - Support from the population is conditional.
   - Intensity of efforts and vastness of means are essential.
3. Charles Callwell's *Ideas for Successful Counterinsurgency*, based on his experience in the Boer War and other British Imperial operations, follow:
   - [Following up] successes...; a single blow will often achieve results, but a succession of blows paralyzes the enemy.
   - Matching the enemy in mobility and inventiveness.

- Collecting actionable intelligence.
- Seizing what the enemy prizes most.

It needs to be remembered that the US Army has experience of COIN operations for more than two centuries, and has been called upon to defeat insurgencies like the Whiskey Rebellion in the eastern United States, the Native Americans on the western plains of the US, the Boxer Rebellion in China, Pancho Villa in Mexico, Augusto Sandino in Nicaragua, and the Viet Cong in Vietnam. The US forces have conducted counterinsurgency operations around the world in Colombia, Somalia, Kosovo, Afghanistan, the Philippines, and Iraq (p. 1-1). The Field Manual Interim, No. 3-24.2 of the US Army discusses different but coordinated Lines of Effort (LOE) during Counterinsurgency (p. 3-11). They are:

Lines of Effort (LOE)

All operations require careful planning and coordination, particularly those involving application of force. The most vital requirement is accurate and timely intelligence. Military forces must be able to communicate with the police and other agencies involved in the operations. During operations, actions must be taken across all the LOEs. Important LOEs and brief actions are (p. 3-11)—

Establish Civil Security: Conduct targeted raids with Host Nation (HN) security forces to attack key insurgent cells.

Establish Civil Control: Conduct investigative training for HN police forces to increase arrests and convictions; establish a block committee to control the population.

Support HN Security Forces: Maximize the number, effectiveness, and use of HN security forces to secure and control the population and to prevent the insurgent's freedom of movement.

Support to Governance: Establish or convene local or tribal council meetings to identify and solve the underlying issues of the insurgency.

***Restore Essential Services*:** Provide projects, such as the restoration of electrical power and sewer systems to blocks that support the government. Projects should provide positive reinforcement of desired behavior.

***Support to Economic and Infrastructure Development*:** Provide funds to city managers to hire additional personnel and initiate economic development projects. Hire from blocks that are neutral, to increase their support for the government.

***Conduct Information Engagement*:** Conduct information engagements to highlight government successes and expose insurgent defeats and excesses.

The LOE covers all dimensions of countering insurgency, such as establishing coordination between the army and all civil agencies, delegating responsibilities and imparting required training to them, actions that have to be taken at each stage, and ensuring the mode of extending mutual support.

Mack (1975)[8] believes that if the masses could be persuaded to support the government rather than the guerrillas, the latter would be cut off from their sources of food, shelter and recruits, and would 'wither on the vine'. But how this could be done is a big question, once people have already supported the insurgents, and made them succeed. To counter it, the government has to prove, through its actions, that it is determined to genuinely execute measures for the welfare of people. The social scientists were liberal in their outlook, which meant in this context that they preferred nonviolent techniques of counterinsurgency to military repression (p.233).

Mack (p. 245) further says that the COIN theory emphasized the 'two front war', i.e. on socio-political front and the military front. In this, the government and the COIN agencies push

[8] Mack, Andrew, 1975; Counterinsurgency in the Third World: Theory and Practice, British Journal of International Studies, Oct., Vol. 1, No. 3, pp. 226-253, Cambridge University Press https://www.jstor.org/stable/20096746

forward programmes for the social and political development, which are generally continuing measures. At the same time, the military actions include short-term measures such as identifying the insurgents, their infrastructural capabilities and strongholds, and conducting operations to neutralize them. It also includes detecting their funding sources, recruitment pattern, procurement of weapons, etc. and taking steps to snap the linkages so that the sources of the rebels dry up and weaken their strengths.

The insurgent groups emphasize on their mode of campaigns and motivating their cadres highly. So, the success of COIN strategy depends on the extent to which the agencies understand the level of motivations of the insurgent groups in different areas, like psychological, economic, political, and so forth, and taking appropriate actions. In brief, the grievances of the people have to be understood and sincere, not lip service, steps need to be taken.

The COIN agencies adopted and still adopt both population-centric as well as enemy-centric approaches depending on the situation. In the former, the focus is on the way in which control is being exercised on the population and the environment, like physical, human and informational. Using different sources, efforts are made to bring changes in the perception and approach of the people in support of the government and its agencies by sincerely implementing developmental programmes and welfare measures. So, to ensure constancy and regularization, managing the people is mandatory. Using force on them during certain situations should be judicious and according to the rule. On the other hand, in the enemy-centric approach, the primary emphasis is on defeating the enemy combatants. Here the school of thought is that defeating the enemy will bring all other issues to normalization, whereas in people-centric approach the concept is how to change the attitude of people in favour of the government to enable establishing peace. Remember, both these are not strictly compartmentalized, but can be used independently or jointly depending on the situation.

However, things do not move as we desire. In majority of the COIN operations that have happened around the world, the insurgents have been successful in securing sympathy and help from the common people. The prime reason is that the failure of the government to meet the needs of the common people led to the breeding of insurgency. Even if the government notices the signs of insurgency in the beginning, serious steps are not taken to nip it in the bud, principally due to their vested interests. Only when full-fledged insurgency has been accomplished, causing serious harm to the state, does the latter wake up from its slumber and initiates action. By that time damage is already done. Common people would have started believing firmly that the government was an utter failure, that no proper development and welfare measures had been carried out, and their political representatives were least bothered about the societal problems, while they themselves led luxurious lives. On the other hand, the insurgent groups would have strengthened their hold by making promises to establish a just society, set examples, people would develop faith in them, and would extended all possible support. In such a scenario, the serious problem faced by the government is to get the cooperation of the people in countering this insurgency. This is an uphill task as the people already have a negative image of the government, and its failurea. When the COIN operations are executed, the agencies use force and intimidation, which further deepens people's 'anger and hate' against the government. The widespread use of torture by the counterinsurgency agencies would create more problems for them. Hence, foreseeing the consequences, the COIN operations must be carried out with utmost care by separating insurgents, so that common people do not suffer.

INDIA

Insurgency in Nagaland was highly influenced by Mao Zedong's ideologies. Mao believed, 'violence and support from the masses were necessary for the achievement of a peaceful communist order. A revolution is an insurrection, an act of violence by which one class overthrows another. The revolutionary war is a war of the masses; it can be waged only by mobilizing the masses and relying on them. Political power grows out of the barrel of a gun.'[9] (the

[9] Asia For Educators; Mao Zedong on War and Revolution, http://

gun being a metaphor for the military). Nagas believed that their territory was never been a part of India, and they did not want to be ruled by India. When the conventional methods of discussions and agreements failed, they adopted the violent path and took up arms. The National Socialist Council of Nagaland (NSCN) was established on the doctrines of Mao Zedong. Quoting Rahmatulla, Kotwal[10] mentions, 'The NSCN has been carrying on an armed struggle to bring an end to Indian suzerainty over the Naga people and to establish a People's Republic of Nagaland based on Mao's ideology.' Raising different issues like the possible disastrous effects of Indian rule on the life of Nagas, lack of development, poverty, economic inequality, etc. the insurgents were able to incite the people, and get their mass support. Through the 'plebiscite' and different campaigns Phizo and his men were able to create awareness among the Nagas and to show that the government forcefully suppressed them using covert violence and there was neither a platform to raise their grievances nor anybody to redress it. Thus, the Indian government was seen as an authoritarian regime that would destroy the Naga culture. This aligned with Mao's ideology. 'For Maoists, the state represents the oppressor; disenchantment with the state is rooted in the grievances of the people. Justification for this violence is the concealed violence of the state.'[11] Another significant factor that supported the mass uprising was the strong intra-clan bonds, wherein the decision taken by the chief of a clan was strictly followed by its members. Thus, Mao's precepts genuinely worked in the framework of insurgency in Nagaland.

All are aware that insurgency is an asymmetrical war, so it is in Nagaland. However, a peculiar facet of Nagaland insurgency is that there are several stakeholders like politicians, government officials, contractors, and so forth who have the secret agenda of continuing with a situation of 'fear of insurgency' for their vested

---

afe.easia.columbia.edu/special/china_1900_mao_war.htm

[10] Kotwal, Dinesh, 2000; The Naga Insurgency: The Past And The Future, IDSA, https://www.idsa-india.org/an-jul-700.html

[11] Ibid.

interests. No doubt, Mao's ideologies do not support creating such environment. But it has to be emphasized that there could be individuals amongst the followers of his philosophy, who in the long run, covertly engage in abuse of power for their private ends. The Communist country – China's Corruption Perception Index (CPI) ranking was 83/198 in 2015, and in 2019 it was 80/180, which was an improvement of 7 places.[12]This shows that corruption does exist in a country even if its regime believes in Mao's doctrines.

Principally, there are two types of insurgencies in India, i.e. secessionist and non-secessionist. The insurgent groups demanding separation from India falls in the former category, e.g. Nagaland. Similar demand was raised by Punjab and Kashmir. On the other hand, there is non-secessionist insurgency that demands restructuring of the present governance or destabilize the government and to replace it with a new system as per the visions of the insurgent groups. This way they want to fulfil the aspirations of the people and eradicate inequality from the society. Naxalism in the red corridor region is an apt example, where the Left Wing Extremists fight for replacing the democratically elected government. Whatever be the aim of the insurgents, both are anti-state, and the government and COIN agencies face the challenge of fighting our own people and to ensure security and integrity of the nation.

Now let us examine how the SWOT approach can be used for preparing plans for COIN operations by the Indian security agencies.

SWOT Analysis

SWOT stands for Strengths, Weaknesses, Opportunities, and Threats. The SWOT framework is creditted to Albert Humphrey,[13] who developed the approach at the Stanford Research Institute

[12] Transparency International, 2019, https://www.transparency.org/en/countries/china#

[13] British Library; What is SWOT Analysis?, https://www.bl.uk/business-and-ip-centre/articles/what-is-swot-analysis#

(SRI), back in the 1960s and early 1970s. Though this approach was used to study the business strategies, this can suitably be used by the security forces for taking decisions in an insurgency-infested situation for carrying out counterinsurgency operations. This can be done by considering two internal variables (Strength, Weakness) and two external variables (Opportunity and Threat).

Strength (Internal)

- India has superior capabilities of Central Armed Police Forces and Army, and advantages over the insurgents.
- These forces have strong administrative back-ups.
- The forces have the power to use legitimate force in any event that endangers national security.
- A substantial quantum of budget is allocated for Defence and Security forces.
- Indian army and security forces have highly dedicated personnel, modern technology and defence equipments.
- These forces have expertise in conventional wars as well as in countering insurgencies in the Northeast and Eastern belt of India.
- By engaging in humanitarian and developmental programs for the civilians, these forces have acquired good level of experiences that can be used for getting moral and strategic support of the civil society. This would help weaken the popular support to the insurgents.
- In case any region of India plans to dismember from the nation, the Indian government gives full freedom to the military and security forces to carry out their operations in a legitimate way and in interest of the nation.
- The Indian Constitution permits the Central government to interfere in the State matters in case the latter fails in preventing the deterioration of the law and order, leads to a chaotic situation and creates threat to the national integrity.
- India could conduct well-planned and coordinated attack.
- India has heavily armed forces and has extensive rough-terrain-combat experience.

Weakness (Internal)

- The first and foremost hurdle on the way to bring solution to the Naga issue is that there is no political will.
- Corruption in public offices is so rampant that politicians, bureaucrats, employees of different levels covertly want the threat to continue, and this has been one of the reasons that strengthened insurgents.
- Intra-group conflict has given birth to several splinter factions, thereby multiplied the number of insurgent groups.
- Insurgents have created a fear psychosis amongst the people, and are engaged in illegal tax collection, extortion, etc.
- Due to fear for life, people simply submit to the dictum of insurgents.
- All these situations have adversely affected the morale of police, government employees, and people.
- The security forces face the disadvantage of identifying the insurgents from the common people.
- The external support the insurgents get from China and Pakistan is a serious issue India faces.
- This has to be considered with utmost care in the backdrop of frequent intrusions made by the Chinese army on the Indian soil in the recent past. They may provoke the insurgent groups to violate the cease fire agreement and to create instability in the country.

Opportunity

(External - Opportunities that the security agencies could exploit from outside)

- This, being an internal security issue of our nation, India could gather support from the international community on the steps it would be taking.
- Since the problem has been going on for several decades, people are tired, and crave peace. This has weakened support to the insurgents, and the government could take advantage of this opportunity.

- Similarly, the demand for 'Nagalim' is also waning as the Nagas of Nagaland do not like the 'authoritarian' approach of the Nagas of Manipur. Further, it is noteworthy that the Indian government has already agreed to provide governance autonomy to the Naga inhabited areas in its 2015 framework agreement along the lines of the Bodoland Territorial Council, to counter the demand for 'Nagalim' by T Muivah. Common people are satisfied with this, but Muivah and likeminded people are opposing the agreement for their vested interests.
- There are several civil/political groups that support the peace initiatives of the Indian government. Indian government should grab this opportunity, carry out COIN operations in Nagaland, which would achieve short-term success.
- In a COIN operation scenario, the security forces could get strategic and infrastructural supports from its neighbouring states, viz., Assam, Arunachal Pradesh, and Manipur.
- This will lead to political success in the long-term and to establish peace and democracy.
- Further, this will help strengthen democratic process, and achieve the ultimate goal of eliminating fear of people, and the development of the state.

Threat

(External - Threats that could come from outside to stop India from achieving its goal)

- The insurgents could get support from China and Pakistan - To counter this threat, India is capable of preventing such supports reaching the insurgents in Nagaland by enhancing security of the state borders and through rigorous intelligence collection.
- All these decades, the insurgents have been able to accumulate colossal funds, weapons and equipments from various sources. However, Indian Intelligence agencies and security forces are capable of dismantling and destroying the infrastructural competences of the insurgents.
- There are several insurgent camps in the State and their

detailed information is available with the Indian intelligence agencies.

- There can be outcry of human rights concern from certain quarters. But, India could counter this issue by justifying it as a national security issue, and by further improving its international relationship with other important countries.
- The possibility of imposing economic sanction on India is very remote, as such sanction would severely affect the poor people, which the developed nations do not want happening, as it would be against humanity. If at all it happens, India is self sufficient to meet such and eventuality.

Why India is not taking strong steps to resolve the issue?

Though insurgency is a state problem as well as a national issue, India looks for a bold political will that has to originate from the State governmen. As State is the primary stakeholder, the initiative has to come from them. Intervention of the centre without the consent of the centre would amount to 'undue interference'. Additionally, the kind of political determination needed is not being manifested by the State.

India does not want another bloodbath. The Centre does not want to violate the ceasefire agreement signed by it and the insurgent groups. The partisan intercession by the Centre could lead to a political turmoil and this will be misused by the insurgent groups leading to a scene of carnage. And this will be disastrous for the people. Certain developments happened in the past, such as a scathing letter written by the Nagaland Governor[14] to the State Chief Minister mentioning that the 'scenario in the State is grim' and that 'law and order has collapsed,' and the lacklustre approach of the latter indicates that the State is not very keen to resolve the

14 Singh Vijaita; Armed Gangs Rule Nagaland: Governor, The Hindu, New Delhi, 25th June, 2020 https://www.thehindu.com/news/national/other-states/nagaland-governor-slams-collapse-of-law-and-order-in-state/article31915402.ece?utm_source=taboola

issue. This does not mean to blame the State. The Centre might be having its own vested interests.

Nevertheless, India believes that when it comes to the integrity of the nation, it has the capability to go to any extent in safeguarding its security. It has strong defence forces, intelligence organisations and all other necessary infrastructures. But, it is the vested interests that desist the Centre and State from moving ahead. The moment such interests are set aside India can easily resolve the problems it faces.

CHAPTER VI

Policy Recommendations

This chapter is divided into 3 Sections, Section-I deals with the security preparedness that have to be taken in an insurgency infested area, Section-II describes about the raising of two new counterinsurgency intelligence and assault units, its structure and functions, and Section-III elaborates the actual counterinsurgency (COIN) operation that has to be carried out in Nagaland.

SECTION - I

SECURITY PREPAREDNESS IN AN INSURGENCY INFESTED REGION

Modus Operandi of Insurgents

Some of the methods of attack by the insurgents are as mentioned below:

a. Laying mines on roads to target security forces
b. Ambushing VIP (Very Important Personage)
c. Ambushing security forces
d. Attacking police stations, snatching away weapons
e. Causing explosion on railway tracks
f. Triggering explosion using remote control device
g. Breaking perimeter security (compound wall/fencing, etc.) and gaining entry
h. Approaching in uniform of security forces/disguise and indiscriminate firing
i. Hurling grenades on police station
j. Intrude in to convoy of security forces, trigger explosion.

There is a need to create high level of awareness amongst security forces engaged in COIN operations about the aforesaid modes of attack and capacitating them in taking precautionary measures.

Counterinsurgency – Background Preparedness

Before carrying out any counterinsurgency (COIN) operation it is very necessary to prepare the atmosphere and making it conducive for the same so that the government agencies get proper cooperation of the citizens. The government strategy should comprise of long and short-term plans. During the last several decades, the fear of insurgency and political situation in Nagaland has reached such a point that the politicians are at the mercy of the insurgents. Obviously, the bureaucrats, government officials, contractors and so on followed suit and became part of the system. Money matters to everybody in different ways. Funding by the Central government to the State in the name of development, threatening and killings by the insurgent organizations, illegal tax collection, extortion at the checkpoints, evolution of culture of corruption in public offices, lack of political will to bring a solution, harnessing vested interests – everything has led to such a chaotic situation that it has become difficult to make sense of things. In such a situation the government must take certain steps to build public support in its favour.

1. Resolute Government mission

Counterinsurgency can be possible only if there is political will and a resolute government mission that is very clear. The government's determination will be certainly a morale boost to the security forces, especially in the context of Nagaland, which has not seen any unyielding political action during the last few decades. The government must have a very clear objective and plans have to be drawn accordingly, to achieve that goal. It must identify strict and honest officers who could head different departments, so as to implement various developmental and welfare programmes of the government. The government, through its deeds, must prove that they are accountable to the people: this effort will help create confidence among the citizens towards the government. A robust administrative system with efficient authorities heading different departments could lead to good governance in all aspects. Security of the people, their economy, food, health, education, shelter, infrastructure and so on come under the ambit of 'welfare', which the government has to give high significance to. Intelligence collection, especially hard intelligence, is a significant aspect of good governance. Equally important is that the government must act on it. Further, such a system will help to identify vulnerabilities in the functioning of different organs of the government and to take corrective steps.

Nagaland, being an insurgency-infested state, a separate agency is needed to collect intelligence exclusively on insurgency, and an armed force to solely counter insurgents, namely Counter Insurgency Intelligence Group (CIIG), and Counter Insurgency Assault Group (CIAG) respectively. Both these forces have to be formed at district level, i.e. they must be present in all the 11 districts of the state. The structure and its functions are discussed in Section II below.

2. Law and Governance

Good governance can be achievable only by following the law and seeking accountability. Deviating from it for vested interests would result in chaos. This is what happened in Nagaland. Politicians, bureaucrats and other government officials in the hierarchical chain found opportunities to accumulate wealth for personal gains in the huge funds that were given to the state by the central government for developmental purposes. Gradually, the number of stakeholders in the funds increased, like agents, contractors, insurgent groups, criminal gangs, etc. and developed in to a vast web. All these evolved into a culture of corruption, least developmental works, and growth of insurgency. Now, if the insurgency has to be stopped, this web has to be dismantled. The political leaders and government authorities must be ready, or be forced, to forgo their vested interests, by strictly implementing the laws. Nobody should be able to twist or misinterpret the law for their personal benefits. This can be achieved by taking immediate and strict punitive actions against the manipulators of law. Such actions will set examples that will deter others from engaging in corruption and malpractices. Moreover, this will help in instilling confidence among the people about their government. So, it is mandatory to implement the law without any prejudice and discrimination in order to ensure the true welfare of the people, for which the politicians were elected to power.

How this can be done is the big question. There should be an all-inclusive plan which then has to be honestly implemented.

3. Comprehensive Plan

Once it is determined to put an end to the insurgency, the government has to formulate a comprehensive plan that incorporates short-term and long-term measures. The plan so prepared should be aimed at all departments, enhancing their infrastructural capabilities, and their mode of action in different contexts. Strong cooperation between civil and military/security forces has to be given highest priority. Duties of each department should be explained explicitly so that no ambiguity exists. This will further facilitate the joint functioning of different departments. Some of the important organs of the government that are directly involved in countering insurgency in Nagaland are Intelligence (Central and State), Central Armed Police Forces, Paramilitary force (Assam Rifles), State Police, Finance Department, Revenue Department, Public Works Department, Health department, etc. The strategy may be such that the intelligence pertaining to different departments should be shared to relevant departments to ensure that all the departments work together.

a) Securing Base area: In an insurgency infested area, it is very necessary that the base area of the security forces is properly secured. Sluggishness in any form would result in serious damage and casualties to the security force. This happens because the insurgents are always on the look out for vulnerabilities within the targets. So, identifying the strength and weakness would enable the security forces to plug the loopholes. Study the area, strength and weakness of the insurgent groups, their infrastructure, funding, political support, sources of information, rapport with the citizens, mode of influencing them, and so on. It is also very important to identify the vital installations and VIPs in the area, and strengthen their security.

b) Secure international border: Nagaland shares 215 kms long border with Myanmar that needs to be properly secured. It needs to be remembered that in addition to Nagaland, other states sharing their border with Myanmar are Arunachal Pradesh (520 kms), Manipur (398 kms), and Mizoram (510 kms.). Enhancing security on Nagaland-Myanmar border would force the insurgents to look for weak sectors on the borders of the other three states and Myanmar. Movement of insurgents across these borders is rampant. So, it is imperative that security on borders of all these four states be strengthened. On the other hand, as the people of Nagaland are threatened and suppressed by the insurgent groups, people do not come out openly against insurgents. So, the government has to work hard to eliminate the fear of the people. The government has to also ensure that the politicians hobnobbing with the insurgents for political convenience, is stopped.

c) Implementation of developmental programs: The success of government counter insurgency efforts mainly depends on the cooperation of the people. To get their support, they must implement developmental programs; make sure that the huge funds that are being poured into the state by the Centre are properly utilized for the exact purpose that they are meant for and ensure security of the personnel engaged in developmental programs.

d) Counter the insurgent propaganda: The government machinery has to evolve new methods to counter the campaign and publicity methods used by the insurgents by raising cultural and social issues. The government efforts would make an impact only if they can prove it on ground. So, the developmental programs and campaigns have to be implemented simultaneously.

Government actions and propaganda should target the recruitment process too so as to cripple the strength of insurgent groups. As such, in the present context, people of Nagaland have lost faith in the old ideologies of insurgent groups. The government should utilise this situation through actions that are beneficial to the common people in order to bring them into ts (government's) fold.

e) Foil Subversion attempts: The moment government starts planning against insurgency, the insurgents, their political sympathizers, as well as others who have vested interests in continuing the menace of insurgency, would join hands to overthrow the present political regime. Hence, the planning process should be done very discreetly. Through intelligence collection, a list of individuals who may create hurdles overtly or covertly, should be prepared. In case they are involved in any crime, case may be registered against them. Similarly, insurgents who are moderate can be convinced and brought into the fold of the government.

As several politicians and government officials in Nagaland are involved in corruption and other crimes, the government could consider giving conditional amnesty to these kind of people. Such a step will help the fence-sitters decide to support the government.

f) Infiltration into the insurgent groups: It is a difficult task to infiltrate the insurgent groups, but if successfully done, it would yield very good results. Tasks like collecting intelligence about the leadership, infrastructure, funding, weaponry, cadre strength, motivation, support from other countries, defense strategy, plans, and other such information, highly valuable for counterinsurgency operations, would be accessed easier through infiltration. Further, it will also help to encourage defection in the organization.

g) Isolate insurgents: The insurgents hide amongst the common people because they get the latter's suppor; hence, they need to be isolates from the common people. This can be done, by creating sources among the common citizens, who will pass on information about the movement of insurgents. It is the responsibility of the government to ensure that the identity of the sources is kept secret because their lives are precious and they are supporting the government cause. The sincerity of the government, their commitment in implementing the developmental programs and its results will certainly play crucial roles in isolating the insurgents. Similarly, infiltration into the insurgent groups can also contribute highly in isolating insurgents from the common people. It needs to be remembered that the insurgency in Nagaland has been going on for long, and hence, the insurgents have now become rather weak, and are depending on funds that are created by threatening government officials and contractors, through extortion of businessmen, checkposts, etc. Common people are also tired of the fearful environment. Considering all these facts, the government would be able to take appropriate steps to counter insurgency.

h) Action at Check posts/Nakas: The extortion happening at all the check posts is generating huge revenue to the insurgent groups, with several politicians, government officials, and criminals taking advantage of this. But the real sufferers are the common people who have to pay more for the essential commodities that are being brought in from neighbouring states. Stern action from the top authority of the state can put an end to the extortion at the checkposts, which can break the financial backbone of the insurgency, and thus, make it wither away. Similarly, resolute actions to stop sharing any portion of the funds meant for development can also dry up the insurgents' income. But, prior to this, the government has to take such steps that ensure security of the citizens.

i) Rehabilitation Programs: The government has rehabilitation programs for the insurgents who surrender, but its execution is not up to the mark. This keeps away the insurgents who intend to surrender. There is a need to implement the rehabilitation programs genuinely as per the policy, so that the surrendered insurgents get proper benefits; this will help in creating divides among the cadres, which in turn may lead to surrender of more insurgents. Only campaigns and lip service will not produce desired results.

j) Security of vital installations: Perimeter security of the vital installations has to be strengthened with compound wall and mounting barbed wire on it. Installing flood lights will enable keeping watch on any activity in that area during night time. Similarly, watch towers will help to see any kind of movement in the surrounding area. To further boost security, CCTV cameras have to be installed at specific distances with display screens in the control room. Moreover, foot as well as vehicle patrolling need to be arranged. Alarm systems should be installed to alert everybody in an emergency situation. The number of entry gate has to be minimum, with proper barricades, checking and frisking equipments, biometric instruments, communication equipments and trained security staff.

Now let us discuss the plan in detail:

i) The prevention of attack against any installation or target depends upon the alertness of the security personnel and the existing strength of security system at the entry point as well as around the perimeter area. Also, the security personnel who are doing patrolling outside the perimeter have to identify certain 'shelters' that can be used in a crisis situation.

ii) Minimum entry point(s) have to be made so that everybody making entry can be checked/frisked properly.

iii) After the main gate, creation of barricades would make the attacker's task of reaching the heart of the installation, more difficult. This will give time to the security personnel to warn and take immediate steps.

iv) The sentries should be properly trained and briefed about the actions to be taken in an emergency.

v) The Legislative Assembly, Secretariat, VVIP bungalows, big complexes, etc. occupy large areas, and in such areas proper security should be arranged in the inner premises too. Installation of sophisticated CCTV cameras would help the control room personnel see the incidents happening outside and issuing proper instructions to take immediate steps.

vi) To avert insurgents entering the vital installation wearing army/police uniforms, the system of specific identification card and/or code words may be evolved.

vii) Quick Reaction Team (QRT) should always be alert to thwart any attack by the insurgents.

viii) All security personnel must carry communication equipments so that message relating to any emergency can be communicated without loss of time.

ix) Security personnel in civil dress can also be used to collect intelligence about the activities of insurgents.

x) Security personnel should undergo proper training and be physically fit to meet any kind of eventuality at any time. They must be capable of handling different kinds of emergency situations.

xi) Security personnel can create awareness amongst the employees about the movement of any suspicious individual or the presence of any doubtful objects.

xii) Every vital installation should have a Standard Operating Procedure (SOP) and the security personnel and the employees have to carry out regular drills of it, which will help them to act in a specific way in case of an attack.

xiii) It is necessary that the security authorites establish good relationship with other agencies like hospitals, ambulance, fire brigade, etc. This will be helpful in an emergency situation.

xiv) In case of an insurgent attack, the main gates should be closed immediately and the QRT team should be alerted.

xv) Inform the police control room instantaneously.

4. Security of VIP/VVIP:

a) It is advisable that VIP/VVIPs do not move into an insurgency affected area. However, in unavoidable circumstances, the security authorities responsible for the VIP/VVIP security have to take all precautionary measures.

b) Advance reccee team should check the route to ensure that everything is clear for the VIP movement.

c) There have been several instances when the insurgents laid mines beneath the road/bridge and targeted the VIP. So, Mine Sweeping/Bomb Disposal Team should clear the route in advance to ensure that there is no danger to the VIP.

d) The VIP convoy must include vehicles with Frequency Jammer to neutralize attempt by insurgents using frequency-operated explosive devices.

e) Insurgents may use any abandoned vehicle on the route to conceal explosives in it to carry out an attack. So, any vehicle lying on the route as 'abandoned' or disguising as under 'repair' should be removed from the route.

f) A Medical team and towing vehicle must be part of the VIP carcade.

5. Bomb Detection & Disposal Squad (BDDS):

In case of an explosion, the BDDS should immediately be informed. Following steps may be taken before their arrival:

i. People should not be allowed to gather around the explosion spot as this will disturb the scene and will create problems in conducting investigation.
ii. Inform the police control room and BDDS team.
iii. If possible, take photos of the scene from a distance, as this will be helpful to the investigating team.

Once the BDDS arrives on the scene, they have to search for any additional bombs in the vicinity, collect fragments, residuals, etc. and send them for laboratory test, determine the type of mechanism used for explosion, and complete all other procedures.

SECTION – II

STRATEGY OF ACTION

Modus Operandi of the Insurgents in Nagaland:

The earlier chapters have discussed the role of culture in encouraging corruption in public offices in Nagaland. We need to also understand, in what ways the insurgents have created fear in the minds of common citizens, businessmen, and employees, which compels them to pay 'illegal taxes', and how the funds meant for developmental projects are diverted to insurgents, the method of extortion at checkposts, and several other issues. The law and order situation in the state has collapsed completely; recently, the Nagaland Governor stated that the "scenario in the State is grim" and that "law and order has collapsed"[1].

[1] Singh, Vijaita, 2020; Armed Gangs Rule Nagaland: Governor, The Hindu, New Delhi, 25th June.

In Nagaland, insurgency is more than seven decades old and the states is still reeling in the grip of insurgents, there is a need for strong political commitment to eliminate the menace. With the increasing tension at the border, between India and China, the Indian government has to be very cautious, keeping in mind that China has always supported cessation activities of the Naga insurgents and provided them with training and weaponary infrastructures. So, it is obvious that the insurgent groups would extend every kind of support to China in their border fight. Hence, India has to fight at both the fronts, i.e. internal and external. To overcome this situation, intelligence collection is of prime importance, followed by counter insurgency operations.

Before initiating such operations, background preparedness is taken up sincerely and systematically completed, as has been explained in the previous section. As mentioned, there should be a unit of **Counter Insurgency Intelligence Group (CIIG)** and **Counter Insurgency Assault Group (CIAG)** in each district of the State. The structure and functions of these units are discussed elaborately below:

Action Plan:

Every District will set up a Counter Insurgency Intelligence Group (CIIG) as per details given below. Structure of the CIIG:

Designation	*Strength*
DySP	1
Police Inspector	1
Police Sub Inspector	2
Assistant Sub Inspector	3
Head Constable	5
Constable	10

Infrastructure of the CIIG:

i) Decide special allowance/one step promotion to those posted in the CIIG. This will encourage police personnel to work in this unit.

ii) Identify dedicated officers/men after verifying their records, seek their willingness and post them in CIIG.

iii) Everyone will function in plain clothes, irrespective of their position.

iv) They will operate from outside the Police Headquarters. Hence, locate appropriate office/residential accommodation for them. As an alternative, premises can be hired.

v) Mobile/telephone Interception facility be created in their office.

vi) Normal looking vehicles may be provided to them.

vii) Modern equipments like Bullet-proof Jackets/helmets, AK 47 rifles, SLRs, NVDs, etc. should be made available to this unit.

Duties of the CIIG:

1) This is an intelligence unit. Yet, unlike other intelligence organizations, CIIG will focus only on insurgents.
2) It is the responsibility of the CIIG to look out for people who have links with insurgent groups. The CIIG personnel have to be placed amongst the locals, people under some disguise. Further, they have to develop sources who are capable of collecting hard intelligence on the plans/movement of the insurgents. The CIIG should ensure that the identity of their sources is kept secret.
3) Regularly visit the hotels in their jurisdiction, check their Guest Registers and verify whether any suspect visited there.
4) Identify suspicious mobile/telephone numbers and place them under surveillance.
5) A databank of the insurgent leaders, cadres, supporters, their details with photographs, camps, activities, etc. have to be prepared.
6) A specific feature of Nagaland insurgency is that its leaders stay in posh bungalows, and police/intelligence agencies are aware of it. This makes the task of carrying out counterinsurgency operations easy, provided proper surveillance is mounted on them.

7) CIIG should have a safe house where they could interrogate insurgents/suspects. The sources can also be met at this place or any other secure place.
8) The cyber cafes need to be instructed to maintain a record register, in which details of people using computer/telephone have to be entered. This will help identify if the cafe has been used for communication by somebody for any kind of insurgency/crime related activity. Sometimes, the insurgents may use such places to communicate with their counterparts inside as well as outside the country.
9) Police have to issue guidelines that if a house is being rented out, details of the person to whom the house has been rented out must be submitted to the nearest police station.
10) Ensure that the dealers of explosives follow all procedures properly, and the merchandises do not reach any wrong hands.
11) Prepare details of the modus operandi of insurgents/criminals extorting money from different stakeholders like businessmen, employees, checkpoints, etc. and those facilitating such actions.
12) The CIIG officials must maintain good rapport with all police station staff because, this being the ground level unit, it could turn out to be a good source of intelligence.
13) Maintain good relationship with the mobile companies in the state.

Counter Insurgency Assault Group (CIAG)

Every district should set up a Counter Insurgency Assault Group (CIAG). The purpose of the CIAG is to reach the spot of any incident, as a first responder and take action before any other force reaches there. This purpose can be accomplished as it is stationed in the district headquarters and its area of operation is the district only, whereas the other forces have to come from outside the district, e.g. the state headquarters. Hence, the CIAG could reach the site within the shortest time. The situation arises when there is need for apprehending an insurgent or an insurgent attack has happened and that has to be neutralized. The structure of the CIAG will be as follows:

Designation	*Strength*
DySP	1
Police Inspector	1
Police Sub Inspector	2
Assistant Sub Inspector	3
Head Constable	5
Constable	20

Infrastructure of the CIAG:

The CIAG in each district will be headed by a DySP and a Police Inspector, with two sections of armed men under them, each headed by a Sub Inspector. The unit can be newly created through recruitment or the personnel can be drawn from other forces on deputation after seeking their willingness and verifying their antecedents. The unit must consist of personnel who have strong physique, courage, good intelligence, well armed and good shooters for this hazardous work, and they must be below 35 years of age. This is an assault squad and their important function is to carry out operations. Decide on special allowance/one step promotion to those posted in the CIAG. This will encourage police personnel to work in this unit. Identify dedicated officers/men after verifying their records, seek their willingness and post them in the CIAG.

Duties of the CIAG:

i) Everyone will be in uniform, armed with modern equipments, like bullet-proof jackets/helmets, AK 47 rifles, SLRs, Gasgun, LMG Grenades, Smoke candles, NVDs, and so on.
ii) They should regularly practice the use and maintenance of these weapons.
iii) They will have bullet-proof vehicles for movement.
iv) They will regularly undergo strenuous physical training and conduct mock drills.

v) They must be provided with latest communication systems (wireless sets, mobile, telephone, etc.) for quick passing of messages.They must be expert in hostage rescue operations.
vi) The unit should be fully prepared for hostage rescue operations, cordon and search operation.
vii) This unit, most importantly, must maintain good relationship with state level and national level intelligence and action agencies, civilian agencies like medical, fire brigade, etc.

CIAG will be carrying out the ground operation principally on the basis of the intelligence collected by the CIIG. Hence, it is necessary that there should be close coordination between these two agencies. It is also to be borne in mind that there should be cooperation with other state level and national level agencies (e.g. State Intelligence, IB, etc.) in conducting the real operation. Furthermore, the CIAG may carry out an operation on the basis of intelligence inputs of the state and central agencies also. Hence, there should be regular inter-agency meetings, exchange of intelligence, and close coordinations. At the same time, the role of civilian agencies like mobile companies, health department, fire brigade, etc. cannot be set aside. So, there should be a network of different agencies and exchange of intelligence as per 'need-to-know' and 'necessary-to-act' basis.

Intelligence-Led Policing

Good relationship between common people and the police is one of the conditions that helps in collecting intelligence. The police station has a significant role in this as it always come in contact with common people and criminals. And this interaction can be properly utilized to collect intelligence about insurgent activities. But, as a prior condition, the police have to establish good rapport with people and win their confidence. Hence, if properly managed, this unit could be productively used for collecting intelligence and formulating strategies against insurgents. For functional facility, it is advisable to divide the jurisdiction of the police station in small areas and entrust the responsibility of collecting intelligence on insurgents' movement/activities to the Constable/Head Constable. All necessary information related to the insurgents, their movement, capability, etc. have to be collected, and surveillance has to be mounted on them.

State-level Nakabandis

As Nagaland is an insurgency infested state, any counterinsurgency operation requires route *Nakabandis* (checkpoints, blockades) to prevent the movement of insurgents. Identify routes that the insurgents may use and select suitable points where *Nakabandi* can be mounted. It is for the police of the jurisdiction to decide whether to keep some of them permanently or temporarily. Office of the Superintendent of Police at district level and the Director General of Police at State level may ensure that the establishment of CIIG and CIAG is carried out appropriately and their functioning is maintained suitably so that they contribute significantly in containing insurgency in Nagaland.

SECTION - III

COUNTERINSURGENCY OPERATION

No insurgency is identical, and hence, plans of Counterinsurgency (COIN) at each place have to be specifically suited to that setting, i.e. it has to be area-specific. This is so because the insurgent organizations, its mission, structure, functioning, internal and external support, landscape in which they operate, government against which they are fighting, their own as well as the government's capabilities and vulnerabilities, and so on are different from one another. Hence, the COIN also has to be setting-specific. Nagaland has special nature of insurgency that needs a specific COIN plan to address this threat. This is especially true in the context of this threat that has been prevailing for more than seven decades, and where certain actions of the government have indirectly supported insurgency, and so on. This part discusses the actions that have to be carried out to wean away insurgency from this state.

Resolute Political Will:

The first and foremost factor needed for containing insurgency is the unwavering political will in a government to bring an end to the insurgency. Such a determination would enable the government to use its vast resources appropriately to achieve the objectives. Insurgency has disturbed the functioning of the government and its agencies according to the prevailing laws and procedures. So it is the political determination that could revive the functioning of different departments and agencies suitable for a democratic set up. Different schemes and programmes need to be planned with care considering the available infrastructure and real ground situation, and these can be executed only with strong political will.

How is this possible today in a state like Nagaland? Corruption is high in the state and the huge funds that are pouring in are shared from politicians to bureaucrats to officials to contractors to insurgents to extortionist criminals. All those connected with the network are happy, except the common people at whose expense the benefitted are relishing. Along with various other factors, corruption in public offices is one of the reasons for the survival of insurgency. So, controlling corruption in government offices will have its impact on insurgency. However, this will be possible only if the head of the state is determined to contain corruption, either willingly or under duress. The power structure in Nagaland is such that it extends unlimited privilege and impunity to certain elites as mentioned above, and they misuse their power for their vested interests. Consequently, the state could not achieve its holistic development. At the same time, it is also noticed that certain policies of the government indirectly supported the survival of the insurgency. In such a situation, expecting any stern action from the State government to eliminate insurgency would be simply delusional. On the other hand, if the Central government puts pressure on the State government to take drastic steps against insurgency, this would lead to speculations and allegations about the Centre's interference. Hence, the only way out is the forceful intervention of the Centre on account of the utter failure of the state to maintain law and peace, running of parallel government in the state by insurgents and criminal groups, frequent violent brawls on the Indo-China border, China's support to the Naga insurgents and their reciprocation to China. Immediately after the Centre's intervention, following actions need to be taken.

Plan the Operation

This is our nation's internal security issue, and hence, we should not allow other nations' meddling or international pressures. Also remember that the Nagas of other states will not come forward with the demand for 'Nagalim' (Greater Nagaland) as everybody is craving for peace. At the same time, Nagas of Nagaland will not ask for 'Nagalim', as they do not like the authoritative approach of Nagas of other states, like Manipur. As NSCN-IM is dominated by Tankhul Nagas of Manipur, 'Nagaland tribes may not be willing to accept their leadership.'[2] The Indian government has already agreed to provide governance autonomy to the Naga inhabited areas in its 2015 framework agreement, along the lines of the Bodoland Territorial Council, to counter the demand for 'Nagalim' by T Muivah. Common people are satisfied with this, but Muivah and likeminded people are opposing the agreement for their vested interests. So, it is not the common people, but the faction of insurgent groups that have to be targeted by the government and the security forces, which can be done with unyielding political will.

a. Prepare the list of insurgent leaders, politicians, IAS/IPS officers, government officials, contractors, etc. who support insurgency.
b. Prepare the structural details of all insurgent groups (area-wise), location of their camps, weaponry they posses, specifics of its leaders and members, and keep surveillance on their movement. A large number of Nagas from Manipur have crossed over to Nagaland, settled, and are involved in violent criminal activities. Their details can be prepared by

[2] Wouters, JP Jelle, 2018; In the shadows of Naga insurgency, Odford University Press, p. 278.

the Intelligence Bureau. Similarly, details of infrastructural capabilities of Naga insurgents in Myanmar and their links with individuals in India can be prepared by the R&AW agents in that country.

ACTION

- Identify the spots and deploy sufficient armed forces (CAPF/Army), and keep a good number in 'reserve' position.
- Carry out surprise midnight swoop-downs on the targets.
- Cordon off all the insurgent camps, be it in rural/urban/forest areas; do not allow the insurgents to escape. Firing from their side has to be retaliated to, properly. Also efforts have to be made to arrest them.
- Carry out COIN/raids on the insurgent leaders. Also conduct raids on politicians, officials, contractors, etc. who support insurgency. Keep certain people under house arrest.
- Put behind bars, the criminal gangsters.
- Conduct rigorous intelligence gathering, surveillance and reconnaissance. Ensure that highest secrecy is maintained throughout the planning stages.
- Snap all mobile communication systems.
- Deploy sufficient forces at all check points to ensure stoppage of illegal taxation.
- Stop the Central funding for a brief period, so that the insurgent groups will not be able to do their extortion business in government offices. Seek accountability when the funding is resumed.

Post Operation Steps

After the Centre's interposition, there is a need to convince the people that the actions taken were for their own benefit. Hold every politician and authority accountable for their position and action. Some of the important steps that need to be taken are mentioned below:

(I) Disentangle people from the fear (II) Strengthen border

security (III) Enhance intelligence capability (IV) Strengthen State Vigilance & Anti Corruption (V) Reinforce relationship with neighbouring countries – China, Myanmar, Bangladesh, Pakistan, (VI) Political Alignment (VII) Accountability of politicians, bureaucrats, officials, police, contractors, (VIII) Focus on people's welfare, (IX) Police Modernization, (X) Countering Propaganda of Insurgents, (XI) Rehabilitation programs.

Now let us elaborate these steps:

I. Disentangle people from the fear: The insurgents have an upper hand in the situation in Nagaland because the people support them, due to fear. So, if the government intends to win the insurgency, they must get cooperation of majority of the people. This support can be achieved only when the population would realize that the government is sincerely implementing pro-people programmes, counter-insurgency measures, and that the government would defeat insurgency. This is possible through a holistic approach - by implementing different developmental programmes related to political, economic, social, and military. Purpose of this approach is 'winning the hearts and minds' of the people, as Mockaitis was quoted by Dixon (2009)[3] that refers to a situation wherein 'a clear understanding that military force is useful only in conjunction with a policy of economic and political development that attacks the causes of unrest.' Perceptibly, less force is to be used, and through appropriate steps people are to be convinced, won over, and persuaded to eschew violent thinking for long-lasting peace. The principal idea is to bring the people into the fold of the government, emotionally as well as rationally. Strengthening police department, making them accountable and ensuring that they work for the welfare of people will have serious positive impact on the faith of the people on the government and

[3] Dixon, Paul, 2009; 'Hearts and Minds'? British Counter-Insurgency from Malaya to Iraq, Journal of Strategic Studies, Routledge, Online, June 26, p. 361. https://www.tandfonline.com/doi/pdf/10.1080/01402390902928172

its machineries.

Bear in mind that the State administration (politicians and government officials) is indirectly supporting insurgents mainly due to two reasons, (1) for fear of their own lives, and (2) prevailing condition enables them to fulfill their vested interests. So, the fear has to be eliminated with iron hand by the government machinaries.

a. **Strengthening Police Department**: Carefully identify a non-corrupt IPS officer who has a clean and efficient service record, for the post of Director General of Police in Nagaland state. If need, bring such accomplished officer on deputation to Nagaland from the Centre or other state. First he has to focus on taking people out of the shadow of the fear of insurgents, because then only the law enforcement agencies and the government can win over the confidence of the people, which is very necessary for bringing the law and order situation of the state to normalcy. Simultaneously, there is a need for instilling confidence amongst the police and security forces in the state through different programmes and trainings, so that they get the message that the Government as well as the Police department seek accountability. Deploy security forces in large numbers at sensitive/important places with strict directions that they are for maintaining peace, and no unruly/undisciplined behaviour will be tolerated in any kind of situations. Presence of security forces and their 'helping role' will enhance faith of the common people in the government and help reducing fear.
b. **Actions at the State Entry Points:** Police presence and strict actions need to be ensured at the Checkposts. Establishing CCTV cameras, their proper maintenance, screening, and taking strict action against the defaulters can reduce illegal activities at these points. Take immediate action on the officials who engage in corruption/manipulation.
c. **Extortion:** Government, police and intelligence agencies are fully aware how insurgents threaten business people, extort illegal taxation, how money from government offices are

collected forcefully. Trap those money collectors and take action according to law.

d. **Infrastructural Development:** Contracts have to be given for the construction of roads, buildings, bridges, etc. through online competitive bidding so that there is complete transparency. Make sure that the work is completed within the stipulated time period. It is the responsibility of the government to provide security to the contractors and labourers and that they are covered under the life insurance.

e. **Spend funds for developmental projects:** Direct all departments to spend funds for developmental projects with accountability, and evolve mechanisms for continuous and regular supervisios, implement the Government of India's developmental programs in rural areas in such a way that the benefits go genuinely down to the local levels, and increase daily wages of rural labourers.

II. Strengthen security of Nagaland borders: Nagaland has borders with Arunachal Pradesh, Assam, Manipur and Myanmar. Borders with these three Indian states have to be strengthened with CAPF and state police forces, whereas border with Myanmar has to be further strengthened with Assam Rifles and Special Frontier Force so that movement of Naga insurgents across the borders can be completely stopped. Similarly, support from other countries to the insurgents in the form of infiltration and smuggling of weapons can be prevented. If the government finds suitable, Border Electronically Dominated QRT Interception Technique (BOLD-QIT) under the Comprehensive Integrated Border Management system (CIBMS) can be used on the India-Myanmar border. However, the challenges are its exorbitant cost, lack of technical expertise, operation and maintenance, and so on.

III. Revitalise Intelligence agencies: The present State Intelligence under the Inspector General of Police (INT) is dealing with a variety of activities that are detrimental or unfavourable for the proper governance of the state, e.g. political, insurgency, economic, employees, teachers, students, labourers, activities at inter-state and international borders, and so on. Personnel of Subsidiary Intelligence Bureau (under the Intelligence Bureau, Central), State Intelligence (State level), and Local Intelligence (District level) are active in the state. Presently, personnel of these agencies are collecting intelligence on all the aforesaid domains. It is necessary that the intelligence so collected should be carefully verified, processed and the actionable intelligence be sent to the appropriate authority, to ensure that right action is taken on it.

COunter INTELligence PROgram (COINTELPRO)

COINTELPRO is the covert projects that are being executed against certain individuals in the national interest and to prevent them from continuing the anti-national activities.

Steps by the intelligence agencies:

Clearly understand that the demand of insurgent group is to (a) break away from India, or (b) to continue with the threat of insurgency, so that they could amass wealth through different means, like 'cuts' from funds for development, illegal tax collection, extortion, and so on. India cannot agree on any of these demands, and hence it becomes necessary to take firm one-sided step. The only way is to forcefully break the insurgents' ties with foreign countries like China, Pakistan, and Myanmar, restrict their movements, desiccate their sources of finance, put behind bars their active supporters in India, make them desperate and wean off their strength. Register cases under the UAPA/Anticorruption Act against all those (government and non-government personnel irrespective of their positions) directly or indirectly supporting insurgency and making money. Also remember that China will use all opportunities to support insurgent groups to act against India.

IV. Strengthen State Vigilance & Anti Corruption: There are several reasons for the prevalence of insurgency in Nagaland, and one amongst them is corruption in government offices. Any kind of threat to the state can be eliminated only with a strong political will. As the government offices in the state of Nagaland have been reeling under corruption for several decades, and because a culture of corruption has been evolved in these offices, a large number of government servants are enjoying its benefit and do not want to be devoid of the same. Even the politicians enjoy the benefit of the existing situation. In this background, a strong political will only can save the situation and common people.

Identify non corrupt senior police officer to head the Vigilance Commission, or make the present Chief of Vigilance Commission accountable to her/his position, provide her/him all infrastructure to run the department according to the rules, and encourage her/him to take action against erring officers of any department. Issue directions to bring judges, prosecutors and police together to work on registration of new cases, speedy trials of old and new cases, and immediate and strict action on the court verdict.

Because the state government offices have been experiencing the menace of corruption for decades and a culture of corruption has been evolved, there is need to have a mechanism that can keep watch on anti-national individuals and take strict action against them. Setting examples of a few cases would send message across all the politicians/employees that now the government means business and no lethargy or misappropriation would be tolerated. It has to be ensured that the innocent and straight forward employees are not made the scapegoat. Similarly, those who do commendable job have to be appreciated and rewarded. Campaign through media may be initiated seeking cooperation of employees and common people in establishing corruption-free governance.

V. Reinforce relationship with neighbouring countries – China, Pakistan, Myanmar, Bangladesh: With the violent brawls continuing on Indo-China border, expecting an improved relationship between both these countries could be a unreal. Similar is the relationship with Pakistan too. However, diplomatic efforts have to be continued. On the other hand, stronger ties have to be established between India, Myanmar and Bangladesh. Recent past has witnessed good cooperation on the part of Myanmar in the context of strengthening border security and restricting movement of Naga insurgents across the border. Strengthen the border with China and Pakistan, so that no movement of insurgents across the border is possible.

VI. Political Alignment: Give position to the leaders of majority community in the Ministry, Boards, etc. so that people of that community support the government initiatives. To appease those involved in violence, the government can make symbolic promises and persuade them to refrain from it, and tacitly provide impunity for some time.

VII. Focus on people's welfare: Developmental projects have to be strictly executed so that the common people genuinely experience the benefits. Spend the funds for constructing roads, bridges, dispensaries, schools, houses for homeless, PDS, drinking water, electricity, irrigation and agricultural facilities, ensuring rights and entitlements of forest dwellers, improving communication system – construction of mobile towers, and so on. The government needs to identify major category of people engaged in insurgency and if steps are taken to offer reservations to that category in government jobs, it will help weakening the insurgent groups.

IX. Police modernization: Enhance the strength of police, if needed, recruit retired army personnel to fill the vacancies in an emergency situation, and thereafter conduct new recruitment process. Make available modern firearms, communication equipments, vehicles, etc. to the police, and if required establish new police stations. It is necessary to give emphasis on beat system and intelligence-led policing. With beat system, police in an allotted territory come in close contact with the community that enables the former to get advance information on any suspicious movement, and thereby taking preventive measures. There must be transparency in the police recruitment, and values of honesty and anticorruption must be given significance during the training stage itself. Refresher training on these subjects may be imparted to those who are already in service. Simply imparting training will be of no use if others, specifically senior officers, are not following the path of trustworthiness and uprightness. Police as well as common people must have faith in the functioning of the State Vigilance and Anticorruption wing. The government has to 'take steps to enhance the functional capability of this wing.

X. Countering Propaganda of Insurgents: It is the fear created by the insurgents that makes them succeed in their extortion business. In the initial stage, using their powerful propaganda, the insurgents succeed in showing the people that the government had failed to fulfil their aspirations. This and various other factors helped them get the sympathy and support of the common people in a big way. Gradually, the insurgents succeeded in converting this support in to their economic benefit. Now it is for the government to counter their propaganda, bring out the truth of the happenings on the ground, the lives of life of the insurgent leaders bought with the extortion money, sufferings of the common people, and so on. It is not that the people are unaware of these developments. But taking up these issues and showing the people the true picture of the insurgents will certainly bring positive changes in their attitude towards the government. It is equally important that the government carries out the welfare and developmental programs with utmost sincerity. Promises without action will only benefit the insurgents.

XI. Rehabilitation program: The government must take actions to genuinely implement the rehabilitation programs for the surrendered insurgents. Incentives for them need to be raised and impunity could be consdered for them under certain conditions. This will encourage more insurgents to come forward and surrender. The surrendered can be interviewed to collect intelligence about their group, leaders, funding, infrastructural facilities, future plans, and various other aspects. Intelligence so collected helps the security agencies in formulating plans for the counterinsurgency operations.

Conclusion

This study started with the question – Is there any relationship between culture and corruption in Nagaland government offices, and what is the link between corruption and insurgency in the State? As this is a pioneer study in this domain, research methodology is very important to prove the relationship, and hence, analysis of both primary data as well as secondary data is used to authenticate the findings.

In the first part of the methodology, considering the complexities of the study topic, hesitation of the people to cooperate, shortage of time and so on, the respondents were selected using purposive sampling method, questionnaire schedule was prepared with 5-point Likert scale answers (Strongly Disagree, Disagree, Can't Say, Agree, and Strongly Agree) and administered to the academicians, students, and government employees (total 142 respondents) during the field work in Nagaland. The data thus collected was analysed using SPSS and the Mean, Standard deviation, Skewness, Kurtosis, Chi square, and P-value were calculated. Moreover, discussions were held with a few police officers and former IB official in Nagaland, and their versions were incorporated at appropriate places.

In the second part of the methodology, 41 pieces of literature were identified, that dealt with culture, corruption and insurgency in Nagaland. Pertinent texts, opinions, statements, speeches, phrases, concepts, and words that directly or indirectly implied any link between Naga culture and corruption in government offices, and/or between corruption in public offices and insurgency in the state, were identified. From these, specific variables wih meanings relevant to the study (24) were selected and interpreted (Concept categorization) using Relational Content Analysis method. Thereafter, frequency of these variables was calculated. By using Pearson's correlation tool, relationship between variables was calculated. With an aim to further validate the correlation, the large number of variables was reduced to fewer numbers of factors using Factor Analysis and Rotated Component Matrix. Further, the researcher felt it necessary to explore whether the findings have got any relationship with Hofstede's cultural dimension of Power Distance. Hence, using the Thematic approach, the above mentioned statements/opinions/discussions/ speeches, that contained similar meanings, were used to formulate certain themes that showed the relationship between culture and corruption. These themes have been put into six categories, which are inter-linked. After formulating these themes, it was found that these (themes) have relationship with Hofstede's cultural dimension of Power Distance. Probing the prevalence of disparity in the society and its acceptance by the people proved the existence of high power distance in Naga society.

Chapter I discusses the brief of insurgency in the Northeast and Nagaland, the problem statement, review of literature, objectives of the study, hypothesis, and research methodology. Being a pioneer study of this nature in India, the researcher used both analysis of primary as well as secondary data to justify the findings.

In **Chapter II**, analysis of primary data shows that 92 per cent of the respondents, in varying degrees (strongly agree/agree), agreed that the government officials/employees misused their power to illegally favour their family/clan members, whereas 75 per cent of the respondents agreed that a government official not doing illegal favours to his family/clan lost his prestige in his clan. 97 per cent of the respondents agreed that corruption was practiced in government offices in Nagaland, 88 per cent of the respondents consented that there was a culture of corruption in government offices, while 83 per cent of the respondents were of the opinion that people have accepted corruption as a way of life. 47 per cent of the respondents did not believe that the Vigilance & Anti-Corruption agency in Nagaland was able to contain corruption.

85 per cent of the respondents were of the opinion that those who accumulated wealth through any means were given high respect in the society, and 62 per cent of the respondents opined that people prefer such government jobs where there was opportunity to make extra illegal money. While 38 per cent of the respondents agreed that the Nagas carry in their minds the bitterness against the atrocities carried out on them by the Indian army in the beginning of insurgency, 51 per cent of the respondents said that Nagas were loyal to the Indian government. This shows that, according to the respondents, people have accepted and imbibed these societal maladies in their life.

The study did not find a strong and direct relationship between culture and corruption in government offices. However, it can be said that certain cultural elements have an 'obscure' relationship with the practice of corruption in public offices.

Analysis of the secondary data brought out certain themes, such as (1) a semblance of relationship between culture and corruption in government offices in Nagaland, (2) 'culture of corruption' in government offices has permeated in the society leading to the creation of social and economic disparity, (3) the impression that the internalization of values and social pressures encouraged the government servants to adopt corrupt practices in their offices, (4) custom of giving high respect to people who accumulated wealth by any means, (5) preference for such government jobs that enabled amassing extra illegal money, and (6) the Moral Economy of Resentment existed, and used corruption to get its 'compensation'. All these indirectly indicate a relationship between culture and corruption.

Further in-depth analysis of the above themes revealed that certain cultural elements e.g. strong intra-family/clan bond encouraged its people to support their clan members (they were considered to be 'our' men) in government offices when the latter faced any serious/difficult situations, like involvement in corruption, absenteeism from duty, and so forth. At the same time, people expect that the government employee should help his family/clan members in office matters, even by misusing official power. People give high respect to those who become rich by any means, even if it is through illegal ways. This richness gave them vast power in the society that nobody dared to raise voice against their illegal deeds. It is possible that such belief system could be the reason that encourages officials to engage in corrupt practices.

After statehood, pouring in of huge funds for development caused heightened corruption in government offices, resulting in a 'culture of corruption.' This might have gradually permeated into the lives of common people, forcing them to accept corruption as a way of life. As a whole, anti-corruption values seem to not be held very strongly, and people are looking for different avenues to become rich by any means. People adopt various methods to secure government jobs, like influencing politicians and higher authorities, back door appointments, etc. Amongst government jobs, there is high competition for the ones that enabled getting extra illegal income.

Further, the government employees, from their experiences, would have found that the corrupt are being imitated nearly by all, the bribe is easy and big, there is least risk of being caught, and if at all trapped, there are several escape routes. So, their decision to be corrupt may have been influenced by the behaviors of the majority, after a kind of risk/reward evaluation. All these indicate the possibility of a relationship between culture and corruption in public life. Manifestation of corruption in different forms has created inequality in society, thereby leading to the prevalence of high power distance in the society. It is seen that people suffer a lot as development is very slow, essential goods are highly expensive, the poor are hard hit, live under threat of life, do not dare to speak against those responsible for such maladies, and a 'culture of silence' prevails, which indirectly supports corruption and other wrong doings. This 'culture of silence' has a relationship with the strong intra-family/clan ties (not raising voice against wrong-doers who are 'our' people). There is a need for the people to understand its consequences and to speak about it in the open forum. No doubt, there had been a few events/incidents in which people vehemently opposed the prevailing corrupt system, but it was not strong enough to bring the required change. No doubt, sincere initiatives from the government could help bettering the system as well as the life of the common citizens.

It needs to be reiterated that there are several reasons for corruption. But here the researcher is looking only the role of culture in precipitating corruption in public offices.

Chapter III deals with corruption and insurgency in Nagaland, and the relationship between both these variables. The research methodology adopted in Chapter II was similarly used in this chapter also, to establish the link between corruption and insurgency in the state. The chapter starts with the methods adopted by the Naga National Council to influence the people to get their support, like money, manpower, logistics, and so on in the initial stage of insurgency. The insurgents bent, interpreted and demonstrated the prevailing belief system in such a way that the people started to believe that the Indian rule will destroy their culture, they will be forced to change their life style, food habits, and there will be complete anarchy. Following such propaganda and the demands made by the insurgents, people started to contribute money as well as one male member from each household. At the same time, people had highest regards and faith in the strong leadership of A Z Phizo. On the other hand, the imposition of AFSPA and tyrannies unleashed by the Indian armed forces generated huge anger and hate against India. All these enraged the people and more and more youths came forward to join the insurgency, which helped strengthening their cadres and fight against India.

Findings of the primary data analysis show that majority of the respondents (64 per cent) agreed that corruption has got links with insurgency in the state, insurgents got their 'cut' from the funds given to the government offices (73 per cent), and corruption in government offices has encouraged insurgency in the state (72 per cent). Further, the successive reports of the CAG have authenticated the prevalence of massive corruption in public offices in the State.

Similar results were found in the secondary data analysis too. It becomes apparent that rampant corruption in public offices had been one of the factors that strengthened insurgency in the

State. Around the world it is seen that the prevalence of corruption is one of the preconditions for the growth of insurgency. The linkage of corruption and insurgency is observed in all countries where insurgency had thrived or is still prevailing. The same is true with Nagaland too. The huge funds poured into the state by the Centre, have given opportunity to politicians, bureaucrats, contractors, agents, and so on to grab money according to their vested interests. The role of the political parties that ruled from Delhi is also significant in helping spread corruption. At the same time, the insurgents, using threat, forced the government offices to spare 'rebel cuts' for them. This way the government funds, meant for development, were used by the insurgent groups to strengthen themselves. Illegal tax, extortion, etc. also became huge sources of income for the insurgent groups. There have been constant accusation of the politicians sponsoring, supporting and receiving kickback from certain insurgent groups. There is 'culture of corruption' in government offices to get any work done, which has earned Nagaland the dubious distinction of 'the symbol of corruption,' 'paradise of corruption,' 'whirlpool of rampant corruption,' and corruption has come to be seen as the 'very norm of government and governance.' All these show that corruption is one of the factors that strengthened insurgency in Nagaland. It needs to be mentioned here that the limitations of the researcher mentioned earlier are applicable here too, in this chapter and throughout the study.

Chapter IV deals with the connectedness between the government and people in Nagaland. It is the prime responsibility of the government to ensure welfare of its people. When the government does not or is incapable of executing the developmental programs, it directly affects the welfare of people. This, in the long run, also reduces the trust of the people in their government and its machineries. It is necessary that the government is transparent and accountable in its functioning. It is 'bad governance', whatever be the reasons, that causes variety of tribulations in the society, and hence, every nation puts serious efforts to ensure 'good governance.'

Primary data shows that people are tired of corruption and

fear for their lives. They expect that the government would take steps to minimize corruption in public offices, contain insurgency, execute developmental programmes, initiate welfare measures for bettering lives of citizens, and maintain transparency and accountability in its work. Such actions will help people have faith in their government and strengthen the relationship between the two. A good number of respondents (30 per cent) agreed with the statement that the State government has taken steps to minimize corruption in government offices. However, when enquired about the impact of those steps, a mere 4 per cent of the respondents agreed that the State government succeeded in controlling corruption in government offices. Similarly, only 17 per cent of the respondents believed that Civic organizations like Public Action Committee/Nagaland Public Rights Awareness & Action Forum/ACAUT have succeeded in containing corruption. Likewise, only 20 per cent of the respondents stated that the present Central government's policies helped in confidence building between people and the Central government, and a mere 12 per cent held that the present State government's policies helped in confidence building between people and the State government. While a meagre 11 per cent of the respondents believed that the State bureaucracy had taken steps to contain corruption in public offices, only 23 per cent of the respondents agreed that the Nagaland government had taken steps to prevent 'illegal tax' collection. All these statements are related to the steps that the government had taken for providing better facilities to the people, which could enhance the faith and relationship between both. However, the lower percentage of respondents agreeing with the statements has shown that the actions of the government were very weak, or were simply formalities, and that it could not make a significant impact on majority of the people. And hence, the people did not have faith in the functioning of the government and there existed a gulf in the relationship between both. To recall Frédéric Boehm,[1]

[1] Boehm, F., 2015; Democracy and Corruption, Dimensión Empresarial, 13(2), p. 75-85, JEL: K42, P16, P17, DOI: http://dx.doi.org/10.15665/rde.v13i2.558

corruption in government adversely affects development, and if the government officials entrusted with the responsibility to work for public interest, are abusing their power for their personal gains, the citizens will lose trust in their government.

It has already been seen in chapter II and III that there is a culture of corruption in public offices; corruption has been one factor that has supported insurgency and extortion, and the government has only been partially successful in containing these dangers in the state. It is the common people who suffer in the absence of development, welfare measures, and live under threat. They submitted to the prevailing situation as there was no alternative available to them. All these could cause dissatisfaction and disconnect amongst the people towards the government.

Chapter V discusses the theoretical perspectives of counterinsurgency with special reference to the US and India. The US has the experience of conducting COIN operations in foreign countries, whereas India has carried out such operations inside the country, and that in Sri Lanka. In the 1960s and 70s, the US Army experimented different counter insurgency approaches in Vietnam – from 'pacification' to 'search and destroy.' But the subsequent failures forced them to focus on advanced technologies. Due to their utter failure in the Vietnam war, the US adopted a 'low profile' approach, and decided to 'help another nation fight the war but not to fight the war for them.' The Field Manual Interim, No. 3-24.2 of the US Army discusses different but coordinated Lines of Effort (LOE) during COIN operations.

Coming to the Indian context, insurgency in Nagaland was highly influenced by Mao Zedong's ideologies, who believed that violence and support from the masses were necessary for the achievement of a revolution to overthrow the existing power system. A common factor in the COIN theory of the US and India is that both emphasized on 'two front war,' i.e. on socio-political front and the military front. In this, the government and the COIN agencies push forward programmes for the social and political development, which are generally continuing measures. At the same time, the military actions include short-term measures such as identifying the insurgents, their infrastructural capabilities and strongholds, and conduct operations to neutralize them.

The mode in which SWOT approach can be used for preparing plans for COIN operations by the Indian security agencies has been narrated briefly.

Chapter VI deliberates on Policy Recommendations. This chapter has 3 Sections, Section-I deals with the security preparedness that have to be taken in an insurgency infested area; Section-II elaborates on raising of two new counterinsurgency intelligence and assault units, its structure and functions; and Section-III describes the actual counterinsurgency operation that has to be carried out in Nagaland.

Finally, there is the Conclusion, References and Appendix.

To end the deliberation, it is important to mention that there is an 'obscure' relationship between the cultural elements and corruption in government offices in Nagaland. At the same time there is a relationship between corruption in public offices and insurgency in the state, and there exists high power distance in the society. There is a big chasm in the relationship between the government and people. Certain cultural elements facilitate corruption, and corruption facilitated insurgency, showing that the *facilitation theory* is significant in the context of Nagaland. Due to the sluggishness in implementing developmental programmes and welfare measures, people suffer a lot, live under fear, and struggle between aspirations, threat and despair.

There are a variety of reasons for the prevalence of corruption and insurgency, whereas this study has dealt with only two factors, i.e. culture and corruption respectively.

The Supreme Court order on Extortion and Insurgency:

The primary and secondary data analysis shows the relationship between corruption in public offices and insurgency in the state. Corruption enables insurgents to manipulate matters in their favour, influence officials, and the money thus extorted is used for insurgency. However, the Supreme court[2] in its order on

[2] The Leaflet, 2021, SC rules payment of extortion money does not

9/4/2021 ruled, 'payment of extortion money did not amount to terror funding under the Unlawful Activities (Prevention) [UAPA] Act,' and granted bail to businessman Sudesh Kedia accused of providing financial support to the Tritiya Prastuti Committee (TPC), a splinter group of the Communist Party of India (Maoist).

While delivering the order on Criminal Appeal Nos . 314-315 of 2021 (arising out of SLP (Crl.) Nos. 6259-6260 of 2020), the Supreme court observed, 'The submission made on behalf of the Appellant (statement recorded under Section 164 Cr.PC) that he was a victim and he was forced to pay the levy as demanded by the organization was not accepted by the Special court. The Special Court was convinced with the contention of the prosecution that apart from the meeting with the members of the terrorist organization, the Appellant had also paid huge amount of money to them.'

The Supreme court further stated, 'It is the bounden duty of the Court to apply its mind to examine the entire material on record for the purpose of satisfying itself, whether a prima facie case is made out against the accused or not. We have gone through the material on record and are satisfied that the Appellant is entitled for bail and that the Special Court and High Court erred in not granting bail to the Appellant.'

While issuing bail to the Appellant, the Supreme Court said, 'We make it clear that these findings are restricted only for the purpose of grant of bail to the Appellant and the trial court shall not be influenced by these observations during trial.' 'Appellant is directed to be released on bail subject to the satisfaction of the Special Court.'

It may be recalled that the appellant did not get bail from the Special court and the High court because they did not take seriously the matter that the appellant was the victim and had been forced to give extortion money. The courts only recorded that he had given money to terror group, but ignored the 'coerced' situation. The courts could have directed the investigating agency to arrest the extortionists on the basis of the statement given by the

---

amount to terror funding, 9th April, https://www.theleaflet.in/sc-rules-payment-of-extortion-money-does-not-amount-to-terror-funding/#

victim Appellant so that such crime could have been contained. Similarly, the Supreme Court could have issued instructions to the law enforcement agencies to take steps to arrest the extortionists, which could have helped to contain this menace. But, the Supreme Court was looking only at the point whether the appellant should be released on bail or not. After this order, there is possibility that the terrorist groups justify and strengthen their extortion business under the guise that the extortion victims 'giving money' are not supporting insurgency, it may be treated as 'donation' that can be given by anybody and accepted by anybody.

The NIA in its chargesheet has said, 'coal traders/transporters were paying cash to Shanti Sah Sanchalan Samiti, Central Coalfield Limited, village committees and TPC operatives for carrying on their business smoothly.' In a second supplementary charge-sheet it further said that the Appellant 'had attended meetings with TPC leaders and had paid levy to TPC leader Akraman (A14) CCL employees and village committee members from his current account. In view of the payments made by him an inference was drawn that the Appellant colluded with the members of the terrorist gang (TPC) and was a party to a criminal conspiracy to raise funds for a terrorist gang.'

In fact, the NIA, and prior to it, the concerned investigating police officials should have gone after the extortionists on the basis of the statement given by the Appellant, instead of terming him a conspirator, and thereby dubbing his paying money to extortionists, as funding terrorism.

Now, as far as my present study is concerned, the findings remain the way it is because it is based on primary and secondary data analysis. There are several cases in Nagaland wherein the businessmen, government employees and so on are forced to give extortion money to the insurgent groups, who use it for strengthening insurgency. Justifying this, the insurgents have said that they needed funds to cater to their cadres stationed in different countries. We have seen in chapter one that how the NSCN (IM) had justified their acts saying 'Peace talks require money. We have coordination offices in 10 countries and thousands of armed men from Nagaland deployed there. We cannot call them back or stop sending them rations and other necessary supplies.' Here, it is noteworthy that the investigating agencies have to conduct balanced and prudent investigation so as to bring out the linkages between different stakeholders of insurgency. Further, the Supreme Court had made it clear that its findings were restricted only for the purpose of granting bail to the appellant, and it should not influence the trial.

Researcher's Viewpoint:

While the findings of chapter II show the 'obscure' relationship between cultural elements and corruption in public offices, the researcher believes that this finding may be applicable to those who have political connections, are rich, and who wield power in society, and generalizations cannot be made. The reasons are: (1) the sample population is very small (142), (2) it represents only one field, i.e. academia, (3) respondents are principally from only one place, i.e. Kohima, (4) the number of sample literature is miniscule (41), and (5) could not spend more time for field work due to time constraints. For proving a hypothesis and generalizing the findings on larger population, the project must be able to cover cities, towns and villages in Nagaland that would require lots of resources and time.

Nonetheless, the findings cannot be out rightly rejected. This being an indication towards the relationship, a larger study could certainly bring out the link between Naga culture and corruption in government offices. It needs to be remembered that there is a lot of frustration among the people, especially youths, over the prevailing corruption in different quarters and illegal taxations by several factions of insurgent groups. The massive rally organized by ACAUT in 2013 and similar rally held by the Public Action Committee (PAC) of the Naga Council, Dimapur in 2018, in which thousands of citizens from all walks of life attended, was evidence of such discontentment against the governance.

The researcher assumes that there are 4 categories of economic strata in Nagaland, (1) upper class, i.e. rich and powerful, (2) middle class, (3) lower middle class, and (4) poor. The findings of this study may be applicable only to those who fall in the first category. It was felt that when the respondents were answering, they had the rich and powerful at the back of their mind, and hence, the aforesaid frustration and exaggeration in their replies. And that the relationship between culture and corruption that came out in the form of findings, is only indirect and could be the 'spin-off effect' of strong intra family/clan bonding and/or the reaction against the corrupt and powerful. Here emerges an important question – Are there two cultures? Possibly yes. One followed by the corrupt and the rich, and the other, honesty – those who still follow the Nagas' truthful traditional culture.

There is no doubt about the strong intra family/clan ties amongst the Nagas. Family/clan members give high significance to the family/clan bond and therefore support government officials of their clan, who engage in corrupt practices, and even justify them. Further, in reciprocation, the cultural obligation of the government officials to help same family/clan members even by misusing official power can be seen as the 'justified use of power' by the officials belonging to the same clan. This happens when the official believes that he has the moral responsibility to help his own people, even if by misusing his official powers. But it becomes a problem when the level of misuse goes beyond acceptable limits. On the other hand, according to the respondents, the belief that the officials who did not (mis)use their power for the benefit of their clan members were of no use and did not deserve any respect, could also have encouraged corruption. Thus, the official justifies the use of his power for the benefit of his clan members, which also gives him high respect amongst them. Favouritism towards own caste/clan members can be witnessed in other Indian societies too. Thus, there could be the possibility that kinship and social bond got embedded with corruption in public offices, and this acted as a vicious cycle, both strengthening each other. It is equally important to mention here that the respect given to those who have become rich through dishonest means, is only hype for gaining material benefits, due to fear factor that they (riches) may harm them, and internalizing the belief that the 'end justifies the means'. And these are the changes that have happened in the approach of a lot of Nagas in the recent past; this running behind wealth and power.

Due to the strong family/clan bond and obligations, there are possibilities that the misuse of official powers may get transformed into their cultural mandate. That is why it is mentioned that these could be the spin-off effect of strong ties amongst the members of family and clan. Another facet is that the culture of corruption that prevails in the office environment could impact the behaviour of the officials. This may further influence the cost/benefit assessment of corruption by the officials, and the weak internalization of anticorruption values. The prevalence of high power distance in the society forces people to give respect to those who have become rich and powerful, and others may be wanting to imitate them. The study further shows that people gave more preference to such government jobs that enabled getting extra illegal income, and there was moral economy of resentment. Huge funding by the Central government might have led to a 'culture of corruption' in government offices and a subsequent lower importance being accorded to following the rules. When we look at the spin-off effects as facilitating factors for the growth of corruption in government offices, it also validates the facilitation theory in the context of Nagaland.

These findings are restricted only with reference to the small sample population and lesser number of literature referred, and hence, could not be generalized. However, the results can be used as a base for conducting a larger study with bigger universe for generalization.

A few Suggestions

When enquired about the causes of corruption, majority of the respondents said that it was the political issue, which was followed by moral, social and cultural issues. As the latter three come under cultural aspects, it can be said that the main causes of corruption are cultural and political factors. When enquired further, it was found that greed for power and money, strong family/clan ties and mutual favouritism, absence of moral values, tribalism, lack of accountability and punitive measures, and inefficient bureaucracy were some of the reasons for corruption. In brief, weak (low level) democracy, fewer civil participation, and lesser political transparency, lead to corruption. So, there is a need for initiating steps in these domains to bring down corruption.

This can be done by bringing transparency in governance, empowering citizens by allowing access to information, free and fair election, stopping backdoor appointments and punishing those responsible for it, disposal of corruption cases at the earliest and taking stern action on those found guilty and thereby setting examples, eliminating power of appointment by ministers, encouraging private industries to reduce unemployment, taking strict actions against absenteeism in government offices and use of technologies, supporting honest and upright officials/political leaders, strict vigilance on the financial matters of all officials, stern implementation of anticorruption policies, and making Lokayukta more accountable. Further, there is a need for the government to create a conducive and secure environment so that people could come out and break their silence.

At the same time, we cannot ignore the role of social relationship. It needs to be emphasized that the social relationship is given high significance and is deep-rooted in the Naga culture, and mutual help is an essential part of it. Being so, misusing the official power for one's clan is considered as a help that strengthens the relationship, but not looked upon as corruption. So, in today's time if corruption has to be controlled, there is a need to devise methods that are capable of changing their belief systems.

To contain corruption and insurgency, it is necessary to have accountable governance and this requires strong political determination. It is equally important to implement developmental projects genuinely, prevent illegal tax collection and extortion, take precise counterinsurgency steps, meet demands of insurgents in a proportionate way, ensure determined mobilization of people against insurgency, educate children not to take up arms, create job opportunities as most join insurgency due to unemployment, stop politicians using insurgents during elections and check their movements, respect Naga aspirations, create feeling of belonging amongst Nagas towards India through various programs, mutual respect, and willingness to work together for the betterment of the society and nation. All these include short as well as long-term steps by the government with firm determination.

References

1. Ackerman, Rose, Susan; 1978; Corruption: A Study in Political Economy, Academic Press Inc. Sandiego.
2. An Introduction to Content Analysis, http://www.umsl.edu/~wilmarthp/mrpc-web-resources/content-analysis.pdf
3. Anand VK, 1981; Insurgency and Counter-Insurgency, Deep & Deep Publications, New Delhi.
4. Aram, M, 1974; Peace in Nagaland, Arnold-Heinemann Publishers (India) Pvt. Ltd., New Delhi, p. 303.
5. Asia For Educators; Mao Zedong on War and Revolution, http://afe.easia.columbia.edu/special/china_1900_mao_war.htm
6. Babatunde Akanji, 2017; The Relationship Between Culture and Corruption in Nigeria – Prospecting Culture Change in Dealing with this 'Big Black Hole', The Romanian Economic Journal, Year XX no. 63, March.
7. Barr, Abigail & Serra, Danila, 2010; Corruption and Culture: An Experimental Analysis, Journal of Public Economics 94, 2010, p.862-863.
8. Baruah Sanjib Kr; 2011; NSCN on Arms Buying Spree, Building Cadre; 18th Jan, https://www.hindustantimes.com/delhi-news/nscn-on-arms-buying-spree-building-cadre/story-2gQE76CuZ95rTSiDzjSEmJ.html
9. Bhattacharjee JB, 2007; Roots of Insurgency in Northeast India, Akansha Publishing House, New Delhi.
10. Biesanz, Mavis Hiltunen and Biesanz, John, 1973; Introduction to Sociology, Second edition, Prentice-Hall Inc., New Jersey, p-54.
11. Boehm, F., 2015; Democracy and Corruption, Dimensión

Empresarial, 13(2), p. 75-85, JEL: K42, P16, P17, DOI: http://dx.doi.org/10.15665/rde.v13i2.558

12. British Journal of International Studies , Cambridge University Press, Vol. 1, No. 3, Oct., pp. 226-253, https://www.jstor.org/stable/20096746
13. Cameron Lisa, Chaudhuri Ananish, Erkal Nisvan, Gangadharan Lata, 2005; Do Attitudes Towards Corruption Differ Across Cultures? Experimental Evidence from Australia, India, Indonesia and Singapore, https://papers.ssrn.com/sol3/papers.cfm?abstract_id=778464
14. Carnegie Endowment for International Peace, 2014; Corruption: The Unrecognized Threat to International Security,
http://carnegieendowment.org/files/corruption_and_security.pdf
15. Chabova,Kristyna;Normsandvaluesconnectedtocorruption: Is there difference between post-communist countries and the rest of Europe? https://www.europeansocialsurvey.org/docs/about/conference/CHABOVA_Norms-and-Values-corruption.pdf
16. Chandola Harish, 2013; The Naga Story: First Armed Struggle in India, Chicken neck, New Delhi,
17. Chandrika Singh, 2004; Naga Politics: A Critical Account, Mittal Publications, New Delhi
18. Chasie, Charles, 2005; Nagaland in Transition; Indian International Centre, Quarterly journal, Vol. 32, No. 2/3, https://www.jstor.org/stable/23006032?seq=1#metadata_info_tab_contents
Corruption, https://www.etymonline.com/word/corrupt, https://www.vocabulary.com/dictionary/corruption, http://www.corruptie.org/en/corruption/what-is-corruption/
Culture, https://study.com/academy/lesson/the-five-basic-characteristics-of-cultures.html
19. Daniels, A Michael and Greguras, J Gart, 2014; Exploring the nature of Power Distance: Implications for Micro- and Macro-level Theories, Processes, and Outcomes, Journal of Management, Vol. 40, No. 5, July.
20. Department of the Army, 2009; Tactics in Counterinsurgency,

Field Manual Interim, No. 3-24.2, Headquarters, Washington DC, March, https://fas.org/irp/doddir/army/fmi3-24-2.pdf

21. Dey Kallol; 2018; Illegal taxation continues to haunt Nagaland, government employees deride NIA; 7th January, http://indianexpress.com/article/north-east-india/nagaland/illegal-taxation-continues-to-haunt-nagaland-government-employees-deride-national-investigation-agency-4951172/
22. Didier Fassin, 2017; The Moral Economy of Resentment, https://piirs.princeton.edu/event/moral-economy-resentment
23. Dixon, Paul, 2009; 'Hearts and Minds'? British Counter-Insurgency from Malaya to Iraq, Journal of Strategic Studies, Routledge, Online, June 26, p.361.
24. Eastern Mirror News, 2015; Police Corruption: Kyong students want action against Home ministers, November 17, http://www.easternmirrornagaland.com/police-corruption-kyong-students-want-action-against-home-ministers/
25. Eastern Mirror, 2019; Nagaland: PAC takes 'illegal collection' issue to governor's doorstep, 9th September, https://www.easternmirrornagaland.com/nagaland-pac-takes-illegal-collection-issue-to-governors-doorstep/
26. Economic Times, 2015; Misappropriation of funds worth Rs 12.79 crore for disabled children in Nagaland, 19th February, https://economictimes.indiatimes.com/news/politics-and-nation/misappropriation-of-funds-orth-rs-12-79-crore-for-disabled-children-in-nagaland/articleshow/46299832.cms?from=mdr
27. Ethnic, https://www.etymonline.com/word/ethnic https://www.dictionary.com/browse/ethnic
28. Ezung, Zarenthung; 2012; Corruption and Its Impact on Development: A Case Study of Nagaland, International Journal of Rural Studies (IJRS) vol. 19 no. 1, April, http://www.vri-online.org.uk/ijrs/April2012/Corruption%20and%20its% 20impact %20on%20development%20in%20Nagaland%20India.pdf
29. Firstpost, 2018; NIA probes large-scale extortion, illegal tax collection by NSCN-K, arrests 3 senior Nagaland govt

officials, 26th March, https://www.firstpost.com/india/nia-probes-large-scale-extortion-illegal-tax-collection-by-nscn-k-arrests-3-senior-nagaland-govt-officials-4405343.html

30. Foco Theory, Dictionary of Revolutionary Marxism, http://www.massline.org/Dictionary/FO.htm
31. Freedom House, 2019, https://www.transparency.org/news/feature/cpi_2018_global_analysis
32. Geertz, Clifford, 1973; The Interpretation of Cultures: Selected Essays, New York: Basic Books, Inc., Publishers.
33. Gogoi, Dilip, 2016; Unheeded Hinterland: Identity and Sovereignty in Northeast India, South Asia Edition, Routledge India.
34. Gonzalex-Trejo,Eli Samuel, 2007; Corruption and Culture: A Relationship Comparison Between 1996 and 2004, Central Business Review, vol.XXVI, No. 1-2, p. 23.
35. Greenbook Directory, https://www.greenbook.org/marketing-research/how-to-interpret-standard-deviation-and-standard-error-in-survey-research-03377
36. Guide to the Analysis of Insurgency, 2012, US Government, https://www.hsdl.org/?abstract&did=713599
37. Hofstede, Geert, 2001; Culture's Consequences: Comparing Values, Behaviours, Institutions and Organisations across Nations, Sage, London, p.9.
38. Hofstede, Geert, 2011; Dimensionalizing Cultures: The Hofstede Model in Context; Online Readings in Psychology and Culture, 2(1), p. 9, https://doi.org/10.9707/2307-0919.1014, https://scholarworks.gvsu.edu/cgi/viewcontent.cgi?article=1014&context=orpc
39. Hofstede-insights, https://www.hofstede-insights.com/country/india/
40. Hoggart, Richard, 1964; Culture, https://www.google.com/search?q=etymology+of+word+culture&rlz=1C1CHBD_enIN848IN848&oq=etymology+of+term+culture&aqs=chrome.1.69i57j0l2.13343j0j8&sourceid=chrome&ie=UTF-8
41. Horam Mashangthei, 1975; Naga Polity, BR Publishing Corporation, Delhi
42. Horam Mashangthei, 1977; Social and Cultural Life of

Nagas, BR Publishing Corporation, Delhi, https://www.tandfonline.com/doi/pdf/10.1080/01402390902928172

43. Hussain, Wasbir, Insurgency in India's Northeast Cross-border Links and Strategic Alliances, https://www.satp.org/satporgtp/publication/faultlines/volume17/wasbir.htm#_ftn35
44. Indian Express, 2015; Everything you need to know about Nagaland insurgency, 4th August, http://indianexpress.com/article/india/india-others/everything-you-need-to-know-about-nagaland-insurgency-and-the-efforts-to-solve/
45. Jamir SC, 2016; A Naga's Quest for Fulfillment, Bhubaneswar, Apurba, p. 121-122
46. Jeemon Jacob, 2017; The story of Nagaland cop who turned Kerala billionaire, India Today,14th June, https://www.indiatoday.in/india/kerala/story/nagaland-cop-turned-kerala-billionaire-mkr-pillai-sreevalsam-business-group-982715-2017-06-14
47. Juacaba, S Rodrigo, 2018; The contingency effect of national culture on corruption, Masters dissertation, https://pdfs.semanticscholar.org/702d/773ac43f5380f34df237a9608cf1c8e190cc.pdf
48. Kamuzora A; 2008; Research Methods for Business and Social Studies, Morogoro Mzumbe Book Project.
49. Kashyap S Gupta & Swami Praveen, 2015; Explained: Everything you need to know about Nagaland insurgency, The Indian Express, 4th August, https://indianexpress.com/article/india/india-others/everything-you-need-to-know-about-nagaland-insurgency-and-the-efforts-to-solve/
50. Ketholesie, 2015; British Policy Towards Annexation of the Naga Hills; International Journal of Engineering, Management, Humanities and Social Sciences Paradigms (IJEMHS), Volume 13, Issue 01, http://www.ijemhs.com/Published%20Paper/Volume%2013/Issue%2001/IJES%2011/IJEMHSJune 2015_55_57_Keth.pdf
51. Klitgaard, Robert, 2017; On Culture and Corruption; BSG Working Paper, BSG-WP-2017/020 July, https://www.bsg.ox.ac.uk/sites/default/files/2018-05/BSG-WP-2017-020.pdf

52. Kothari C R; 2004; Research Methodology; New Age International (P) Ltd., Publishers, New Delhi
53. Kotwal, Dinesh, 2000; The Naga Insurgency: The Past And The Future; Strategic Analysis, Volume 24, Issue-4, Taylor & Francis Online, https://www.tandfonline.com/doi/abs/10.1080/09700160008455245
54. Krieger, Tim and Meierrieks, Daniel, 2019; Income inequality, redistribution and domestic terrorism, Elsevier, World Development, Volume 116, April 2019, Pages 125-136.
55. Kurtosis, https://www.spcforexcel.com/knowledge/basic-statistics/are-skewness-and-kurtosis-useful-statistics#kurtosis
56. List of recognized Naga tribes in Nagaland, https://dpar.nagaland.gov.in/list-of-recognized-nagascheduled-tribes-certificate/
57. Luithui, Luingam and Haksar, Nandita, 1984; Nagaland File: A Question of Human Rights, Lancer International, New Delhi.
58. Mack, Andrew, 1975; Counterinsurgency in the Third World: Theory and Practice, British Journal of International Studies, Cambridge University Press, Oct., Vol. 1, No. 3, https://www.jstor.org/stable/20096746
59. MacLachlan, Karolina, 2018; Corruption and Conflict: Hand in Glove, NATO Review, 6th December, https://www.nato.int/docu/review/2018/Also-in-2018/corruption-and-conflict-hand-in-glove-nato-defense-security/EN/index.htm
60. Manchanda, Rita & Bose, Tapan, 2011; Expanding the Middle Space in the Naga Peace Process, Economic and Political Weekly, December 31, Vol xlvi No 53, p. 58.
61. Manoj, Anand, 2018; NIA Claims Former Nagaland CM Zeliang help in funding terror, Deccan Chronicle, 19th March, https://www.deccanchronicle.com/nation/current-affairs/190318/nia-claims-former-nagaland-cm-zeliang-help-in-funding-terror.html
62. Maslow; Positive Psychology, https://positivepsychology.com/self-esteem/

63. Mate, S Haukhanlian, 2014; Traditional Administrative System and Customary Laws of the Thangkhals, Akansha Publishing House, New Delhi
64. Matters India, 2014; Present Situation of Nagaland, 15th December, http://mattersindia.com/2014/12/present-situation-of-nagaland/
65. Misra, Udayon, 1978; The Naga National Question, Economic and Political Weekly, Vol. 13, No. 14, 8th April, https://www.jstor.org/stable/4366506?seq=1#metadata_info_tab_contents
66. Misra, Udayon, 2014; India's North-East, Oxford University Press, New Delhi
67. Morung Express News, 2015; Nagaland Health Sector in Shambles?, 30th November, http://morungexpress.com/nagaland-health-sector-in-shambles/
68. Naga, http://morungexpress.com/origin-of-the-word-naga/, https://nagalandgk.com/origin-of-the-word-naga/
69. Nagaland Backgrounder, 2001; South Asia Terrorism Portal (SATP), http://old.satp.org/satporgtp/countries/india/states/nagaland/backgrounder/index.html
70. Nagaland Post, 2018; Holy Crime and Saintly Corruption in Nagaland!, 25th September, http://www.nagalandpost.com/holy-crime-and-saintly-corruption-in-nagaland/182190.html
71. Nagaland Post, 2019; Corruption has hampered overall growth: SVC, 29th October, http://www.nagalandpost.com/corruption-has-hampered-overall-growth-svc/184184.html
72. Nagaland Post, 2019; Promote and preserve rich culture: Temjen Imna, 15th August, http://www.nagalandpost.com/promote-and-preserve-rich-culture-temjen-imna/201849.html
73. Nagaland Post, 2020; HC serves notice on state govt: ACAUT, PAC, BAN File PIL with HC against rampant illegal taxations, 11th December, http://www.nagalandpost.com/hc-serves-notice-on-state-govt/225942.html
74. Neil J. Salkind, 2010; Mean, Encyclopedia of Research Design, Sage Research Methods, https://methods.sagepub.

com/Reference/encyc-of-research-design/n236.xml

75. News18; 2016; 70 NSCN-IM Cadre Attack Imphal Security Posts, Snatch 20 Weapons, 17th December, https://www.news18.com/news/india/70-nscn-im-cadre-attack-imphal-security-posts-snatch-20-weapons-1324276.html
76. Nienu V, 2015; Naga Cultural Milieu: An Adaptation to Mountain Ecosystem, Dorylus Publishing Group (DPG), California.
77. Nixon Doctrine, President Richard Nixon, November 3, 1969, http://cf.linnbenton.edu/artcom/social_science/clarkd/upload/Nixon%20Doctrine.pdf
78. Northeast Window, 2018; Dynamics of Political Corruption in Nagaland, 10th February,http://www.thenortheastwindow.com/2018/02/dynamics-political-corruption-nagaland/
79. Nuh VK, 2016; The Naga Chronicle, 2nd revised edition, Regency Publications, New Delhi.
80. Paul J Lavrakas, 2008; Encyclopedia of Survey Research Methods, Sage, https://methods.sagepub.com/Reference/encyclopedia-of-survey-research-methods, https://www.statisticssolutions.com/factor-analysis-sem-factor-analysis/
81. Pillai S K; 2001; Anatomy of an Insurgency Ethnicity & Identity in Nagaland; SATP, http://www.satp.org/satporgtp/publication/faultlines/volume3/fault3-enpillaif.htm#33
82. Press Trust of India, 2018; Nagaland Congress mocks PM promise of corruption-free govt; in company with 'most corrupt leaders', PTI@moneycontrolcom, https://www.moneycontrol.com/news/india/nagaland-congress-mocks-pm-promise-of-corruption-free-govt-in-company-with-most-corrupt-leaders-2515149.html
83. Purkayastha, Rakhal, 2007; 3rd Presentation, *in* Roots of Insurgency in Northeast India, Ed. Bhattacharjee JB, Akansha Publishing House, New Delhi
84. Rajshekhar, M & Chakravarty, Ipsita; 2018; What does the new 'historic' Naga peace accord have that the Shillong Accord of 1975 did not?; 5th August 2015, https://scroll.in/article/746319/what-does-the-new-historic-naga-peace-accord-have-that-the-shillong-accord-of-1975-did-not

85. Rammohan, EN, 2003; The Naga Insurgency – Part I, USI Journal, July – September, https://usiofindia.org/publication/usi-journal/the-naga-insurgency-part-i/
86. Rao Abhimanyu & Charles Mwirigi K, 2019; Critical evaluation of armed forces (special powers) act, 1958: Sovereignty first, Research Review Journals, vol. 4, issue 2, February, https://rrjournals.com/wp-content/uploads/2019/02/125-129_RRIJM190402029.pdf
87. Ray, Ayesha, 2016; Culture, Context and Capability: American and Indian Counterinsurgency Approaches, ISDA Monograph Series, No. 57, December.
88. Rediff Interview, https://www.rediff.com/news/2001/jun/25inter.htm
89. Robert Tiba (Robert Tiba foundation), 2013; History and Culture of the Maram Nagas, Akansha Publishing House, New Delhi
90. Rodrigo Santiago Juaçaba, 2018; The Contingency Effect of National Culture on Corruption; Master's dissertation submitted to the Department of Geography at the Norwegian University of Science and Technology.
91. Santoshini, Sarita; 2016; In India's Nagaland, a tale of taxes and corruption; 14th April, https://www.aljazeera.com/indepth/features/2016/04/india-nagaland-drowning-taxes-corruption-160411062725238.html
92. Seleim Ahmed and Bontis Nick, 2009; The relationship between culture and corruption: A cross-national study, Journal of Intellectual Capital, Vol. 10 No. 1, pp. 165-184, Emerald Group Publishing Limited. https://www.emerald.com/insight/content/doi/10.1108/14691930910922978/full/html
93. Shumaker and Longsdorf , http://www.duhaime.org/LegalDictionary/C/Corruption.aspx
94. Singh, Vijaita, 2020; Armed Gangs Rule Nagaland: Governor, The Hindu, New Delhi, 25th June. https://www.thehindu.com/news/national/other-states/nagaland-governor-slams-collapse-of-law-and-order-in-state/article31915402.ece?utm_source=taboola

95. Skewness, https://www.spcforexcel.com/knowledge/basic-statistics/are-skewness-and-kurtosis-useful-statistics#skewness
96. Special Inspector General for Afghanistan Reconstruction-SIGAR, 2018; Corruption in Conflict, September, https://www.sigar.mil/interactive-reports/corruption-in-conflict/index.html
97. State Vigilance Commission, Government of Nagaland, 2016, https://dpar.nagaland.gov.in/state-vigilance-commission/
98. Stephen Taylor, India Business Etiquette & Culture; Geert Hofstede Analysis for India, https://www.cyborlink.com/besite/india.htm
99. Study.com, https://study.com/academy/lesson/writing-research-questions-purpose-examples.html
100. Taylor, Edward, Burnett, 1871; Primitive Culture: Researches into the Development of Mythology, Philosophy, Religion, Art, and Custom, Vol.1, Dover Publications, Inc., Mineola, New York.
101. Teets Jessica & Chenoweth Erica; 2009; To Bribe or to Bomb: Do Corruption and Terrorism Go Together?; *in* Corruption, Global Security, and World Order, Ed. Robert I Rotberg, Brookings Institution Press, Washington DC.
102. Tehelka Magazine, 2010; Gandhi supported the Naga desire for independence, Quoting Thinoselie Keyho, Nagalim voice, Vol 7, Issue 43, 30th October, http://www.nagalimvoice.com/interviews/%E2%80%98gandhi-supported-the-naga-desire-for-independence%E2%80%99/
103. Temjensosang, 2013; Self-Governing Institutions of Nagas, Akansha Publishing House, New Delhi
104. Temsula Ao, 2006; These Hills Called Home: Stories from the War Zone, Zubaan, New Delhi, p.x.
105. The Morung Express, 2011; Do you believe that Nagaland is the 'corruption capital' of India?, 7th November, http://morungexpress.com/do-you-believe-nagaland-corruption-capital-india
106. The Morung Express, 2015; Wangtin, Tikhak Form 'NSCN (Reformation); 6th April, http://morungexpress.com/wangtin-tikhak-form-nscn-reformation/

107. The Morung Express, 2018; Naga Plebiscite Day is 67 years Old, 16th May.
108. The Morung Express, 2019; Walls of Nagaland are broken: Dr SC Jamir, 20th August, http://morungexpress.com/walls-nagaland-are-broken-dr-sc-jamir
109. The Northeast Today; 2018; NIA stumbles upon evidence of Zeliang's involvement in terror funding case; 19th March, https://thenortheasttoday.com/nagaland-nia-stumbles-upon-evidence-of-zeliangs-involvement-in-terror-funding-case/
110. Thomas, Hayden H, 2007; Whast is the difference between insurgency and terrorism? 28th Feb, https://usiraq.procon.org/view.answers.php?questionID=000931
111. Tinyi, Venüsa and Nienu, Chothazo, 2018; Making Sense of Corruption in Nagaland: A Culturalist Interpretation, *in* Jelle JP Wouters and Zhoto Tunyi (ed.) Democracy in Nagaland: Tribes, Traditions, and Tensions, Highlander Books, p. 176, http://www.highlanderbooks.org
112. Transparency International, 2019, https://www.transparency.org/en/countries/china#
113. Treston, Wheat, 2011; The Difference between Terrorists and Insurgents, World Report News, 26th December, http://www.worldreportnews.com/us-foreign-policy-archived/the-difference-between-terrorists-and-insurgents
114. UNI, 2018; Nagaland Governor calls people to fight corruption, 29th October, http://www.uniindia.com/nagaland-governor-calls-people-to-fight-corruption/east/news/1391805.html
115. Unnithan, Sandeep; 2011; Chinese agents smuggle arms to revive militancy in north-eastern India, 28th May,
116. https://www.indiatoday.in/magazine/investigation/story/20110606-chinese-agents-smuggle-arms-to-spread-militancy-in-north-east-746248-2011-05-28
117. US Government, 2012; Guide to the Analysis of Insurgency, https://www.hsdl.org/?abstract&did=713599, https://shodhganga.inflibnet.ac.in/bitstream/10603/116506/9/09_chapter%204.pdf

118. US Military Academy training manual, "Insurgents vs. Guerrillas vs. Terrorists", https://usiraq.procon.org/sourcefiles/InsurgentsvsTerrorists.pdf
119. USC Libraries, http://libguides.usc.edu/writingguide/literaturereview, http://libguides.usc.edu/writingguide/theoreticalframework
120. Usman, Umaru, 2017; Impact of Corruption on Insurgency in the North-Eastern Region of Nigeria, IOSR Journal of Business Management, Vol. 19, Issue 1, Ver. I, January, p. 19-25.
121. Vannucci, Alberto, 2015; Three paradigms for the analysis of corruption, Labour and Law Issues, vol.1, no.2, ISSN: 2421-2695.
122. Verrier, Elwin, 1961; Nagaland, Research Department, Adviser's Secretariat, Shillong.
123. Victoria, Nkemdilim Ogbuehl, 2018; Corruption and Escalating Boko Haram Insurgency in Nigeria, Research & Reviews: Journal of Social Sciences, Vol. 4, Issue 3, October.
124. Vijayalakshmi V, 2013; Transparency, Accountability, and Governance: Local Government in Kerala and Karnataka, *in* Local Governance in India, *Ed. by* Niraja Gopal Jayal, Amit Prakash, Pradeep K Sharma, Oxford University Press, New Delhi
125. Wittek, Rafael, 2013; Rational Choice Theory, *in* Theory in Social and Cultural Anthropology : An Encyclopedia Account: Sage Publications, Inc., January, p. 688.
126. World Report News, http://www.worldreportnews.com/us-foreign-policy-archived/the-difference-between-terrorists-and-insurgents
127. Wouters, Jelle JP, 2018; In the Shadows of Naga Insurgency, Oxford University Press, New Delhi.
128. Yap Kioe Sheng, The United Nations Economic and Social Commission for Asia and the Pacific; What is Good Governance?, https://www.unescap.org/sites/default/files/good-governance.pdf
129. Yonuo, Asoso, 1948; The Rising Nagas, Manas Publications, Delhi.

Appendix

CAG Report for the year 1978-79, Government of Nagaland:

- Purchases of surgical equipments for police battalion hospitals were made without prior approval.
- Police uniform clothes worth Rs. 4.76 lakhs was purchased without actual demand.
- Forest department had spent Rs. 0.99 lakh (1974) for the purchase of fencing material, but there was no record to show that the material had been received.
- Misappropriation of funds was done in the medical department which led to the registration of case and arrest of the cashier. But the government did not take conduct further investigation of procedural failures to fix responsibility and to make good the loss.
- In the construction of a tourist lodge at Kohima, the work was entrusted to a contractor and Rs. 3.97 lakhs was spent and it remained incomplete. As per the condition, an amount of Rs. 0.83 lakh had to be levied from the contractor, but it was not done.

CAG Report for the year 1979-80, Government of Nagaland:

- Misappropriation of money was made by the Rural Development department
- The purchase of vegetable ghee in improper way by the police department led to incurring extra expenditure of Rs. 1.32 lakhs.

- Unauthorized advance payment for purchase of jeeps was made by the Agriculture/ Planning and Coordination/Geology and Mining departments.
- Blocking of development funds was done by Medical department. Improper purchasing of nursing sundries resulted in excess payment of Rs. 0.40 lakh.
- Records of Accounts for site records, tenders and agreements of schemes, etc. were not maintained by the Public Health Engineering department.
- Irregularities in construction of stone masonry reservoir dam were found.
- In the Wokha Public Works division, materials worth Rs. 5.55 lakhs was not received.

CAG Report for the year 1980-81, Government of Nagaland:

- Avoidable extra expenditures were made of Rs. 0.43 lakh in respect of purchase of projector by the Director, Information, publicity and tourism.
- Prisons department made avoidable extra expenditure of Rs. 45,210/- in the purchase of fire extinguishing equipments.
- Irregularities were practiced in the construction of state stadium at Dimapur.
- Fraudulent payment of Rs. 10,800/- was made by the Public Works Division, Phek.
- There was a loss of Rs. 0.73 lakh at Phek district Agar mahal due to misappropriation.
- Irregularities were found in the sale of molasses that led to the loss of Rs. 0.36 lakh.

CAG Report for the year 1983-84, Government of Nagaland:

- The Rural Development Department, while implementing the Centrally sponsored Integrated Rural Development Program (IRDP), without conducting proper household survey, provided a subsidy of Rs. 14.65 lakh to such households, whose income was higher and thus ineligible for subsidy.

- No receipt and issue accounts of the materials valuing Rs. 4.66 lakh received by the State Family Welfare Bureau in the office of the Director of Health Services during 1976-77 to 1979-80 from the Government of India kept.
- The audio-visual equipment purchased in 1982 and 1983 for Rs. 1.19 lakhs to exhibit films in rural areas remained unutilized.
- Extra/excess expenditure on irregular purchase of surgical gloves/ophthalmic equipments caused Rs. 0.86 lakh.
- Improper procuring and utilization of road metal led to the loss of Rs. 0.50 lakh.

CAG Report for the year 1984-85, Government of Nagaland:

- In 1983, three cases of theft took place in police armoury wherein ammunitions and rifles were stolen. Though FIRs were registered, no action was taken to fix the responsibility.
- Misappropriation of Rs. 0.31 lakh was detected at the office of the Directorate of Administrative Training Institute.
- Irregularities were reported in the Public Distribution System. Wheat or wholemeal atta was never distributed to ration card holders.
- The infructuous purchase of a generator for the chilling plant of the Rural Dairy Project, Dimapur incurred Rs. 0.55 lakh.
- The non-acceptance of the lowest rate by the Works and Housing department in the purchase of Hexagonal mesh of triple twisted galvanized iron sausage wire resulted in an extra expenditure of Rs. 24 lakhs.

CAG Report for the Year 1988-89, Government of Nagaland:

- Recoveries of loans were not effected in 99.69 per cent and 74.42 per cent of cases in Kophima and Zunheboto district respectively during 1980-81 to 1984-85 in the Low Income Group Housing Scheme.
- The deployment of 12 out of 14 jeeps (cost Rs. 11.64 lakhs) purchased during 1981-82 and 1982-83 was not available on record.

- There was an irregular payment of land compensation of Rs. 7.36 lakhs to a private individual on acquisition of government land which had been given to him earlier purely for temporary cultivation purpose.
- Non-acceptance of lower offered rates of a firm resulted in an avoidable extra expenditure of Rs. 115.55 lakhs in the Scheme of Augmentation of Water Supply at Mokokchung, Phase II.
- Between October 1985 and September 1988, the Executive Engineer, PWD, Dimapur purchase items of store worth Rs. 520.60 lakhs, although the balance of stock was sufficient to meet the demands for the next 5 to 10 years.

CAG Report for the Year 1989-90, Government of Nagaland:

- Excess payment of Rs. 61.82 lakhs was made to a contractor in connection with the work of construction of power house of Dikhu Hydro Electric Project.
- Infructuous/unfruitful expenditure of Rs. 41.15 lakhs was incurred on account of salaries of the staff, repairs to plant, machinery and building of the Seasoning and Treatment Plant at Dimapur during 1985-82 which did not function.
- Stock materials worth Rs. 302.66 lakhs were purchased by the Police Engineering Project Division, Chumukedima during October 1987 to September 1989 for construction of residential buildings. The materials were not utilised as the land for construction of the buildings had not been acquired.
- Physical verification of stock of various godowns under the Director of Food and Civil Supplies revealed shortage of 0.30 lakh quintals of rice valuing Rs. 79.42 lakhs.
- Arrears amounting to Rs. 198.70 lakhs were kept out of records in the Sales Tax arrears collection.

CAG Report for the Year 1990-91, Government of Nagaland:

- Under Lift Irrigation Scheme, 18 pumpsets valuing Rs. 1.97 lakhs were issued during the period from May 1987 to December 1990 to 18 individuals on loan basis, which were not recovered.

- Though the office cum plant for the Pasteurisation Plant at Mokokchung was completed at a cost of Rs. 11.23 lakhs in September 1988, the work orders for supply of plant and machinery were issued to a contractor in March 1990, that is after 18 months of completion of the building. Upto March 1991 the contractor was paid Rs. 22.96 lakhs, but the plant was not commissioned.
- An extra expenditure of Rs. 7.61 lakhs was incurred in purchase of medicines at higher rates by the DH&FW during December 1985 to March 1987.
- The Nagaland State Transport Department sustained loss of Rs. 182.50 lakhs in operation of a helicopter service during September 1987 to February 1989.
- Registrar of Cooperative societies encashed a bank draft for Rs. 9 lakhs and paid to the Chairman, MARCOFED, Dimapur for purchase of blankets. Neither the blankets were purchased nor the money was accounted for in the account of MARCOFED.

CAG Report for the Year 1991-92, Government of Nagaland:

- There was an excess expenditure of Rs. 789.72 lakhs for purchase of power at higher rates due to non-construction of HT lines in time.
- Rs. 22.66 lakhs being the value of medicines and hospital equipment were paid to suppliers by the Directorate of Health and Family Welfare without entries in the stock registers in evidence of receipt of the materials.
- An avoidable extra expenditure of Rs. 83.01 lakhs was incurred by the PHED on procurement of GI pipes due to granting of enhancement in rates. Another extra expenditure of Rs. 22.81 lakhs was also incurred by the department due to non-acceptance of lowest rates.
- There was a fraudulent withdrawal of Rs. 1.75 lakhs in the Working Division, PHED, Dimapur through a missing cheque leaf.
- There was a loss of revenue of Rs. 305.20 lakhs during October 1991 to April 1992 due to non-realisation of guaranteed profit from the Organising Agents of State Lotteries.

CAG Report for the Year 1993-94, Government of Nagaland:

- In contravention to the provisions of the Jawahar Rojgar Yojana manual works costing Rs. 454.46 lakhs were executed through contractors and other intermediate agencies other than the VDBs for which the department paid directly to these contractors.
- There was an extra expenditure of Rs. 20.29 lakhs on procurement of spare parts for vehicle during 1990-94 by the GM, Nagaland State Transport, Dimapur.
- Executive Engineer, Public Health Engineering Division, Dimapur made payment of Rs. 224.27 lakhs to a supplier for water supply fitting without receipt of the materials at site.
- Executive Engineer, Civil Administration Works Division, Kohima paid to a contractor Rs. 19.30 lakhs against the value of work of Rs. 6.87 lakhs executed.
- Director of State Lotteries did not forfeit and encash bank guarantees of Rs. 140 lakhs furnished by an organising agent of state lotteries against whom government dues of Rs. 924.56 lakhs was outstanding. Instead, the department released bank guarantees for Rs. 120 lakhs in1993.

CAG Report for the Year 1995-96, Government of Nagaland:

- Under the Employment Assurance Scheme, payment of wages amounting Rs. 39.05 lakhs were not made directly to the labourers, instead the same were made to third parties including political leaders, office bearers of a political party and government officials. The disbursing officers could not confirm whether wages had actually reached the labourers through the third party.
- The fictitious/double payments of Rs. 39.78 lakhs were facilitated by non-adherence of prescribed scheme norm by the implementing agencies and issue of fake completion certificates by the BDOs. The Director RD expressed his ignorance of all such happenings indicating that there was a total system failure at all levels of implementation of the scheme.

- Under the National AIDS Control Programme, as against the GOI's supply of equipment/materials worth Rs. 36.20 lakhs to the blood banks in Nagaland, the department had recorded receipt of only 2 refrigerators and 2 air conditioners. No action was taken to ascertain the whereabouts of the remaining equipment/materials.
- Under the Community Development Programme, an amount of Rs. 24.92 lakhs was sanctioned as grants-in-aid. BDO, Wakching retained 6.13 lakhs with him and shown as spent, for which there were no supporting documents.
- Executive Engineer, Police Engineering Project, Alichen drew a sum of Rs. 37.30 lakhs through 25 cheques in October 1994 and paid this amount to fictitious contractors/suppliers against fictitious charges.

CAG Report for the Year 1996-97, Government of Nagaland:

- No transparency in the implementation of the Members of Parliament Local Area Development Scheme in the state because 54 per cent (Rs. 272.95 lakhs) spent on social forestry/ horticulture, construction of roads (Rs. 69.77 lakhs), minor irrigation projects (Rs. 25.18 lakhs), and these were not supported with the details of locations/areas and technical estimates.
- Under Calamity Relief Fund, claims worth Rs. 171 lakhs for relief measures were entertained during the years 1990-97 without proper authentication and receipt of certificates of disbursements.
- Central assistance of Rs. 16.12 lakhs was irregularly claimed and obtained by submitting grossly inflated progress reports by the Director of Agriculture (DOA).
- The DOA reported distribution of 15,000 minikits valuing Rs. 20 lakhs to the farmers during 1992-97 against the distribution of 5602 minikits at a cost of Rs. 5.13 lakhs.
- An amount of Rs. 2.15 crore was spent for plantation works during 1992-96 by 4 Divisional Forest Officers, but no documents were maintained.

CAG Report for the Year 1998-99, Government of Nagaland:

- In the absence of proper accounts, veracity of distribution of 3,37,849 MTs of PDS commodities valued at Rs.220.60 crore by the FP Shops/stockists during 1995-99 to the beneficiaries could not be verified in audit. Thus, the possibility of diversion of these PDS commodities to open market could not be ruled out.
- Physical verification of 3 godowns conducted between March 1995 and July 1997 by a Board constituted by the Department revealed shortage of 298.61 MTs fine/superfine rice valued at Rs.0.18 crore.
- 23360.40 quintals of rice worth Rs.2.46 crore was lifted and claimed to have been distributed during months when schools were not in session. During 1996-99, 3737.10 quintals of inferior rice was delivered by carriage contractors in Kohima Block against lifting of fine rice from FCI godowns at Dimapur. By accepting inferior rice against superior rice, undue benefit of Rs.0.17 crore was extended to the contractors.
- The Inspector General of Prisons unauthorisedly diverted Rs.33.42 lakh out of the funds meant for the implementation of "Modernisation of Prison Administration" which included an advance payment of Rs.6 lakh to a supplier who neither delivered the materials nor refunded the money.
- In respect of payment of Rs.1.35 crore made by the Director of School Education towards supply of books/furniture, there was no evidence for the supply of these articles and the possibility of misappropriation of the money could not be ruled out.